Today in African-American History

366 Days of Historical Events and Accomplishments

To; Sam

Always remember how Brilliant you are. Please enjoy reading the Book.

Michael A. Carson

Copyright © 2018 by Michael A. Carson

Double Infinity Publishing
P. O. Box 55 Grayson, GA 30017

Printed in the United States of America

Today in African-American History

Contributing Research Editor: Shenika H. Carson
Research Assistant: Matthew A. Carson
Cover Design: Double Infinity Publishing
Design Director: Shenika H. Carson

ISBN-13: 978-0692178041
ISBN-10: 069217804X

Double Infinity Publishing books may be purchased in bulk at a special discount for sales promotion, corporate gifts, fund-raising or educational purposes. For details, contact the Special Sales Department, Double Infinity Publishing, P.O. Box 55 Grayson, GA. 30017 or by email: DoubleInfinityPublishing1@Gmail.com.

DEDICATION

This book is dedicated to the love of my life, my beautiful wife Shenika, thank you for all of your love and support. To my son Matthew, who inspires me to continue my search for knowledge, I love you and I am very proud of you.

To the next generation of African-American innovators who continue to thrive, push the limits and challenge themselves to create new ideas and write the next chapter in world history.

African-American Inventions That Changed The World

Influential Inventors and Their Revolutionary Creations

Michael A. Carson

Double Infinity Publishing

CONTENTS

INTRODUCTION   1

1. January   2 - 32

2. February   33 - 61

3. March   62 - 92

4. April   93 - 122

5. May   123 - 153

6. June   154 - 183

7. July   184 - 214

8. August   215 - 245

9. September   246 - 275

10. October   276 - 306

11. November   307 - 336

12. December   337 - 367

INDEX   369 - 392

SOURCES   395

ACKNOWLEDGEMENTS   397

ABOUT THE AUTHOR   399

INTRODUCTION

Every year Black History Month sparks an annual debate about the use of the month of February to celebrate the history and accomplishments of African-Americans. Although February provides an amazing opportunity to celebrate and acknowledge the achievements of African-Americans throughout history, it's also important to honor African-American history during the other eleven months of the year as well.

While Black History Month is synonymous with prominent figures such as Dr. Martin Luther King Jr., Harriet Tubman, Rosa Parks, Muhammad Ali, Jackie Robinson, Maya Angelou and President Barack Obama, there are countless other African-Americans who have made a profound impact in history.

The best way to extend the spirit of Black History Month is to continue recognizing each day of the year with other significant contributions African-Americans have made in our society and the world.

The incredible men and women featured in this book have contributed to the fields of Education, Science, Technology, Politics, Law, Medicine, Sports and Entertainment, to name a few. This book features their accomplishments for all 366 days of the year.

Recognizing the accomplishments of African-Americans began in 1926 with Negro History Week, a commemoration launched by Historian, Dr. Carter G. Woodson. He chose the second week of February to coincide with and pay homage to the birthdays of President Abraham Lincoln and Frederick Douglass. He credited the two for bringing an end to slavery in America. The Federal Government officially recognized Black History Month in conjunction with the 1976 United States Bicentennial Celebration.

On this Day in History...

January 1st

1863 - President Abraham Lincoln signed the Emancipation Proclamation, a Presidential Proclamation and Executive Order issued to changed the federal legal status of more than 3.5 million enslaved African-Americans in the designated areas of the South from slave to free.

1916 - The first issue of "The Journal of African-American History" was published, formerly known as "The Journal of Negro History," a quarterly academic journal covering African-American life and history. Founded by Dr. Carter G. Woodson, this journal published original scholarly articles on all aspects of the African-American experience.

1966 - The first observance of the seventh day of Kwanzaa, "Imani," which means "Faith" was observed. The celebration honors African Heritage in African-American Culture.

1967 - The Black Panther Party for Self Defense opened its first official Headquarters in Oakland, CA., it was originally co-founded in 1966, by Huey P. Newton and Bobby Seale.

1990 - David Dinkins became the first African-American Mayor of New York City. He began his political career by serving as the Manhattan Borough President before becoming Mayor. His administration made significant accomplishments in lowering New York City's crime rate and increasing the size of the New York Police Department.

2011 - The Oprah Winfrey Channel (OWN), named after the former Daytime Talk-Show Host, Oprah Winfrey, debuted on cable television in more than 80 million households.

On this Day in History...

January 2nd

1800 - A group of free African-American citizens living in Philadelphia, PA., submitted a petition to the United States Congress to repeal the Fugitive Slave Act of 1793, in order to end the slave trade and abolish slavery. Although the petition was rejected, it was the beginning of the long-term campaign to abolish slavery in America.

1875 - Abolitionist, Mary Ellen Pleasant earned her title as the "Mother" of California's early civil rights movement. She worked on the Underground Railroad across many States and then helped bring it to California during the Gold Rush Era. Pleasant established several restaurants for California miners, she made a fortune through her various businesses and became one of the richest and most powerful people in the state of California. Pleasant was a real estate innovator and millionaire, she also helped to establish the Bank of California.

1904 - George Edwin Taylor became the first African-American to run for President of the United States on a minority party ticket "The National Negro Liberty Party." In 1908, he also delivered the Keynote Address to the "Union Convention of Black Political Leagues" that was held in Denver, CO.

1965 - In an effort to bring the issue of Voting Rights to national attention, Dr. Martin Luther King, Jr., launched a voter registration drive in Alabama and organized a march from the City of Selma to the State's Capital of Montgomery.

1975 - Walter Washington became the first ever elected Mayor of Washington D.C., he was also the only Mayor of D.C., appointed by the President.

On this Day in History...

January 3rd

1624 - William Tucker was the first African child born in the 13 British Colonies. His birth symbolized the beginning of a distant African-American identity along the eastern coast of what would eventually become the United States. He was born in Jamestown, Virginia. There were 22 Africans who lived in Virginia at the time of Tucker's birth. In 1619, they all worked under indentured servitude contracts. These men and women were not slaves because Virginia's General Assembly had not yet worked out the terms for enslavement in the colony. Consequently these first Africans in Virginia received the same rights, duties, privileges, responsibilities and punishments as their Caucasian indentured counterparts from Great Britain.

1961 - Robert C. Henry became the first African-American Mayor elected to head an American City, which was Springfield, Ohio. Although this achievement is frequently overshadowed by fellow Mayor Carl B. Stokes, who was the first African-American elected as Mayor of a major U.S. City, Cleveland, Ohio in 1967.

1979 - Hazel W. Johnson became the first African-American woman to be promoted to the rank of General in the United States Army. She was also the Director of the Walter Reed Army Institute of Nursing.

1989 - The Arsenio Hall Show premiered, it was the first regular scheduled nightly talk show to be hosted by an African-American.

2005 - Senator Barack Obama was sworn into office and became the 5th African-American to serve in the United States Senate, he represented the State of Illinois.

On this Day in History...

January 4th

1893 - Nancy Green, a former slave from Montgomery County, KY., became the first "Aunt Jemima" and the world's first living trademark. She made her debut at the age of fifty-nine, in Chicago, IL., at an exposition where she worked and served pancakes in a booth.

1943 - Illinois Congressman, William L. Dawson became the first African-American Vice Chairman of the Democratic National Committee.

1971 - The Congressional Black Caucus was established. Serving as a Political Organization made up of the African-American members of the United States Congress, it provides awareness and alliances across racial, political and social lines. While race and party affiliation are not official requirements for membership, most of its members have been African-American and most of them Democrats.

1971 - Author, Activist and Professor, Angela Davis was arraigned on murder, kidnapping and conspiracy charges in Marin County, CA. Davis was alleged to have played a role in a courthouse shooting, she was later acquitted.

2007 - Actress, Queen Latifah (Dana Owens) become the first Hip-Hop Artist inducted into the Hollywood Walk of Fame and awarded a star on Hollywood Boulevard..

2018 - Jordan Greenway became the first African-American Hockey Player to ever be listed to a U.S. Olympic Hockey roster. He was a member of the United States Olympic Hockey Team for the Winter Olympics in Pyeongchang.

On this Day in History...

January 5th

1908 - Allensworth, California became the first all African-American township, founded and financed by African-Americans. Created by Colonel Allen Allensworth, the town was built with the intention of establishing a self-sufficient City where African-Americans could create a better life for themselves outside of segregated U.S. society. Today the site is known as "Colonel Allensworth State Historic Park."

1911 - Kappa Alpha Psi Fraternity was founded on the campus of Indiana University.

1948 - Inventor and Botanist, George Washington Carver was commemorated on the U.S. postage stamp. Carver was appointed to Director of Agricultural Research at Tuskegee Institute, where he revolutionized agriculture in the Southern region of the United States, transforming its economy. He famously developed more than 500 uses from peanuts, soybeans and sweet potatoes. He produced such items such as soap, ink, hand lotion, glue, medicines, plastics and adhesives just to name a few. He was commemorated on the stamp once again in 1998.

2007 - Philanthropist, Oprah Winfrey opened "The Oprah Winfrey Leadership Academy for Girls (OWLAG) boarding school in South Africa. The school has transformed the lives of hundreds of students in grades 8-12, providing them with the educational and emotional tools to realize their dreams of pursuing careers in such illustrious fields as medicine, public service and architecture. When Winfrey visits the school, she spends at least a week on campus, conducting fireside chats with each student and teaching what she calls her Life Lessons 101 course.

On this Day in History...

January 6th

1869 - Howard University Law School classes began, the institution became first African-American Law School in the Nation.

1891 - Jazz, an African-American Musical form was born, this new sound originated out of the Blues, Ragtime and Marching Bands in Louisiana. Charles "Buddy" Bolden became the first person to form a Jazz band in New Orleans. He has been called the "Patriarch of Jazz," due to his fierce driving tone, he was known as "King Bolden."

1919 - The first two African-American women in the United States were appointed as Police Officers, Cora I. Parchment, by the New York Police Department and Georgia Ann Robinson, by the Los Angeles Police Department.

1972 - Actress, Dancer, Poet and Civil Rights Activist, Maya Angelou became the first African-American woman to have an Original Screenplay produced, "Georgia, Georgia," which she directed. She published several books of poetry and was credited with a list of plays, movies and television shows spanning over fifty years. She received dozens of awards and more than 50 Honorary Degrees. Angelou was also the first African-American woman to have a Nonfiction book on the best-seller list.

1984 - Robert Nelson C. Nix Jr., became the first African-American Chief Justice of the Pennsylvania Supreme Court. He is also the son of Robert Nelson C. Nix Sr., the first African-American to represent Pennsylvania in the House of Representatives.

On this Day in History...

January 7th

1873 - When the Tennessee Legislature convened, Sampson W. Keeble was elected as the first African-American member of the State House of Representatives.

1890 - Inventor, William Purvis was awarded a U.S. Patent for his invention of the Fountain Pen.

1995 - Atlanta Hawks Head Coach, Lenny Wilkens, became the winningest Coach in National Basketball Association (NBA) history. He won his 939th game as a Head Coach, surpassing the record of Red Auerbach, Legendary Coach of the Boston Celtics, who had 938 career wins. Wilkins retired from coaching in 2005 with 1,332 career victories. As a NBA player, he was a thirteen-time All Star and inducted into the Naismith Memorial Basketball Hall of Fame in 1989.

2002 - Shirley Franklin was sworn in as the first African-American woman Mayor of Atlanta, GA. Throughout her career, Franklin served as the Commissioner of Cultural Affairs under Mayor Maynard Jackson. She was also named Chief Administrative Officer and City Manager under Mayor Andrew Young.

2003 - Associate Justice of the Supreme Court of the United States, Thurgood Marshall was commemorated on the U.S. postage stamp.

2005 - One of the most celebrated Singers of the 20th century, Marian Anderson was commemorated on the U.S. postage stamp. Anderson was also awarded the Presidential Medal of Freedom in 1963 by President John F. Kennedy, a Grammy Lifetime Achievement Award in 1965 and the Congressional Gold Medal in 1977.

On this Day in History...

January 8th

1804 - Lemuel Haynes became the first African-American in the United States to receive an Honorary Degree. Middlebury College in Vermont awarded Haynes a Masters Degree at its second commencement. He was an early anti-slavery advocate, writer and speaker on the topic years before Frederick Douglass. He also advocated against the colonization movement, arguing that people of African descent living in the United States should be entitled to the same rights as others.

1867 - Congress overrides President Andrew Johnson's veto of a bill granting all adult male citizens of the District of Columbia the right to vote, the bill became a law. This was the first law in American history that granted African-American men the right to vote. According to terms of the legislation, every male citizen of the City twenty-one years of age or older has the right to vote.

1927 - Wesley A. Williams became the first African-American Officer in the New York City Fire Department.

1931 - William G. Still became the first African-American to have a symphony performed by a major orchestra, he conducted the Los Angeles Philharmonic and the New York City Opera.

1995 - Hal Jackson became first African-American inducted into the Radio Hall of Fame. In 2003, he was also awarded the Pioneer Award by the Rhythm & Blues Foundation. Throughout Jackson's career, he broke a number of color barriers in radio broadcasting.

1996 - Willie L. Brown was sworn in as the first African-American Mayor of San Francisco, CA.

On this Day in History...

January 9th

1840 - Former slave, Benjamin Bradley became the first person to develop a working model of a Steam Engine for a War Ship. While working at the Annapolis Naval Academy, Bradley was unable to patent his invention, he then sold it and used the proceeds to purchase his freedom.

1866 - (HBCU) Fisk University was founded in Nashville, T.N. The school was named in honor of General Clinton B. Fisk of the Tennessee Freedmen's Bureau, who provided the new institution. The University opened its doors to newly freed slaves and held its first classes. The first students ranged from ages seven to seventy, they had an extraordinary thirst for learning.

1869 - Ebenezer Don Carlos Bassett became the first African-American Diplomat, he was appointed United States Ambassador to Haiti. Prior to his appointment, he was Principal of a Philadelphia, PA., Institute.

1916 - Phi Beta Sigma Fraternity was founded on the campus of Howard University.

1997 - Vernon Baker became the first and only living African-American to receive the United States highest battlefield honor, "The Medal of Honor," for service in World War II. Baker was given the award along with posthumous awards to six other African-American soldiers. The seven men had previously been denied the Medal because they were African-American. Baker received the award because of his heroic service in Italy. He was also awarded the United States second-highest battlefield honor, "The Distinguished Service Cross." Baker has also received the Bronze Star and a Purple Heart awards.

On this Day in History...

January 10th

1946 - Astronomer and Physicist, Walter S. McAfee and his team participated in successfully calculating the speed of the Moon. They sent a radar pulse transmission towards the Moon; two and a half seconds later, they received a faint signal back, proving that transmissions from Earth could cross over vast distances into Outer Space.

1954 - Norma Merrick Sklarek became the first African-American woman registered Architect in the State New York State. In 1962, she then became the first African-American woman Architect licensed in the State of California, she was also the first woman "Fellow" of the American Institute of Architects. In 1985, Sklarek founded her own Architectural Firm, Siegel, Sklarek, Diamond.

1957 - The Southern Christian Leadership Conference (SCLC) was founded. Sixty African-American Ministers and Civil Rights Leaders met in Atlanta, GA., in an effort to replicate the successful strategy and tactics of the recently concluded Montgomery, AL., bus boycott. Dr. Martin Luther King Jr., was chosen as the first President of this new group dedicated to abolishing legalized segregation and ending the disfranchisement of African-American Southerners in a nonviolent manner. The SCLC also addressed the racial issues of war and poverty.

1980 - J. Clay Smith Jr., became the first African-American President of the Federal Bar Association, an organization for Federal Lawyers. In 1981, he was also named him as Interim Chair of the Equal Employment Opportunity Commission.

2007 - Jazz Singer, who was often referred to as the "First Lady of Song" Ella Fitzgerald was commemorated on the U.S. postage stamp.

On this Day in History...

January 11th

1773 - Phillis Wheatley became the first published African-American woman Poet, with her book "Poems on Various Subjects, Religious and Moral." The publication brought her fame both in England and the American Colonies. Figures such as President George Washington praised her work, he personally told her that "The style and manner of your poetry exhibits a striking proof of your great poetical talents."

1909 - Arctic Explorer, Matthew A. Henson became the first African-American to successfully have an expedition to the North Pole. He was an invaluable member of his team, training others on handling the weather and building sledges. Henson was also commemorated on the U.S. postage stamp in 1986.

1954 - Eugene K. Jones became the first Executive Secretary of the National Urban League, he was also one the seven co-founders of Alpha Phi Alpha Fraternity.

1957 - Jackie "Moms" Mabley became the first African-American woman Comedian to have a best selling record. Mabley was one of the most successful entertainers of the "Chitlin Circuit," at the height of her career she was earning $10,000 a week at The Apollo Theater in Harlem, N.Y. She also became known to a wider Caucasian audience, playing Carnegie Hall in 1962. She was billed as "The Funniest Woman in the World," she tackled topics too edgy for most mainstream comics.

1976 - Baseball Legend, Hank Aaron was awarded the 60th NAACP Spingarn Medal for his achievements in Baseball, establishing the "home run" record of "715" and for "Outstanding Sportsmanship." Aaron would go on to hit "755" "home runs" in his career.

On this Day in History...

January 12th

1896 - John Shippen became the first African-American Professional Golf Player to play in the U.S. Open at the age of sixteen. After his debut, Shippen played in five more U.S. Opens, his best finish was a tie for fifth place in 1902.

1939 - Singer and Actress, Ethel Waters became the first African-American Singer to appear on television, she was also the first to star and appear in her own show "The Ethel Waters Show." Waters was the second African-American, after Hattie McDaniel, to be nominated for an Academy Award. She was also the first African-American woman to be nominated for an Emmy Award in 1962.

1948 - The United States Supreme Court decision "Sipuel vs Oklahoma State Board of Regents" required that all State Funded Law Schools must open their doors to African-American Students and all other citizens.

1959 - Motown Records was founded by former Auto-Worker, Berry Gordy Jr., in Detroit, MI. Motown Records would become the most successful record label in history owned and operated by African-Americans. After co-writing hits for Smokey Robinson and Jackie Wilson, Gordy purchased a house at 2648 West Grand Boulevard and began operating Tamla Records (later Incorporated as Motown). The home was named "Hitsville USA," it served not only as a recording studio, but also as the label's headquarters.

1995 - Singer, Songwriter and Record Producer, Al Green was inducted into the Rock & Roll Hall of Fame. Green was best known for recording a series of Soul hit singles in the early 1970's. He also earned a Grammy Lifetime Achievement Award in 2002.

On this Day in History...

January 13th

1869 - The Colored National Labor Union (CNLU) was formed by African-Americans wanting to organize their labor collectively on a national level. Frederick Douglass was elected as its first President.

1913 - Delta Sigma Theta Sorority Incorporated was founded on the campus of Howard University.

1919 - James Wormley Jones became the first African-American FBI Special Agent. Throughout his career, Jones was also a Police Officer with the Washington Metropolitan Police Department and World War I Veteran.

1931 - Known as the "Father of Gospel," Thomas Dorsey founded the first Gospel Choir in the world with Theodore Frye at Chicago's Ebenezer Baptist Church. He established the first music Publishing Firm, "Dorsey Music,"dedicated only to Gospel Music in 1932. Dorsey wrote more than two-thousand Blues and Gospel songs during his lifetime. "Precious Lord, Take My Hand" has been declared one of the most profound expressions of Christian Faith ever published.

1966 - Lucius D. Amerson became the first African-American Sheriff in the South. He was elected to office in Macon County, AL. He was elected to Sheriff the year after the passage of the Voting Rights Act of 1965, which removed many barriers that kept African-Americans from voting.

1990 - L. Douglas Wilder was sworn in as the 66th Governor for the State of Virginia, he became the first African-American U.S. Governor since Reconstruction. Throughout his military career, Wilder also served in the United States Army during the Korean War.

On this Day in History...

January 14th

1754 - Mt. Pisgah African Methodist Episcopal Church in Elsinboro, N.J., was founded. This is the oldest continuously operating African-American Church in the United States. The Church was founded by Rueben Cuff, the son of a former slave who began preaching to a African-American congregation in the early 1700's.

1921 - "Black Swan Records" became the first record company owned and operated by African-Americans. The label was established by Henry Pace, who was an Owner of a music publishing company with W. C. Handy. In spring 1921, Ethel Waters recorded the company's first hit, "Down Home Blues/Oh, Daddy." Based in Harlem, New York, Black Swan Records specialized in Jazz and Blues, during its first six months the company reportedly sold more than half a million records.

1950 - Jackie Robinson signed a one year deal with the Brooklyn Dodgers. The contract guaranteed the thirty-one year-old $35,000, making him the highest paid player in the franchise.

1975 - Attorney and Politician, William Thaddeus "Bill" Coleman Jr., was named the fourth U.S. Secretary of Transportation, he became the second African-American to serve in a United States Cabinet position. As an Attorney, Coleman played a major role in significant civil rights cases.

1976 - Johnnie Mae Gibson became the first African-American woman Agent with the Federal Bureau of Investigation (FBI). Gibson's early undercover work in fugitive, organized crime and political corruption helped her develop an outstanding arrest record and establish a reputation as a highly skilled professional.

On this Day in History...

January 15th

1908 - Alpha Kappa Alpha Sorority became the first African-American Sorority, it was founded on the campus of Howard University.

1929 - Dr. Martin Luther King Jr., Baptist Minister and Activist who became the most visible spokesperson and leader in the civil rights movement from 1954 through 1968, was born on this date. He is best known for his role in the advancement of civil rights using the tactics of nonviolence and civil disobedience based on his Christian beliefs as well as being inspired by the nonviolent activism of Mahatma Gandhi.

1962 - The Chicago Cubs signed John Jordan "Buck" O'Neil as a Coach, making him the first African-American Coach on a Major League Baseball Team. A notable "First-Baseman" in the Negro Leagues, O'Neil served for several years also as a Scout.

1972 - Jerome H. Holland became the first African-American to serve on the Board of Directors for the New York Stock Exchange. Throughout his career, Holland received a Ph.D. from the University of Pennsylvania, he was also appointed as President of Delaware State College. In 1960, he took over as President of Hampton Institute. Nine years later, Holland was named as the Ambassador to Sweden. After serving as a Diplomat, he returned to the United States and served on the boards of eleven major U.S. Corporations.

1998 - Civil Rights Veteran, James Farmer was one of fifteen men and women awarded the Presidential Medal of Freedom by President Clinton. He was the National Director of the Congress of Racial Equality during the 1960's and was one of the most influential Leaders of the Civil Rights Movement throughout its most turbulent decade.

On this Day in History...

January 16th

1930 - Ophelia DeVore-Mitchell became one of the first African-American Models in the United States, she enrolled in the Vogue School of Modeling at the age of seventeen. She modeled for several years before deciding to help other African-American women overcome stereotypes and succeed in the field. In 1948, she started the Ophelia DeVore School of Self-Development and Modeling. She also initiated a fashion column for the Pittsburgh Courier and created a line of cosmetics. In 1959, she began publishing a weekly African-American newspaper in Columbus, GA. During her career, Mitchell served on boards and committees under four Presidents, including the advisory committee on the arts for the Kennedy Center for the Performing Arts.

1979 - Benjamin F. Gibson became the first African-American Federal Judge in the Western District in the State of Michigan.

1983 - Dr. Martin Luther King Jr., Day was signed into Law as an American Federal Holiday marking the birthday of Dr. Martin Luther King Jr., it is observed on the third Monday of January each year, which is around Dr. King's birthday, January 15th. The holiday is similar to holidays set under the Uniform Monday Holiday Act.

1986 - Dr. Martin Luther King, Jr., became the first African-American to have a bronze bust permanently displayed in the halls of the United States Capital Building. The bronze sculpture is 36 inches high on a 66-inch high Belgian black marble base.

1991 - Singer and Songwriter, Wilson Pickett, who was a major figure in the development of American Soul Music, was inducted into the Rock & Roll Hall of Fame.

On this Day in History...

January 17th

1916 - Charles Young became the first African-American Serviceman to become a Colonel in the U.S. Army.

1931 - Actor, James Earl Jones was born, his career has spanned more than sixty years. He has been described as one of America's most distinguished and versatile actors, he has also been considered as one of the Greatest Actors in American History.

1942 - Activist and three-time World Heavyweight Boxing Champion, Cassius Marcellus Clay Jr., (Muhammad Ali) was born in Louisville, Kentucky. He is widely regarded as one of the most significant and celebrated sports figures of the 20th century. Early on in his career, Ali was known as an inspiring, controversial and polarizing figure both inside and outside the ring.

1964 - First Lady of the United States from 2009 to 2017, Michelle Obama was born. She is married to the 44th President of the United States, Barack Obama and she is the first African-American First Lady. She is also the most educated First Lady in American history, she skipped second grade, graduated Salutatorian at her magnet High School and has two Ivy League Degrees from Princeton and Harvard Law School.

1990 - Doo-Wop, Jazz, Soul and R&B group from Detroit, MI., "The Four Tops," were inducted into the Rock & Roll Hall of Fame. The group helped define the City's Motown Sound of the 1960's.

1990 - Vocal group "The Platters," were inducted into the Rock & Roll Hall of Fame. They were one of the most successful groups of the early Rock & Roll Era.

On this Day in History...

January 18th

1888 - Abolitionist, Author and Orator, Frederick Douglass became the first African-American to be nominated as a Presidential Candidate at the Republican Convention, he received one vote.

1966 - President Lyndon B. Johnson appointed Dr. Robert Clifton Weaver as the first African-American Secretary of Housing and Urban Development (H.U.D). Weaver became the first African-American appointed to a U.S. Cabinet-Level Position. H.U.D., was a new agency established by Johnson's Administration.

1975 - Television Sitcom, "The Jeffersons" premiered its first episode, the show was a major success that lasted 11 seasons with 253 episodes. The Jeffersons is one of the longest running sitcoms with an African-American cast, it was the first show to feature an interracial married couple. They became the first interracial couple to kiss on television.

1989 - Singer, Songwriter, Record Producer, Arranger and Talent Scout, Otis Redding was inducted into the Rock & Roll Hall of Fame. He is considered one of the greatest Singers in the history of American Popular Music as well as a seminal Artist in Soul Music and Rhythm & Blues.

1989 - Vocal group, The Temptations were inducted into the Rock & Hall of Fame. The group released a series of successful singles and albums with Motown Records during the 1960's and 1970's.

1989 - Musician and Singer, Stevie Wonder was inducted into the Rock & Roll Hall of Fame. Wonder is considered to be one of the most successful musical performers of the 20th century.

On this Day in History...

January 19th

1969 - The Parks Sausage Company became the first African-American owned company to be publicly owned and traded on the stock market (NASDAQ). In 1951, the company was founded in Baltimore, MD., by Henry G. Parks Jr., a marketing graduate of Ohio State University. Parks Sausage would become an iconic company for its "More Park Sausages Mom, Please" campaign, marking one of the most memorable slogans in advertising history.

1979 - The first two Hip-Hop records were recorded, "King Tim III - Personality Jock," (this song is often cited as the first commercially released Hip-Hop song) by Brooklyn group "the Fatback Band," and "Rapper's Delight," by "The Sugar Hill Gang." Bronx-style Rapping can be traced back to 1976, but was not recorded until 1979. Hip-Hop has evolved into a multi-billion dollar industry worldwide.

1988 - Multitalented woman singing group, "The Supremes" were inducted into the Rock & Roll Hall of Fame. They were a Premier Act of Motown Records during the 1960's. They were the most commercially successful Motown Act and America's most successful vocal group.

1999 - African-American Leader, Human Rights Activist and prominent figure in the Nation of Islam, Malcolm X was commemorated on the U.S. postage stamp.

2004 - Cathy Hughes, who founded the largest African-American owned Broadcasting Company, Radio One, launched the Television Station TV One. The station aired African-American entertainment, lifestyle and scripted shows in more than two-million households.

On this Day in History...

January 20th

1949 - Lionel Hampton became the first African-American Musician to perform at a Presidential Inauguration, for President Harry S. Truman. On April 17, 2002, Hampton's 94th birthday, the U.S. Congress honored him by passing a resolution describing him as one of the all-time great Jazz Musicians.

1953 - Opera Singer and Choral Director, Dorothy Maynor became the first African-American to sing at a Presidential Inauguration, she sang "The Star Spangled Banner" at Dwight D. Eisenhower's swearing-in as President of the United States.

1977 - Patricia R. Harris became the first African-American woman to hold a Cabinet Position. President Jimmy Carter appointed her to U.S. Secretary of Housing and Urban Development. Harris previously served as United States Ambassador to Luxembourg under President Lyndon B. Johnson, which made her the first African-American woman to represent the United States as an Ambassador. Harris was also was commemorated on the U.S. postage stamp in 2002.

2009 - President Barack Obama became the first African-American President of the United States of America. He was sworn in as the 44th President and took the oath of office using the same bible President Abraham Lincoln used when he was sworn in as President during his 1861 inauguration. Obama also became the first African-American to secure the nomination of any major national political party. He was sworn in for a second time on this date in 2013 after being re-elected as President in 2012.

On this Day in History...

January 21st

1987 - Singer, Guitarist, Songwriter and Music Producer, Bo Diddley was inducted into the Rock & Roll Hall of Fame. Diddley played a key role in the transition from the Blues to Rock & Roll, he also influenced many Artists, including "The Beatles" and "Rolling Stones."

1987 - Singer and Songwriter, Aretha Franklin became the first woman ever inducted into the Rock & Roll Hall of Fame. Franklin has won a total of 18 Grammy Awards, she is also one of the best-selling musical Artists of all time, having sold over 75 million records worldwide, she is Known as the Queen of Soul.

1987 - Singer, Songwriter and Record Producer, Marvin Gaye was inducted into the Rock & Roll Hall of Fame. Gaye helped to shape the sound of Motown Records in the 1960's , he was first as an in-house Session Player and later became a Solo Artist with a string of hit songs.

1987 - Blues Singer, Electric Guitarist, Songwriter and Record Producer, B.B. King was inducted into the Rock & Roll Hall of Fame. He reigned as the King of Blues music for more than half a century. Since he began recording in the 1940's, he has released over fifty albums, many of them were classics.

1987 - Singer, Songwriter and Performer, Jackie Wilson was inducted into the Rock & Roll Hall of Fame. Nicknamed "Mr. Excitement," he played an major role in the transition of Rhythm & Blues into Soul. Wilson was considered a master showman and one of the most dynamic and influential Singers and Performers in R&B and Rock & Roll History.

On this Day in History...

January 22nd

1986 - Singer, Musician and one of the pioneers of Rock & Roll Music, Chuck Berry was inducted into the Rock & Roll Hall of Fame. Berry is known as one of the pioneers and the "Father of Rock & Roll."

1986 - Singer, Songwriter, Dancer, Musician and Bandleader, James Brown was inducted into the Rock & Roll Hall of Fame. As a major figure of 20th century Popular Music and Dance, he is often referred to as the "Godfather of Soul." Brown's career that lasted more than five decades, he has influenced the development of several music genres.

1986 - Singer, Songwriter and Composer, Ray Charles, often referred to as "The Genius" was inducted into the Rock & Roll Hall of Fame.

1986 - Singer, Songwriter and Entrepreneur, Sam Cooke was inducted into the Rock & Roll Hall of Fame. Cooke was influential as both a Singer and Composer, he was commonly known as the "King of Soul" for his distinctive vocals and importance within Popular Music.

1986 - Pianist and Singer, Songwriter, Fats Domino was inducted into the Rock & Roll Hall of Fame. Domino was one of the pioneers of Rock & Roll Music. Throughout his career, he who sold more than 65 million records.

1986 - Musician, Songwriter, Singer and Actor, Little Richard (Richard Penniman) was inducted into the Rock & Roll Hall of Fame. His music and charismatic showmanship laid the foundation for Rock & Roll. His music played a key role in the formation of Popular Music genres including Soul and Funk, he also influenced many singers and musicians from Rock, Hip Hop and Rhythm & Blues.

On this Day in History...

January 23rd

1883 - General Surgeon, Dr. Daniel Hale Williams opened Provident Hospital in Chicago, IL., the first interracial facility in the country. This hospital was also one of the first schools to offer nursing for African-American students in the United States. Dr. Williams later became the first Surgeon in the United States to successfully perform an open heart surgery. His patient, James Cornish fully recovered and would go on to live for another 50 years.

1961 - Catherine Britt became the first African-American woman to work at NYU Hospital as a Medical Blood Technician, she was responsible for collecting, labeling and preparing blood, plasma and other components for transfusions in the Operating Room (OR). Britt also interacted with the public by conducting interviews and testing samples to screen potential donors. She personally saved a patient's life abroad, by donating her own blood that was shipped to the Country of Iceland, her blood type matched a patient in desperate need. Britt was an inspiration to her colleagues, she lived her life through faith and was a strong believer in God, she conducted prayer groups with staff and patients. Throughout her career, she continued to serve the citizens of New York City, she became one of the first African-American woman Technicians to work at Coney Island Hospital, Bellevue Hospital, New York Blood Center and Downstate Medical Center. After forty-three years of service, she retired in 2003 and relocated with her family to Garner, N.C.

2001 - Roderick R. Paige became the first African-American as well as the first School Superintendent to serve as the U.S. Secretary of Education.

On this Day in History...

January 24th

1938 - Jack and Jill of America was founded, it was formed by African-American mothers with the idea of bringing together children through educational, social and cultural experiences. Today it has over 230 chapters nationwide, representing over 40,000 family members, it is headquartered in Washington, D.C.

1962 - Jackie Robinson was inducted into the Baseball Hall of Fame. The impact Robinson made on Major League Baseball is one that will be remembered forever. On April 15th each season, every team in the Major League celebrates Jackie Robinson Day in honor of when he truly broke the color barrier in Baseball, becoming the first African-American player in the 20th century to take the field in the Majors.

1972 - Shirley Chisholm became the first African-American candidate for a major party's nomination for President of the United States and the first woman to run for the Democratic Party's Presidential Nomination. In 1968, Chisholm also became the first African-American woman elected to the United States Congress, she represented New York's 12th Congressional District for seven terms, from 1969 to 1983. In 2015, Chisholm was posthumously awarded the Presidential Medal of Freedom by President Barack Obama.

1985 - Los Angeles Mayor, Thomas Bradley was awarded the NAACP Spingarn Medal for becoming a four-term Mayor and overseeing the most successful Summer Olympics in history, which took place in his City in 1984. His 20 years in office marked the longest tenure by any Mayor in the City's history. Bradley's 1973 election made him the second African-American Mayor of a major U.S. City.

On this Day in History...

January 25th

1890 - The National Afro-American League (NAAL) was founded in Chicago, IL., under the leadership of Timothy Thomas Fortune. The focus of the league was to obtain equality, civil rights, education and public accommodations for African-Americans.

1977 - Chuck Berry's song "Johnny B. Goode," and Blind Willie Johnson's 1927 recording, "Dark Was the Night, Cold Was the Ground," were the first songs by African-American recording Artist to be sent out of the solar system. When Voyager I was sent into outer space, it carried a copper phonograph record containing the songs, as well as other musical selections and greetings in over 100 different languages, on the chance that aliens might find it.

1980 - Black Entertainment Television (BET) was launched as the first cable network created for African-American viewers by founder Bob Johnson. Although BET thrived in the 1990's by expanding its viewership and product line, Johnson decided to take the company private in 1998. In 2001, he sold BET to Viacom for $3 billion, making Johnson the first African-American billionaire.

1983 - Michael Jackson's Album "Thriller" became the first to produce five top singles "The Girl is Mine," "Billie Jean," "Beat It," "Wanna Be Startin Somethin," and "Human Nature." The Guinness Book of Records certified his albulm "Thriller," for which Jackson won eight Grammy Awards as the best-selling album to date. Guinness also cited Jackson for winning the most awards (seven) at the American Music Awards in 1984. Michael Jackson began his solo career by acting in the 1977 film, "The Wiz." His enormous record sales and successful concerts earned him the title "King of Pop."

On this Day in History...

January 26th

1939 - George Gibbs became the first African-American to set foot on the continent of Antarctica. He was one of forty U.S. Navy men selected from two thousand applicants. Gibbs he was a member of Admiral Richard Byrd's third expedition to the South Pole from 1939 to 1941. The men sailed on the USS Bear. After a career in the Navy, Gibbs became a civil rights leader in Rochester, New York and helped to organize the local chapter of the NAACP.

1982 - Harold E. Doley Jr., founded Doley Securities, LLC, the oldest African-American owned Investment Banking Firm in the Nation. Doley is the only African-American to have owned a seat on the New York Stock Exchange.

1993 - Mike Espy became the first African-American Secretary of the U.S. Department of Agriculture.

1999 - The International Criminal Police Organization, or Interpol, named Ronald K. Noble to head the organization, making him the first African-American Secretary General. Noble became the highest ranking African-American in the history of law enforcement.

2016 - The Guinness Book of World Records declared that famed Actor, Samuel L. Jackson's films have have generated more than $7.4 billion worldwide at the box office, making him the "Highest-Grossing Actor in History." Jackson has acted in more than 120 films and has been part of the successful Star Wars, Jurassic Park and Marvel franchises. He has also had a successful career as a voice Actor in many animated series and video games.

On this Day in History…

January 27th

1939 - Ethel Waters became the first African-American woman to perform the leading role in a Dramatic Play, "Africana" on Broadway. She made her first public appearance at the age of five, as a Singer in a church program. When she toured with the Broadway Musical "As Thousands Cheer" (1934), she became the first African-American to co-star with Caucasian players below the Mason-Dixon line. Her greatest role came in 1940, when she appeared on stage in "Cabin in the Sky." From 1957 to 1976 she toured with many evangelist and achieved wide recognition for the Gospel Hymn, "His Eye is on the Sparrow."

1961 - Following the successful Russian Satellite Launch, there was pressure on America to send their own into space. Three brilliant African-American women at NASA, Katherine Johnson, Dorothy Vaughan and Mary Jackson served as the brains behind one of the greatest operations in history, the launch of Astronaut, John Glenn into orbit. A stunning achievement that restored the Nation's confidence, turned around the Space Race and galvanized the world. The Motion Picture "Hidden Figures" was released in 2016 to tell their story, it received positive reviews from critics and grossed $236 million worldwide.

1971 - Alan Cedric Page became the first defensive player in the history of the NFL to receive the Most Valuable Player (MVP) Award. Known as the NFL's "Marathon Man," he was the first active NFL player to complete a full 26.2-mile marathon. In his fifteen seasons with the Minnesota Vikings and the Chicago Bears, he never missed a game. Page is a member of both the College Football Hall of Fame (1993) and the Pro Football Hall of Fame (1988). Considered one of the Greatest Defensive Linemen ever to play the game, Page also served as an Associate Justice of the Minnesota Supreme Court.

On this Day in History...

January 28th

1937 - Jazz Legend, Billie "Lady Day" Holiday teamed up with the Artie Shaw Band and toured the country, this was the first time an African-American woman and a Caucasian Band shared the same stage. Jazz Saxophonist, Lester Young nicknamed her "Lady Day." She assumed the name "Billie" from the Movie Star, Billie Dove.

1997 - Benjamin O. Davis Sr., was commemorated on the U.S. postage stamp. In 1940, he was the first African-American to rise through the rank of General in the U.S. Military. His son Benjamin O. Davis Jr., was also the first was the first African-American General Officer in the United States Air Force. He was promoted to Four-Star General by President Bill Clinton in 1998.

1998 - Madam C.J. Walker was commemorated on the U.S. postage stamp, Walker was the inventor of the Hot Comb and a line of African-American Hair Care Products. She was an Entrepreneur, Philanthropist, Political and Social Activist. Her business talent led her to become the first woman in the United States to be a self-made millionaire.

2018 - Singer and Dancer, Tina Turner received the Grammy Lifetime Achievement Award. Turner is one of the world's best-selling recoding Artists of all time, she has been referred to as "The Queen of Rock & Roll." Her combined album and single sales total approximately 200 million copies worldwide. She is noted for her energetic stage presence, powerful vocals and career longevity. According to Guinness Book of World Records, Turner has sold more concert tickets than any other solo performer in history.

On this Day in History...

January 29th

1794 - Richard Allen founded the African Methodist Episcopal Church (AME), the first independent Black Denomination in the United States. Allen was also instrumental in the construction of Bethel Church in Philadelphia, PA., in 1816, it became the Mother Church of the African Methodist Episcopal Church. Elected as First Bishop, Allen focused on organizing a denomination where free African-Americans could worship without racial oppression. He worked to upgrade the social status of the African-American community, organizing Sabbath Schools to teach literacy and promoting national organizations to develop political strategies.

1926 - Attorney, Violette Neatley Anderson became the first African-American woman to practice law before the U.S. Supreme Court.

1963 - Carl T. Roman was named the first African-American Director of the United States Information Agency (USIA), an agency devoted to "Public Diplomacy." President Dwight D. Eisenhower established the agency, which existed from 1953 to 1999.

1993 - Critically acclaimed Author and Professor Emeritus at Princeton University, Toni Morrison became the first African-American to win a Nobel Prize in Literature. Morrison also won the Pulitzer Prize and and the American Book Award in 1988 for Beloved.

2012 - Actress and Author, Quvenzhané Wallis became the youngest Actress ever to receive a nomination for an Academy Award for "Best Actress," for her role as Hushpuppy in the film, "Beasts of the Southern Wild." At the age of nine, she became the first person born in the 21st century nominated for an Academy Award.

On this Day in History...

January 30th

1844 - Richard Theodore Greener became the first African-American graduate of Harvard University. He then took a position as a Professor at the Howard University School of Law. He later served as Dean of Howard Law School from 1878 to 1880. In 1898 Greener was appointed by President William McKinley as General Consul at Bombay, India. Three years later he accepted a post in Vladivostok, Russia. He successfully served as an American representative during the Russo-Japanese War.

1931 - Actress and Contralto Vocalist, Etta Moten Barnett became the first African-American Stars to perform at the White House. She was invited to sing at a White House dinner for President Franklin D. Roosevelt and his guests. In 1933, Barnett also performed in two musical films, "Flying Down to Rio" and "Gold Diggers of 1933."

1977 - The television series "Roots" became the most-watched dramatic show in television history, it aired on ABC as an eight-episode miniseries and 130 million viewers tuned in. Roots received 37 Primetime Emmy Award nominations and won 9, it also won a Golden Globe and a Peabody Award. The series received had unprecedented Nielsen ratings for the finale, which still holds a record as the third highest rated episode for any type of television series and the second most watched overall series finale in U.S. television history. Alex Haley was the first African-American to win a Pulitzer Prize for his book Roots, which the television movie was based. Haley's twelve year venture to track the ancestry of his mothers family led him to Gambia, West Africa where his 4th great-grandfather Kunta Kinte was born. Haley also wrote the Autobiography of Malcolm X in 1964.

On this Day in History...

January 31st

1810 - The African Insurance Company was founded in Philadelphia, PA., it became the first African-American owned insurance company in the United States. The first President was Joseph Randolph, he established several offices in the Philadelphia area. The original purpose of the company, which stayed in business for thirty years, was to provide African-Americans with proper life insurance for final expenses.

1870 - Jefferson F. Long became the first African-American to speak in the House of Representatives as a Congressman. Long was the second African-American member of Congress and the first and only one from the State of Georgia (4th District) during Reconstruction. He was a member to the House of Representatives (41st Congress).

1988 - Professional Football Player, Doug Williams became the first African-American to "Quarterback" a Super Bowl Team. Williams led the Washington Redskins to a 42-10 victory the Denver Broncos in Super Bowl XXII.

1992 - W.E.B. Du Bois was commemorated on the U.S. postage stamp, he is known for being one of the founders of the National Association for the Advancement of Colored People (NAACP) in 1909.

1994 - Actor, Sidney Poitier was inducted into the Hollywood Walk of Fame and awarded a star on Hollywood Boulevard. In 1964, he broke the color barrier in the U.S. Motion-Picture Industry by becoming the first African-American Actor to win an Academy Award for "Best Actor." From 1997 to 2007, he served as the Bahamian Ambassador to Japan. In 2009, Poitier was awarded the Presidential Medal of Freedom, the United States highest civilian honor, by President Barack Obama.

On this Day in History...

February 1st

1865 - Attorney and Abolitionist, John S. Rock, associated with coining the term "Black is Beautiful" became the first African-American Attorney to practice law before the U.S. Supreme Court.

1926 - What is now known as "Black History Month" was first celebrated as "Negro History Week" by Historian, Carter G. Woodson. The Federal Government officially recognized the celebration as Black History Month in conjunction with the 1976 United States Bicentennial Celebration. Woodson chose the month of February to coincide with the birthdays of Abraham Lincoln and Frederick Douglass. He was also commemorated on the U.S. postage stamp on this date in 1984.

1960 - Four African-American College Students sat down at a lunch counter at Woolworth's in Greensboro, N.C., and politely asked for service, their request was refused. When they were asked to leave, they remained in their seats. Their passive resistance and peaceful sit-down helped to ignite a youth-led movement to challenge racial inequality throughout the South.

1978 - Abolitionist and famous "Conductor" of the Underground Railroad, Harriet Tubman was commemorated on the U.S. postage stamp.

1990 - Journalist, Educator and an early Leader in the Civil Rights Movement, Ida B. Wells was commemorated on the U.S. postage stamp. Wells was also one of the founders of the NAACP in 1909.

2002 - Poet, Activist and Novelist, Langston Hughes was commemorated on the U.S. postage stamp, he was one of the earliest innovators of the Art form called "Jazz Poetry." He was also born on this day in 1902.

On this Day in History...

February 2nd

1914 - Genetic Biologist, Academic and Science Writer, Ernest Everett Just became the first African-American awarded the NAACP Spingarn Medal, for his groundbreaking work in cell division and fertilization. Just was also one of the founding members who established the Omega Psi Phi Fraternity on the campus of Howard University.

1948 - President Harry S. Truman sent Congress a special message urging the adoption of a Civil Rights Program, including the creation of a Fair Employment Practices Commission.

1988 - James Weldon Johnson was commemorated on the U.S. postage stamp. Known for his leadership in the NAACP, where he was the Executive Secretary as well as the Operating Officer of the organization. He was appointed under President Theodore Roosevelt as U.S. Consul in Venezuela and Nicaragua. In 1934, he also became the first African-American Professor at New York University.

1989 - U.S. Navy Lieutenant Commander, Evelyn Fields was nominated by President Bill Clinton and confirmed by the Senate to be promoted from Captain to Admiral. She became the first African-American woman to command a Naval Ship. In 1999, Fields was also the first African-American woman Director of the National Oceanic and Atmospheric Administration (NOAA).

2009 - Eric Holder became the 82nd Attorney General of the United States. Serving in the Administration of President Barack Obama, Holder was the first African-American to hold the position of U.S. Attorney General.

On this Day in History...

February 3rd

1623 - William Johnson became the first known African-American child that was Baptized in the United States, he was the son of Isabella and Anthony Johnson of Jamestown, Virginia.

1874 - Blanche K. Bruce became the second African-American elected to the U.S Senate, representing the State of Mississippi. Bruce was born into slavery but escaped as the Civil War began. Years later, he began teaching and founded Missouri's first school for African-American students. He later moved to Mississippi where he held a number of local county positions including Sheriff. While serving as a Senator, Bruce pressed for civil rights not only for African-Americans but also for Native Americans.

1905 - Louisville Western Branch Library became the first Library in the United States to open its doors to African-Americans. When this Kentucky City passed an ordinance in 1902 that created a public library system, some African-American residents challenged the legislation. Activist, Albert E. Meyzeek, began a movement that urged the City's Library Committee to allow African-Americans to have access to the new system. When the new library system opened, its plan called for a branch library for African-American citizens, it was funded by a wealthy Industrialist named, Andrew Carnegie.

1994 - Gospel, R&B, Soul and Pop Singer, Sam Cooke was inducted into the Hollywood Walk of Fame and awarded a star on Hollywood Boulevard. Cooke is considered one of the pioneers and founders of Soul music. He is commonly known as the "King of Soul" for his unmatched vocal abilities and impact and influence on the modern world of music.

On this Day in History...

February 4th

1882 - The Fisk Jubilee Singers, who introduced the Spiritual to the world as an American Art form, became the first African-American Choir to perform at the White House. Their rendition of "Safe in the Arms of Jesus" moved President Chester Arthur to tears. The night before their performance, the singers were denied lodging in every hotel in Washington D.C.

1954 - Civil Rights Activist, Medgar Evers applied for admissions to then segregated "University of Mississippi Law School." When his application was rejected, he became the focus of an NAACP campaign to desegregate the school, a case aided by the United States Supreme Court ruling in the Brown vs. Board of Education case that segregation is unconstitutional. In December of that year, Evers became the NAACP's first Field Officer in Mississippi. He worked for voting rights, economic opportunity, access to public facilities and other changes in the segregated South.

2006 - Warren Moon became the first African-American "Quarterback" inducted into the National Football League Hall of Fame, at the time of his retirement, he held several all-time passing records. He spent the majority of his career with the Houston Oilers, he also played for the Minnesota Vikings, Seattle Seahawks and the Kansas City Chiefs.

2007 - Tony Dungy became the first African-American NFL Head Coach to win the Super Bowl, his Indianapolis Colts defeated the Chicago Bears.

On this Day in History...

February 5th

1760 - Jupiter Hammon became the first known African-American Published Author for the poem, "An Evening Thought: Salvation by Christ with Penitential Cries," published as a broadside.

1785 - Rev. Lemuel Haynes became the first African-American ordained as a Christian Minister in the United States. He was ordained in the Congregational Church, which became the United Church of Christ. Haynes ministered for more than thirty years, drawing people from neighboring communities and hours away. In 2018, the Vermont town of West Rutland honored Haynes the Nation's first ordained African-American Minister with a Historical Landmark Marker.

1913 - Sarah Rector became the first African-American child in the United States to become a millionaire. Born in Indian Territory to Joseph and Rose Rector, their family were members of the Creek Nation. They received a land allotment under the Treaty of 1866 made by the United States with the Five Civilized Tribes. Prior to her parents passing, they leased the land to the Standard Oil Company. As it turned out, they made the right decision, independent oil driller B.B. Jones, produced a "gusher" that brought in 2500 barrels a day. At the age of twelve, Sarah began receiving royalties, then shortly after became a millionaire.

1948 - Journalist, Alice A. Dunnigan became first African-American woman Correspondent to receive White House Credentials as well as the first woman member of the Senate and House of Representatives Press Galleries. Dunnigan was also the first African-American woman reporter to travel with a U.S. President, she traveled with Harry S. Truman's election campaign.

On this Day in History...

February 6th

1978 - Max Robinson became the first African-American Broadcast Network News Anchor in the United States, most notably serving as co-anchor on ABC World News Tonight alongside Frank Reynolds and Peter Jennings. Robinson was also a founder of the National Association of Black Journalists.

1990 - Then Harvard Student and future President of the United States, Barack Obama became the first African-American elected President of the Harvard Law Review.

1993 - Joycelyn Elders became the first African-American and the second woman named Surgeon General of the United States, she was also the Vice Admiral in the Public Health Service Commissioned Corps.

1995 - Walter Payton became the first African-American Team Owner in the Indy Car series. Payton was a "Running Back" who played for the Chicago Bears of the National Football League (NFL) for 13 seasons, he was known around the NFL as "Sweetness." A nine-time Pro Bowl selectee, Payton is remembered as a prolific "Rusher," once holding records for career rushing yards, touchdowns and carries. He was elected into the Pro Football Hall of Fame in 1993 and the College Football Hall of Fame in 1996.

2017 - Actress, Viola Davis became the first African-American woman to earn three Academy Award nominations. She received the Award for "Best Supporting Actress" for her performance opposite Denzel Washington in the film, "Fences." She was previously nominated for "Best Actress" for film, "The Help" in 2012 and "Best Supporting Actress" for the film, "Doubt" in 2009.

On this Day in History...

February 7th

1775 - Prince Hall founded the "Black Freemasonry," known today as Prince Hall Freemasonry. He was an Abolitionist who lobbied for education rights for African-American children and was active in the back-to-Africa movement. Hall formed the African Grand Lodge of North America, he was unanimously elected its Grand Master. Hall was known for his role in creating Black Freemasonry, championing equal education rights and fighting slavery, he was also one of the most influential African-American leaders in the late 1700's.

1867 - (HBCU) Alabama State University was founded in Marion, AL., as a school for African-Americans. The school started as the Lincoln Normal School with $500 raised by nine freed slaves now known as "The Marion Nine," making ASU one of the Nation's oldest institutions of higher education founded for African-Americans.

1982 - Clarence Gaines became the first African-American inducted to the Basketball Hall of Fame as a Coach. He had a forty-seven year career coaching men's College Basketball at Winston-Salem State University in Winston-Salem, NC.

1989 - Ronald H. Brown was elected Chair of the Democratic National Committee, he became the first African-American to head one of the two Major Political Parties.

1992 - Robert Erik Pipkins became the first African-American member of the Olympic Luge Team. He participated in the 1992 Winter Olympics in Albertville, France and the 1994 Winter Olympics in Lillehammer, Norway. He is also the first African-American to compete in a Luge International Competition.

On this Day in History...

February 8th

1960 - Jazz Trumpeter and Singer, Louis Armstrong was inducted into the Hollywood Walk of Fame and awarded a star on Hollywood Boulevard. Armstrong was a foundational influence on Jazz, shifting the music's focus from collective improvisation to solo performers.

1960 - Singer, Actor and Social Activist, Harry Belafonte was inducted into the Hollywood Walk of Fame and awarded a star on Hollywood Boulevard. Belafonte is one of the most successful Pop Singers in history, popularizing the Caribbean Musical Style with an international audience in the 1950's.

1986 - Oprah Winfrey became the first African-American woman to Host a Nationally Syndicated Talk Show. "The Oprah Winfrey Show" was the highest-rated television program of its kind in history, it was nationally syndicated from 1986 to 2011 in Chicago, IL. Known as the "Queen of Media," Winfrey has built a multi-billion dollar media empire and ranked as one of the greatest Philanthropist in American history. She is also the first African-American woman in television and film to own her own production company. Winfrey has been ranked as the most influential woman in the world. In 2013, she was awarded the Presidential Medal of Freedom by President Barack Obama as well as Honorary Doctorate Degrees from Duke and Harvard.

1990 - One of the most celebrated and profound Singers of the 20th century, Marian Anderson was inducted into the Hollywood Walk of Fame and awarded a star on Hollywood Boulevard. Throughout her career, Anderson broke barriers for many African-American musicians.

On this Day in History...

February 9th

1941 - Colonel, Frederick Drew Gregory became the first African-American Astronaut Commander of the Space Shuttle, he was the nephew of famed Dr. Charles Richard Drew, Inventor of the Blood Bank.

1944 - Harry S. McAlpin became the first African-American Correspondent to be admitted to a White House press conference. He was a correspondent for the National Negro Press Association and the Atlanta Daily World.

1956 - Don Newcombe of the Brooklyn Dodgers became the first African-American to win the Cy Young Award as the top Pitcher in Major League Baseball (MLB), in the award's inaugural year.

1995 - Jazz Legend, Benny Carter was inducted into the Hollywood Walk of Fame and awarded a star on Hollywood Boulevard. Carter was a major figure in Jazz for over sixty years. The National Endowment for the Arts honored Carter with its highest honor, the NEA Jazz Masters Award. He was also awarded the Grammy Lifetime Achievement Award and the National Medal of Arts, presented by President Bill Clinton.

1995 - Bernard Anthony Harris Jr., became the first African-American Astronaut to walk in space. He logged over 200 hours in space, completed 129 orbits and traveled over 2.9 million miles. He joined NASA's Johnson Space Center as a Clinical Scientist and Flight Surgeon, he conducted clinical investigations of space adaptation and developed countermeasures for extended duration space flights.

On this Day in History...

February 10th

1943 - "Sister" Rosetta Tharpe became the first African-American to take Gospel music into a secular setting when she performed at the Apollo Theater. She was the first great recording star of Gospel Music and among the first Gospel musicians to appeal to Rhythm & Blues and Rock & Roll audiences. Tharpe was later referred to as "the Original Soul Sister" and "the Godmother of Rock & Roll."

1947 - Nathaniel and Arthur Bronner, with the help of their sister, Emma Bronner, started "Bronner Bros." in Atlanta GA., as a way to teach Cosmetology at the local YMCA. About 300 people attended the first show, as the attendance grew, it continued to move to larger venues. In 1967, Bronner Bros., signed a contract with the new Hyatt Regency Hotel and the show was held there annually for the next twenty years. During this time, the Bronners secured a number of popular guest speakers, including Dr. Martin Luther King, Jr., Jackie Robinson, Dick Gregory and Dr. Benjamin Mays.

1966 - Economist and Educator, Andrew Brimmer was appointed by President Lyndon B. Johnson to serve as the first African-American Governor of the Federal Reserve Board.

1973 - Margaret A. Haywood became the first woman to head the United Church of Christ, she was also the first African-American woman to lead a major religious denomination in the United States.

1974 - The single largest donation from an African-American organization was the sum of $132,000 donated by Links Inc., to the United Negro College Fund.

On this Day in History...

February 11th

1641 - Mathias De Sousa, an African indentured servant who came from England with Lord Baltimore was elected to Maryland's General Assembly. He was the only African-American in history to serve in the Colonial Maryland Legislature as well as sit in any legislative body in what would become the United States.

1935 - Mary McLeod Bethune was awarded the NAACP's Spingarn Medal for her outstanding leadership and service to education. She was founder and President of Bethune-Cookman College.

1958 - Ruth C. Taylor became the first African-American Flight Attendant, she was selected from 800 applicants. During her career, she broke through racial barriers and discrimination. At age of twenty-five, Taylor was hired by Mohawk Airlines, she was assigned to travel between New York, Massachusetts and Michigan.

1990 - South Africa's Nationalist Leader, Nelson Mandela was released from prison after twenty-seven years. In 1994, he was elected President of South Africa. His administration focused on dismantling the legacy of apartheid by tackling institutionalized racism and fostering racial reconciliation.

2009 - Lisa Jackson became the first African-American woman Administrator of the Environmental Protection Agency (EPA). As the head of the the Environmental Protection Agency, Jackson was responsible for enforcing the Nation's Clean Air and Clean Water Acts, as well as numerous other environmental statutes. Jackson was nominated by President Barack Obama and confirmed by the U.S. Senate.

On this Day in History...

February 12th

1865 - Henry Highland Garnet was an African-American Abolitionist, Minister, Educator and Orator. Having escaped with his family as a child from slavery in Maryland, he grew up in New York City. Garnet became the first African-American to preach a sermon in the U.S. Capitol, he delivered a memorial sermon on the abolishment of slavery at services in the House of Representatives.

1900 - James Weldon Johnson wrote the lyrics and his brother John Johnson composed the music for the song, "Lift Every Voice and Sing" in celebration of the birthday of President Abraham Lincoln. The song became immensely popular in the African-American community and became known as the "Black National Anthem."

1909 - The National Association for the Advancement of Colored People (NAACP) was founded. The call for the organizational meeting was issued on 100th anniversary of President Abraham Lincoln's birth.

1945 - Olivia J. Hooker became the first African-American woman to enter the U.S. Coast Guard, she became a Semper Paratus Always Ready (SPAR), a member of the United States Coast Guard Women's Reserve during World War II. She earned the Yeoman, Second Class rank during her service. For her years of service, Hooker has two Coast Guard buildings named in her honor, she later went on to be a Psychologist and a Professor at Fordham University. Hooker was a survivor of the Tulsa Massacre of Black Wall Street of 1921, she was six years old at the time. She later became a founder of the Tulsa Race Riot Commission in hopes of demanding reparations for the riot's survivors. President Barack Obama has called Hooker an inspiration.

On this Day in History...

February 13th

1863 - Robert E. Smalls of Charleston, S.C., became the first and only African-American to be commissioned a Captain in the U.S. Navy during the Civil War. In 1875, he was also elected as a member of the the U.S. House of Representatives from South Carolina's 5th District.

1870 - (HBCU) Allen University was founded in Columbia S.C., by the African Methodist Episcopal Church. Five years after the American Civil War, there was a significant expansion of the African Methodist Episcopal Church in the former Confederate States. Allen University grew out of the church's desire to educate newly freed slaves and to ensure a well-trained clergy for the African Methodist Episcopal Church.

1920 - Andrew "Rube" Foster organized the first successful African-American Professional Baseball League, the National Association of Professional Baseball Clubs, usually called the Negro National League. Foster, a former Pitcher, was known as the "Father of the Negro Leagues." In 1981, he was inducted to the National Baseball Hall of Fame. In 2001, a set of two U.S. postage stamps bearing the images of Negro Leagues Baseball and Rube Foster were issued.

1923 - Professional Basketball Team, "The Renaissance" was organized in Harlem, N.Y. All of the players on the team were African-American and they were one of the most dominant Basketball Teams in history. During the 1932-33 regular season, they had a record of 120-8 which included an 88 game consecutive win streak. In 1939, they won their first Professional Basketball Championship when they beat the Oshkosh All-Stars in the World Professional Basketball Tournament in Chicago, IL.

On this Day in History...

February 14th

1845 - Master Juba (William Henry Lane) became the first African-American Dance Star. He took his stage name from the African Dance, "The Juba." Lane won the "King of All Dancers" Title after three challenge contests. He toured with three Caucasian minstrels, receiving top billing and garnered acclaim for his 1848 performance in London. He is credited as one of the most influential figures in the creation of American Tap Dance.

1920 - Mamie Smith became the first African-American woman to make a Record. She recorded "You Can't Keep a Good Man Down" and "This Thing Called Love." Smith was a vaudeville singer, dancer, pianist and actress. As a Vaudeville Singer she performed in various styles, including Jazz and Blues. She also recorded, "It's Right Here for You" and "Crazy Blues" which was the first Blues song ever recorded. "Crazy Blues" sold 790,000 copies in the first year.

1965 - Emlen "The Gremlin" Tunnel became the first African-American Player/Coach in the National Football League (NFL), he played professionally for the New York Giants. Tunnel was also the first African-American inducted into the Pro Football Hall of Fame.

1967 - Abolitionist, Author, Orator and perhaps the most influential man of the 19th century, Frederick Douglass was commemorated on the U.S. postage stamp.

1993 - Rodney Earl Slater became the first African-American U.S. Secretary of Transportation. Slater was also was the first African-American Federal Highway Administrator.

On this Day in History...

February 15th

1869 - Fanny Jackson Coppin became the first African-American woman School Principal in the United States. She served as Principal of the Institute for Colored Youth (now Cheyney University of Pennsylvania). Along with being an educator, Copping was a missionary and a life long advocate for higher education for women.

1873 - Bishop, Patrick Healy became President of Georgetown University, making him the first African-American to preside over a predominately Caucasian University. He was also the first African-American to become a Jesuit Priest.

1913 - Bert Williams became the first African-American Actor to Star in a Motion Picture, he played the lead role in the film, "Darktown Jubilee,"

1920 - The first African-American Heavyweight Champion, Jack Johnson opened the "Club Deluxe" in Harlem, NYC. Two years later, a local gangster named Owney Madden bought the club and changed the name to the "Cotton Club." The club featured many popular African-American entertainers of the era, including Duke Ellington, Louis Armstrong, Count Basie, Ethel Waters, Billie Holiday and Lena Horne.

1980 - Benjamin Banneker was commemorated on the U.S postal stamp. Banneker invented the first ever clock in the United States at the age of twenty-one. In 1791, President George Washington asked Banneker to survey and design the plans for the layout of Washington D.C., many of the buildings and monuments he designed still exist today. Banneker was also a Scientist, Author and he became the first African-American to create a popular series of Almanacs.

On this Day in History...

February 16th

1653 - African-American workers built a wall across Manhattan Island to protect against a British or Pirate invasion. The site of the wall is now Wall Street, an eight-block-long street running roughly northwest to southeast from Broadway to South Street in New York City.

1817 - Francis Johnson became the first African-American Bandleader and Composer to publish sheet music. In 1837, he also became the first American to perform before royalty, he appeared before Queen Victoria in England.

1941 - Jacob Lawrence Jr., became the first African-American Artist that was represented by a New York City Gallery, helping to set a standard for future generations of African-American Artists. His work is characterized by small-scale genre paintings of African-Americans and their political and social struggles.

2012 - Antron Brown became the first African-American Drag Racer to win the the Top Fuel Dragsters Championship. Top Fuel Dragsters are the fastest accelerating racing cars in the world, with competitors reaching speeds of 335 miles per hour and finishing at 1,000 feet. Brown has also won the Championships in in 2015 and 2016.

2018 - The Motion Picture "Black Panther" was released. Shortly after, it became the highest grossing Comic Book Superhero Movie in film history, it was also the first movie with a predominately African-American cast to earn $1 billion worldwide. Ryan Coogler became the second African-American Director of a $1 billion grossing movie, joining F. Gary Gray, who was the first. Gray directed the film, "The Fate of the Furious," which was released in 2017.

On this Day in History...

February 17th

1877 - President Rutherford B. Hayes appointed Frederick Douglass as the first African-American U.S. Marshal. His jurisdiction was the District of Columbia. While occupying this position, Douglass continued to strengthened the hold of African-American civil servants in government positions in the Nation's Capital.

1919 - Author and Film Director, Oscar Micheaux released his first film, "The Homesteader," in Chicago, IL. Over the next four decades, Micheaux produced and directed 24 silent films and 19 sound films, making him the most prolific African-American Filmmaker of the 20th century.

1927 - The Harlem Globetrotters Basketball Team was founded in Chicago, IL. The original team was called the "Savoy Big Five," named after Chicago's famous Savoy Ballroom, where they played many of their early games. The Harlem Globetrotters have played in over 115 countries for more than 120 million fans. They have scored over 20,000 victories, with only 332 losses. They surpass every other team in the history of sports for number of games played. Today they are best known for their wildly-entertaining comedic routines and ball-handling skills on the court and of course the famous song, "Sweet Georgia Brown."

2000 - The White House displayed the bust of Civil Rights Leader Dr. Martin Luther King Jr., in commemoration of Black History Month. This marked the first time that an image of an African-American person was displayed in public spaces of the White House. The bronze bust by Artist, Charles Austin was on extended loan from the Smithsonian Institution's National Portrait Gallery, he sculpted the bust in 1970.

On this Day in History...

February 18th

1867 - (HBCU) Morehouse College was founded. Originally established as Augusta Theological Institute in the basement of Springfield Baptist Church in Augusta, GA., which is the oldest independent African-American Church in the United States. The school's primary purpose was to prepare African-American men for ministry and teaching. Morehouse College is currently located on a 66-acre campus in Atlanta, GA., it has an international reputation for producing leaders who have influenced national and world history.

1975 - Activist, Attorney and Civil Rights Leader, Margaret Bush Wilson became the first African-American woman to Chair the National Association for the Advancement of Colored Peoples (NAACP) Board of Directors.

1984 - Air Atlanta became the first major Airline in the United States that was owned and operated by African-Americans, it was considered a major success for an African-American business. The Airline's founder, Michael Hollis, then age twenty-nine, raised over $45 million to launch the Airline, he raised more start-up capital for his fledgling Airline than any other African-American Entrepreneur in American history. The company had 400 employees and a fleet of five Boeing 727-100 jets, it serviced Atlanta, New York, Miami and Memphis.

2006 - Shani Davis became the first African-American to win a gold medal in an individual event in the Winter Olympics. He was also the first African-American male to win a gold medal when he competed in the men's 1,000-meter Speed Skating Championship in the 2006 Winter Olympic Games in Turino, Italy.

On this Day in History...

February 19th

1934 - After operating under a number of names, the Apollo Theater opened in Harlem, NYC. Over the years, the Apollo became the most famous performance venue associated with African-American Entertainers in the world. In 1983, both the interior and exterior of the building were designated as New York City Landmarks. The building was also added to the National Register of Historic Places, it is estimated that 1.3 million people visit the Apollo Theater each year.

1957 - Dorothy Height was appointed President of the National Council of Negro Women, a position she held for forty-one years. In 1937, Height met Mary McLeod Bethune, Founder and President of the National Council of Negro Women (NCNW), who later became her mentor. Height led the NCNW during the Civil Rights Era of the 1950's and 1960's. As President, she helped to organize "The March on Washington" in 1963. She has worked with every major civil rights leader of the period, including Dr. Martin Luther King, Jr., Roy Wilkins, Whitney Young, and A. Philip Randolph. She also personally encouraged President Dwight Eisenhower to desegregate public schools and urged President Lyndon B. Johnson to appoint African-American women into Governmental Positions.

1998 - Considered one of the most influential musicians of the 20th century, Miles Davis was inducted into the Hollywood Walk of Fame and awarded a star on Hollywood Boulevard. Davis adopted a variety of musical directions in his fifty year career which kept him at the forefront of a number of major stylistic developments in Jazz.

On this Day in History...

February 20th

1865 - The North Carolina General Assembly incorporated the town of Princeville, NC. Princeville is the oldest town incorporated by African-Americans in the United States, it was established by freed slaves after the Civil War.

1966 - James T. Whitehead Jr., became the first African-American to pilot a U-2 spy plane. In 1967, he became a Flight Engineer for TWA Airlines located at John F. Kennedy International Airport in New York.

1985 - Businessman, Reginald F. Lewis orchestrated the leveraged buyout of Beatrice Foods, he became the first African-American CEO of a billion dollar corporation. During his career, Lewis also desired to support a Museum of African-American Culture. In 2005, "The Reginald F. Lewis Museum of Maryland African-American History & Culture" opened in Baltimore with the support of a $5 million grant from his foundation.

1987 - Jean Baptiste Pointe DuSable was commemorated on the U.S. postage stamp. Regarded as the first permanent resident of what later became Chicago, Illinois, he is known as the "Founder of Chicago." A school, museum, harbor, park and bridge have all been named in his honor. The place where he settled near the mouth of the Chicago River around the 1780's is recognized as a National Historic Landmark, now located in Pioneer Court.

2002 - Vonetta Flowers became the first African-American to win a gold medal in the Winter Olympics. Flowers competed in the two-woman bobsled event at the Winter games in Salt Lake City, Utah..

On this Day in History...

February 21st

1949 - Jazz Trumpeter and Singer, Louis Armstrong became the first African-American to preside over the New Orleans Mardi Gras. His lifelong dream came true when he was selected Mardi Gras King of the Zulu Social Aid and Pleasure Club, that led to his appearance on the cover of Time Magazine. Armstrong was recognized as one of the most influential Jazz Artists of the 20th century. He was a superb showman known for his gravelly and growling vocal style.

1969 - Edith Jacqueline Ingram-Grant became the first African-American woman Judge in the State of the Georgia.

1972 - Los Angeles Lakers "Center" Wilt Chamberlain became the first National Basketball Association (NBA) player to score over 30,000 points during his career.

1974 - The Black Filmmakers Hall of Fame, Inc. (BFHFI), was founded in Oakland, CA., it supports and promotes filmmaking by people of color and preserves the contributions by African-American Artists both before and behind the camera. The Hall of Fame also sponsors advance screenings of films and "The Oscar Micheaux Award," (regarded as the first major African-American feature filmmaker in the United States), the ceremony is held each February in Oakland.

1990 - Jazz Pianist and Vocalist, Nat King Cole was awarded the Grammy Lifetime Achievement Award at the 32nd Annual Grammy Awards.

1990 - Jazz Trumpeter and Composer, Miles Davis was awarded the Grammy Lifetime Achievement Award at the 32nd Annual Grammy Awards.

On this Day in History...

February 22nd

1778 - Boston Businessman, Paul Cuffe along with his brother John Cuffe both refused to pay taxes, due to African-Americans not being allowed to vote. He petitioned the council of Bristol County, Massachusetts to end such taxation without representation. The petition was denied, but his suit was one of the influences that led the Legislature in 1783 to grant voting rights to all free male citizens of the state.

1865 - Martin R. Delany was appointed to a Major in the Union Army by President Abraham Lincoln, making him the highest ranking African-American Officer during the Civil War.

1983 - Songwriter, Producer and Record Executive, Smokey Robinson was inducted into the Hollywood Walk of Fame and awarded a star on Hollywood Boulevard. Robinson was the founder and front man of the Motown vocal group "The Miracles."

1989 - Singer, Dancer and Actress, Lena Horne was awarded the Grammy Lifetime Achievement Award at the 31st Annual Grammy Awards.

2013 - The Harriet Tubman Underground Railroad National Monument site in Church Creek, MD., was proclaimed as a National Monument by President Barack Obama, as part of the American Antiquities Act. Tubman is the Underground Railroad's best known Conductor, she repeatedly risked her life to guide nearly 70 enslaved people north to new lives of freedom. This historical park preserves the same landscapes that Tubman used to carry herself and others away from slavery. The park became one the first of its kind in the United States to honor an African-American woman.

On this Day in History...

February 23rd

1603 - Mathieu Da Costa, a free Seaman and Explorer became the first African-American to reach Canada and visit the region of Port Royal in Nova Scotia. He guided the French through parts of Canada and the Lake Champlain region of what is now New York State.

1869 - Congress sends the Fifteenth Amendment of the Constitution to the States for approval. The Amendment guarantees all African-American males the right to vote.

1878 - Marie S. Williams became the first African-American woman Entertainer to perform at the White House. She presented a musical program for President Rutherford B. Hayes and assembled guests.

1970 - Joseph L. Searles III became the first African-American Trader on the New York Stock Exchange (NYSE) floor.

1973 - Actor, Screenwriter, Director and Composer, Clarence Muse was inducted in the Black Filmmakers Hall of Fame. Muse was also the first African-American to Star in a film. He appeared in more than 150 movies over the span of a fifty-year career.

2000 - Regarded as one of the most influential recording Artists of the 20th century, Legendary Singer and Songwriter, Nina Simone was inducted into the Grammy Hall of Fame. Simone was also an Activist and an active member in the civil rights movement. She employed a broad range of musical styles including Classical, Jazz, Blues, Folk, R&B, Gospel and Pop. In 2018, she was inducted into the Rock & Roll Hall of Fame.

On this Day in History...

February 24th

1837 - (HBCU) Cheyney University of Pennsylvania was founded, it is the Nation's first Historically Black University. The founding of Cheyney University was made possible by Richard Humphreys, a Quaker Philanthropist who bequeathed $10,000, one tenth of his estate, to design and establish a school to educate the descendants of the African Ancestry. Having witnessed the struggles of African-Americans competing unsuccessfully for jobs, he became interested in their plight.

1966 - Emmett "Ash" Ashford became the first African-American Umpire in Major League Baseball. Ashford went on to umpire both an All-Star Game (1967) and a World Series (1970), before the American League's mandatory age retirement policy caught up with him at age of fifty-five.

1980 - Willie Davenport and Jeff Gadley became the first two African-American Athletes to participate in the Winter Olympics on the U.S. Bobsled Team. Both Athletes were Track and Field stars, Davenport also competed in hurdles at the 1964, 1968, 1972 and 1976 Summer Olympics Games. He is the only African-American Athlete to compete in both the Summer and Winter Olympics.

1987 - Singer, Songwriter and Musician, Ray Charles was awarded the Grammy Lifetime Achievement Award at the 29th Annual Grammy Awards.

1987 - Jazz Musician, Singer and Songwriter, Billie Holiday was awarded the Grammy Lifetime Achievement Award at the 29th Annual Grammy Awards.

On this Day in History...

February 25th

1870 - Hiram Revels became the first African-American elected to serve in the United States Senate, he represented the State of Mississippi. During reconstruction, he became an outspoken opponent to racial segregation. Although Revels served in the Senate for just a year, he broke new ground for African-Americans in politics.

1964 - Cassius Clay defeated Sonny Liston in the 7th round and became the Heavyweight Champion of the World at the age of twenty-two. Liston was the most intimidating fighter of his day, Clay began taunting and provoking Liston almost immediately after the two agreed to fight. He purchased a bus and had it emblazoned with the words "Liston Must Go In Eight." On the day of the contract signing, he drove it to Liston's home in Denver, waking the champion up at 3:00 a.m., shouting, "Come on out of there, I'm gonna whip you now." Their second fight was in May 1965, which Clay won with a first-round knockout.

1987 - Singer, Songwriter, Dancer, Musician, Producer and Bandleader, James Brown was awarded the Grammy Lifetime Achievement Award at the 29th Annual Grammy Awards.

1987 - Rock Guitarist, Singer and Songwriter, Jimi Hendrix was awarded the Grammy Lifetime Achievement Award at the 29th Annual Grammy Awards.

2007 - Forest Whitaker became the fourth African-American Actor to receive an Academy Award for "Best Actor" for the film, "The Last King of Scotland."

On this Day in History...

February 26th

1964 - Heavyweight Champion of the World, Cassius Clay changed his name to Muhammad Ali, as he accepted Islam as his new religion. Muhammad Ali's conversion to Islam in many ways defined his career and legacy as a fighter with conviction. He went on to become an icon for Muslim's worldwide.

1966 - Actress, Nichelle Nichols became one of the first African-American woman characters on television that was not portrayed as a Servant, playing the groundbreaking role as Communications Officer Lieutenant Uhura aboard the USS Enterprise in the television series "Star Trek." During the first year of the series, Nichols was tempted to leave the show in order to pursue a Broadway career, however, a conversation with Dr. Martin Luther King Jr., changed her mind. She has said that King personally encouraged her to stay on the show, telling her that he was a big fan of Star Trek. He told her "do not give up, because you are a role model for all African-American children and young women across the Country."

2009 - Composer, Pianist and Jazz Musician, Duke Ellington was prominently featured on a U.S. coin. The quarter he was featured on was released into circulation representing the District of Columbia.

2011 - Sanford Carson became a Master Mechanic for the National Association for Stock Car Auto Racing (NASCAR) in Charlotte, NC. He serves as a Technician who could perform a wide variety of repairs and maintenance related work on stock cars used in NASCAR Races. Earlier in his career, he joined the Trucking Industry, he was a 2nd generation member of an elite organization "The Teamsters," who championed for freight drivers and warehouse workers.

On this Day in History...

February 27th

1830 - African-American Delegates from New York, Pennsylvania, Maryland, Delaware and Virginia met in Philadelphia in the first of a series of National Negro Conventions to devise ways to challenge slavery in the South and racial discrimination in the North.

1926 - Theodore "Tiger" Flowers became the first African-American Middleweight Champion of the World, he defeated Harry Greb in 15 rounds and won the title in New York City.

1988 - Figure Skater, Debi Thomas became the first African-American to win a medal (bronze) at the Winter Olympic Games in Calgary, Canada. Thomas was also the first African-American woman to hold the United States and World Figure Skating Championships.

2002 - Jazz Pianist and Bandleader, Count Basie was awarded the Grammy Lifetime Achievement Award at the 44th Annual Grammy Awards.

2002 - Singer, Songwriter and Record Producer, Al Green was awarded the Grammy Lifetime Achievement Award at the 44th Annual Grammy Awards.

2005 - Actor, Morgan Freeman won an Academy Award for "Best Supporting Actor" for the film, "Million Dollar Baby." Freeman is a five-time Academy Award nominee and five-time Golden Globe Award nominee, he has also won the Golden Globe Award for "Best Actor" for the 1989 film, "Driving Miss Daisy."

2005 - Actor and Comedian, Jamie Foxx became the third African-American Actor to receive an Academy Award for "Best Actor" for the film, "Ray." Foxx is also the first African-American Actor to receive two Academy Award nominations in the same year.

On this Day in History...

February 28th

1768 - Wentworth Cheswell became the first known African-American in the United States to be elected to public office, he was Town Constable in Newmarket, New Hampshire. His grandfather Richard was the first African-American in New Hampshire to own land. A deed shows that Richard purchased 20-acres in 1717.

1962 - Lieutenant Commander, Samuel Lee Gravely Jr., became the first African-American to command a U.S. Warship, he oversaw all operations on 100 Navy ships. He was also in command of 60,000 Sailors and Marines stationed at Pearl Harbor, Hawaii.

1977 - Drew S. Days III became the first African-American Director of the Justice Department's Civil Rights Division.

1984 - The "King of Rock & Roll," Chuck Berry was awarded the Grammy Lifetime Achievement Award at the 26th Annual Grammy Awards.

1984 - Jazz Saxophonist and Composer, Charlie Parker was awarded the Grammy Lifetime Achievement Award at the 26th Annual Grammy Awards.

2015 - Loretta Lynch succeeded Eric Holder and became the 83rd Attorney General of the United States. Serving in the Administration of President Barack Obama, Lynch was the second African-American to hold the position of U.S. Attorney General. She previously held the position for United States Attorney for the Eastern District of New York under both the Clinton and Obama Administrations. As U.S. Attorney, she oversaw Federal Prosecutions in Brooklyn and Queens.

On this Day in History...

February 29th

1915 - "Jelly Roll Blues," by Jelly Roll Morton (Ferdinand Joseph La Menthe) became the first published Jazz Arrangement. Morton was the first true Jazz Composer, he was also the first to notate his Jazz Arrangements.

1940 - Hattie McDaniel became the first African-American to receive an Academy Award, she won "Best Supporting Actress" for her role in the film, "Gone with the Wind." McDaniel appeared in over 300 films during her career. In addition to Acting, she was a radio performer as well as a television star, she was the first African-American woman to sing on radio in the United States. McDaniel has two stars on the Hollywood Walk of Fame, one for her contributions to radio and one for Acting in motion pictures. In 1975, she was inducted into the Black Filmmakers Hall of Fame and in 2006, she became the first African-American Oscar winner honored with a US postage stamp.

1961 - Dr. Samuel L. Kountz became the first African-American in the United States to perform the first successful Kidney Transplant between humans who were not identical twins. He later developed the prototype for the Belzer Kidney Perfusion Machine, a device that can preserve kidneys for up to 50 hours from the time they are taken from a donor's body. This device is now standard equipment in hospitals and research laboratories around the world. In 1975, Dr. Kountz went on "The Today Show" to perform the first live kidney transplant on television, he inspired 20,000 viewers to offer their kidneys to patients who needed them. In addition, his groundbreaking research in the area of tissue typing helped improve the results of kidney transplantation and led to the increased use of kidneys from unrelated donors.

On this Day in History...

March 1st

1871 -   President Ulysses S. Grant appointed James M. Turner as the first African-American Minister Resident and Consul General to the Country of Liberia. In 1866, he was also appointed to teach in Missouri's first tax supported school for African-Americans.

1948 -   William Clarence "Billie" Eckstine became the first African-American Ballad Singer to become successful as a solo Artist independent of a Dance Band. When he recorded such Pop songs as "I Apologize" and "My Foolish Heart," his deep-voice vibrato caused teenagers at every concert to swoon. Eckstine was perhaps the first African-American male Pop idol. He began his singing career with Jazz Orchestras.

1991 -   Formula One Race Car Driver, Willie T. Ribbs became the first African-American to qualify for the Indianapolis 500, he was also the first African-American Driver in NASCAR's Craftsman Truck Series.

1994 -   Rock & Roll Singer and Songwriter, Frankie Lymon was inducted into the Hollywood Walk of Fame and awarded a star on Hollywood Boulevard. Lymon is best known as the lead singer of the New York City-based group "The Teenagers." The film, "Why do fools fall in Love" starring Actor, Larenz Tate opened in 1998, tells the Frankie Lymon story.

1994 -   Singer, Songwriter and Record Producer, Stevie Wonder was inducted into the Hollywood Walk of Fame and awarded a star on Hollywood Boulevard. Wonder has recorded more than 30 U.S. Top Ten hits and received 25 Grammy Awards, he is one of the most-awarded male solo Artists in history and has sold over 100 million records worldwide.

On this Day in History...

March 2nd

1867 - (HBCU) Howard University was founded in Washington D.C. The school was named in honor of General Oliver Howard, a Freedman's Bureau leader and Civil War Hero. In 1874, he served as President of the University. Howard was also instrumental in the establishment of Lincoln Memorial University in the mountains of Tennessee.

1872 - Charlotte E. Ray became the first African-American woman in the United States to become an Attorney, she was also the first woman admitted to practice before the Supreme Court of the District of Columbia. Ray opened her own Law Office and ran advertisements in a newspaper ran by Frederick Douglass. Ray was involved in the women's suffrage movement and joined the newly formed organization "National Association of Colored Women."

1962 - Wilt Chamberlain set the single-game scoring record in the National Basketball Association (NBA) by scoring 100 points for the Philadelphia Warriors, in a 169-147 win over the New York Knicks. Chamberlain is the only player in history to score 100 points in a single NBA game or average more than 40 and 50 points in a season. He was also the first professional player to score more than 4,000 points in a single season. Chamberlain was inducted into the Naismith Memorial Basketball Hall of Fame in 1978 and chosen as one of the 50 greatest players in NBA History in 1996.

1988 - DJ Jazzy Jeff and the Fresh Prince became the first Hip-Hop group to win a Grammy Award for the song "Parents Just Don't Understand." Jeff Townes and Will Smith teamed up in 1987 to form the group. Smith continued to have a successful career in television and movies.

On this Day in History...

March 3rd

1821 - Inventor, Thomas Jennings became the first African-American man to receive a U.S. patent. Jennings was a successful tailor from New York City and he invented "Dry Cleaning." He was an active Abolitionist and the founder of the Legal Rights Association. Jennings was also inducted into the National Inventors Hall of Fame in 2015.

1891 - (HBCU) Elizabeth City State University was founded in Elizabeth City, N.C. Hugh Cale, an African-American Representative in the North Carolina General Assembly sponsored House Bill 383, which established a school for training African-American teachers to teach in the common schools of North Carolina. The bill passed and the origin of Elizabeth City State University was born.

1954 - Jesse Ernest Wilkins Sr., was appointed as the first African-American Assistant Secretary of Labor, President Dwight D. Eisenhower appointed him to this sub-cabinet post. Wilkins was the top-ranking African-American in the Executive Branch at the time. He was also the first African-American Leader of a U.S. Delegation to the International Labor Organization meetings held in Cuba and in Europe.

2016 - Singer, Songwriter and Record Producer, Lionel Richie received the Songwriters Hall of Fame's highest honor, the Johnny Mercer Award. Richie began his career as a member of the Funk and Soul Band "The Commodores." After launching his solo career in 1982, he has sold over 100 million records worldwide, making him one of the world's best-selling Artists of all time. He is also a five-time Grammy Award winner.

On this Day in History...

March 4th

1871 - Robert C. DeLarge was elected to the (42nd) Congress, as a member of the U.S. House of Representatives from South Carolina's 2nd District.

1871 - Benjamin S. Turner was elected to the (42nd) Congress, as a member of the U.S. House of Representatives from Alabama's 1st District.

1871 - Robert B. Elliott was elected to the (42nd - 43rd) Congresses, as a member of the U.S. House of Representatives from South Carolina's 3rd District.

1871 - Josiah Walls was elected to the (42nd - 44th) Congresses, as a member of the U.S. House of Representatives from Florida's 2nd District.

1873 - John R. Lynch was elected to the (43rd) Congress, as a member of the U.S. House of Representatives from Mississippi's 6th District.

1873 - Alonzo J. Ransier was elected to the (43rd) Congress, as a member of the U.S. House of Representatives from South Carolina's 2nd District.

1873 - James T. Rapier was elected to the (43rd) Congress, as a member of the U.S. House of Representatives from Alabama's 2nd District.

1873 - Richard H. Cain was elected to the (43rd) Congress, as a member of the U.S. House of Representatives from South Carolina's 2nd District.

1896 - (HBCU) South Carolina State University was founded in Orangeburg, S.C., as the state's sole Public College for African-American Students.

On this Day in History...

March 5th

1897 - The American Negro Academy (ANA) was founded in Washington, D.C. This organization of African-American intellectuals who through their scholarship and writing were dedicated to the "promotion of Higher Education, Arts and Science for African-Americans as part of the overall struggle for racial equality." The ANA brought together people of African Ancestry from around the world. As an all-male organization, the ANA consisted of those with backgrounds in Law, Medicine, Literature, Religion, and Community Activism.

1948 - William J. Powell founded the Clearview Golf Club, the first integrated Golf course to cater to African-American Golfers, he was also the first African-American to design, construct and own a Professional Golf course in the United States. In 1978, he expanded the course to 18 holes and earned a National Historic Site designation in 2001. Powell was inducted into the National Black Golf Hall of Fame.

1960 - Dancer and Singer, Sammy Davis Jr., was inducted into the Hollywood Walk of Fame and awarded a star on Hollywood Boulevard.

1985 - Dr. Mary McLeod Bethune was commemorated on the U.S. postage stamp. Bethune was an Educator and Activist, she served as President of the National Association of Colored Women and founded the National Council of Negro Women. She started a private school for African-American students in Daytona Beach, Florida which later continued to develop as Bethune-Cookman University. Bethune was also an Adviser to President Franklin D. Roosevelt. Her houses in Washington D.C. and Daytona Beach, Florida are Historic Landmarks.

On this Day in History...

March 6th

1867 - Dr. Robert Tanner Jackson became the first African-American to receive a Doctoral Degree in Dentistry from Harvard University.

1882 - (HBCU) Virginia State University was founded in Petersburg, VA. An African-American Attorney named Alfred W. Harris, who was a State Delegate, introduced the bill that established the University. The first president of the University was John Mercer Langston, former Dean of Howard University's Law School and later elected to Congress as the first African-American Representative from Virginia.

1911 - Samuel Battle became the first African-American Police Officer in New York City. "Big Sam" as he was known, earned the respect of his fellow officers after saving his partners life in the early 1920s. He would later become the first African-American Police Sergeant (1926), Lieutenant (1935) and Parole Commissioner (1941) in New York City.

1999 - Alford L. McMichael became the first African-American Sergeant Major of the United States Marine Corps. He was also the first Senior Non-Commissioned Officer for Allied Command Operations for NATO from 2003 to 2006.

2000 - Country Singer, Charley Pride became the first African-American inducted into the Country Music Hall of Fame. During Pride's extraordinary career, he had twenty-nine major Country hits.

On this Day in History...

March 7th

1945 - Phyllis Mae Dailey became the first African-American woman to serve as a Nurse in the United States Navy.

1960 - Singer, Dancer, Actress and Civil Rights Activist, Lena Horne was inducted into the Hollywood Walk of Fame and awarded two stars on Hollywood Boulevard, for the categories of Motion Pictures and Music. Horne's career spanned over seven decades appearing in Film, Television and Theater.

1964 - Civil Rights Leader, Malcolm X severed all ties with the Nation of Islam and its Leader Elijah Muhammad. Expressing many regrets about his time with them, he embraced Sunni Islam. After a period of travel to Africa and the Middle East, which included completing the Hajj, he became known as el-Hajj Malik el-Shabazz. He repudiated the Nation of Islam, disavowed racism and founded Muslim Mosque Inc., as well as the Organization of Afro-American Unity. He continued to emphasize Pan-Africanism, Black self-determination and self-defense. In 1987, Lenox Avenue in Harlem was co-named Malcolm X Boulevard, in his honor.

1978 - Jill Brown became the first African-American woman to serve as a Pilot for a Major U.S. Commercial Airline (Texas International Airlines). In 1974, she signed up for flight training in the U.S Navy, making her the first African-American woman to be admitted into the program.

1993 - Singer, Songwriter, Actress and Entrepreneur, Patti LaBelle was inducted into the Hollywood Walk of Fame and awarded a star on Hollywood Boulevard.

On this Day in History...

March 8th

1971 - "The Fight of the Century," the first time that two undefeated Boxing Champions fought each other for the Heavyweight Title. WBC/WBA Heavyweight Champion, Joe Frazier (26–0, 23 KOs) and Heavyweight Champion, Muhammad Ali (31–0, 25 KOs) fought at Madison Square Garden in New York City. Both Ali and Frazier had legitimate claims to the Title of World Heavyweight Champion. An undefeated Ali had won the Title from Sonny Liston, which was stripped by Boxing Authorities for his refusing induction into the Armed Forces. In Ali's absence, the undefeated Frazier garnered two Championship belts through defeating Buster Mathis and Jimmy Ellis. The tension and the excitement of the fight was monumental, Frazier won in 15 rounds via unanimous decision. The fight grossed $20 million, each fighter received $2.5 million. They would later fight two more times.

1977 - Henry L. Marsh III became the first African-American Mayor of Richmond, VA. In 1991, he was also elected to the State Senate of Virginia.

1995 - Dr. Lonnie Bristow became the first African-American President of the American Medical Association (AMA). One of Dr. Bristow's main goals as President of the AMA was to address the issue of ethics in the medical community, including implementing ethics courses and questions about ethics on medical licensing exams.

1998 - Vincent W. Patton III became the first African-American Master Chief Petty Officer of the Coast Guard. His career included staff and operational assignments both afloat and ashore throughout the United States and a joint military service assignment in Cuba.

On this Day in History...

March 9th

1891 - (HBCU) North Carolina Agricultural and Technical State University (also known as North Carolina A&T) was founded in Durham, N.C. In 1890, Congress enacted the Morrill Act that mandated "a separate College for the African-Americans." N.C. A&T was established as that school in the State of North Carolina by an Act of the General Assembly. Originally operating in Raleigh as an Annex to Shaw University, the College made a permanent home in Greensboro with the help of local citizens.

1968 - Barbara M. Watson became the first African-American appointed as a United States Assistant Secretary of State. Under President Lyndon B. Johnson, she served as Administrator of the Bureau of Security and Consular Affairs. Watson also severed under President Jimmy Carter's Administration as the Ambassador to Malaysia.

1987 - Ross M. Miller Jr., became the first African-American elected as President of the Southern California Chapter of the American College of Surgeons. Throughout his career, he was also the Governor of the American College of Surgeons. He later became a General Surgeon and Professor of Surgery at the University of California.

1999 - Major, Shawna Rochelle Kimbrell became the first African-American woman Combat Pilot in the United States Air Force. She flew the F-16 Fighting Falcon during combat missions in Operation Northern Watch.

2001 - Kelvin Mack became the first African-American Postmaster for the City of Baltimore, MD. He led a staff of 2,500 members and directed a $375 million budget.

On this Day in History...

March 10th

1837 - Dr. James McCune Smith became the first African-American to earn a Medical Degree, he studied at the African Free School in New York. He was a very successful Physician in New York, with a busy practice and two Pharmacies, where he trained several African-American Pharmacists. Smith was an avid Abolitionist and supporter of the Underground Railroad.

1863 - Daniel A. Payne became the first African-American President of a College in the United States, he was also a major shaper of the African Methodist Episcopal Church (AME). He organized AME's missionary support of free men in the South after the Civil War, the church gained 250,000 new members. AME stressed education and preparation of ministers, they purchased the future site of Wilberforce University for $10,000 and chose Payne to lead as its first President.

1972 - Several thousand African-Americans gathered in Gary, IN., for the first National Black Political Convention. Some of the goals were to raise the number of African-American Politicians elected to office, increase representation and create an agenda for fundamental change.

1975 - Air Force Veteran, who later worked as a Talent Agent, Wallace "Wally" Amos took the advice of some celebrity friends; with a $25,000 investment from Singers, Marvin Gaye and Helen Reddy, he opened a cookie store in Hollywood, CA., naming it "Famous Amos." In the first year he sold $300,000 worth of cookies, followed by more than $1,000,000 in sales in the store's second year of operation. By 1982, the company's revenues reached $12 million in sales. His cookies eventually reached specialty retail stores such as Baskin-Robbins and Starbucks.

On this Day in History...

March 11th

1864 - Dr. Rebecca Davis Lee Crumpler became the first African-American woman to earn a Medical Degree in the United States. She completed the four-year Medical program at the New England Female Medical College in Boston, MA., and awarded a Doctress of Medicine Degree.

1892 - Alonzo "Lonnie" Clayton became the youngest Jockey ever to win the Kentucky Derby, he was fifteen years old. Throughout his career, he won several other major races. Clayton retired to Little Rock, AR., in 1904 where he bought a prominent home known now as the "Engelberger House," which is listed on the National Register of Historic Places.

1945 - Inventor, Dr. Lloyd Augustus Hall received a U.S Patent for inventing a new method of Preserving Food. He was a pioneer in the field of food chemistry who introduced new methods related to curing meats, seasonings, emulsions, bakery products, antioxidants, protein hydrolysates and many other products that keep our food fresh. He has 59 patents related to food preservation. Dr. Hall was inducted into the National Inventors Hall of Fame in 2004.

1959 - Lorraine Hansberry's play "A Raisin in the Sun" opened in New York with Actor, Sidney Poitier in the starring role, making it the first play by an African-American woman to be produced on Broadway. Lloyd Richards directed the play, also making him the first African-American Director of a play on Broadway.

1993 - Ron Brown became the first African-American Secretary of the U.S. Department of Commerce.

On this Day in History...

March 12th

1955 - Jewel S. Lafontant became the first African-American woman named Assistant U.S. Attorney for the Northern Illinois District. President Dwight D. Eisenhower appointed her to the post. In 1973, Lafontant was also the first African-American woman Deputy United States Solicitor General. In 1983, she became a partner in the Law Firm Vedder, Price, Kaufman and Kammholz.

1970 - Samuel R. Pierce Jr., became the first African-American to serve as a General Counsel to the United States Treasury Department. He was also a member of the legal team that defended civil rights leaders. He argued before the United States Supreme Court on behalf of Dr. Martin Luther King Jr., and the New York Times in the important First Amendment case, New York Times vs. Sullivan. In 1980, Pierce was appointed as Secretary of the Department of Housing and Urban Development.

2003 - Comedian, Actor and Director, Chris Rock was inducted into the Hollywood Walk of Fame and awarded a star on Hollywood Boulevard. During his comedic career, Rock has hosted the 77th Academy Awards in 2005 and the 88th in 2016. He has also won four Emmy Awards and three Grammy Awards.

2007 - Grandmaster Flash and the Furious Five became the first Hip-Hop Artists inducted into the Rock & Roll Hall of Fame. Composed of DJ Grandmaster Flash and five Rappers, (Melle Mel, The Kidd Creole, Keef Cowboy, Mr. Ness/Scorpio, and Rahiem), the group was significant in the early development of Hip-Hop Music. They are widely regarded as the most influential Hip-Hop group ever.

On this Day in History...

March 13th

1861 - Historian and Abolitionist, William Cooper Nell became the first African-American to hold a federal position as a Boston, MA., Postal Clerk. In 1855, Nell published "The Colored Patriots of the America Revolution," which was the first substantial historical work by an African-American in America. Nell joined local Abolitionists in their efforts to desegregate all schools in Boston. He continued his anti-slavery efforts by working in the Underground Railroad and becoming one of the founders of a Committee on Vigilance that worked to undermine the Fugitive Slave Act.

1895 - Mary J. Small became the second woman in the United States ordained as a Deacon, she was a member of the African Methodist Episcopal Church (AME). Her status infuriated some of the male clergyman who felt it was inappropriate for women to hold such status. In 1898, she also became the first Methodist woman to be ordained an Elder.

1915 - Joseph E. Trigg became the first African-American Athlete to compete both on a Varsity Rowing and Football Teams at Syracuse University.

1984 - Dr. Mark Dean was awarded his first U.S. patent, which made him instrumental in the invention of the Personal Computer. He holds three of IBM's original nine Personal Computer patents and currently holds more than 20 total patents. Dr. Dean was also inducted into the National Inventors Hall of Fame in 1997.

2013 - Jeh Johnson became the first African-American to be named as the United States Secretary of Homeland Security. He was also the General Counsel of the Department of Defense from 2009 to 2012 during the first Obama Administration.

On this Day in History...

March 14th

1955 - Mahalia Jackson was inducted into the Gospel Music Hall of Fame. Known as the "Queen of Gospel" she is revered as one of the greatest musical figures in U.S. History. She became one of Gospel music's all-time greats, known for her powerful voice that cultivated a global following. President John F. Kennedy requested she sing at his inauguration. Jackson was also an active supporter of the Civil Rights Movement. She sang at the March on Washington in 1963 at the request of her friend, Dr. Martin Luther King, Jr., performing "I Been Buked and I Been Scorned."

1957 - Clinton E. Knox became the first African-American Secretary to the United States Mission to the North Atlantic Treaty Organization (NATO). He held post in Haiti, Dahomey, Honduras and France.

1972 - Benjamin L. Hooks became the first African-American Commissioner of the Federal Communications Commission (FCC). Hooks was also a Civil Rights Leader, Baptist Minister and practicing Attorney who served as Executive Director of the National Association for the Advancement of Colored People (NAACP) from 1977 to 1992.

1980 - Record Producer, Quincy Jones was inducted into the Hollywood Walk of Fame and awarded a star on Hollywood Boulevard. His career spanned over six decades in the Entertainment Industry. Jones has a record 79 Grammy Award nominations and awarded a total of 28, including a Grammy Legend Award in 1991.

1993 - Hazel Rollings O'Leary became the the first woman and first African-American to serve as the United States Secretary of Energy. O'Leary also served as the President of Fisk University during her career.

On this Day in History...

March 15th

1875 - Bass Reeves was sworn in as a Federal Deputy Marshal in Fort Smith, AR., making him the first African-American Federal Law Enforcement Officer on the early Western Frontier. For thirty-two years he was a Deputy U.S. Marshal in Native-American Territory and served with the Muskogee Police Department. Reeves worked in the Federal Territory that later became Oklahoma. Known as the real "Lone Ranger," he was credited with arresting more than 3,000 felons. He shot and killed 14 outlaws in self-defense during his career.

1897 - Solomon Carter Fuller Jr., became the first African-American Psychiatrist in the United States, he was also one of the first African-American Physicians to teach on the faculty at the University of Boston School of Medicine.

1963 - Jazz Musician, Duke Ellington was awarded the Grammy Lifetime Achievement Award at the 5th Annual Grammy Awards.

1972 - Gospel Singer, Mahalia Jackson was awarded the Grammy Lifetime Achievement Award at the 14th Annual Grammy Awards.

1972 - Jazz Trumpeter, Louis Armstrong was awarded the Grammy Lifetime Achievement Award at the 14th Annual Grammy Awards.

1997 - Thurgood Marshall Jr., son of Supreme Court Justice, Thurgood Marshall, became the first African-American to serve as Cabinet Secretary. He was named Assistant to President Bill Clinton and was the highest-ranking African-American in the White House. Marshall was also Deputy Counsel and Director of Legislative Affairs in the Office of the Vice President.

On this Day in History...

March 16th

1940 - Husband and wife team, Willa Brown-Chappell and Cornelius Coffey established the first flying school owned and operated by African-Americans, it was called the "Coffey School of Aeronautics" at Harlem Airport in Southwest Chicago, IL.

1972 - Mother Bethel African Methodist Episcopal (AME) Church was added to the National Register of Historic Places. Founded in Philadelphia PA., in 1793, it is the is the oldest AME Church in the Nation. After the American Civil War, the church sent missionaries to the South in order to help freedmen build many new churches in the region.

1974 - A monument honoring the life and contribution of Dr. Mary McLeod Bethune was built in Washington, D.C. This was the first statue of an African-American erected on public land in the Nation's Capital. Bethune was a Humanitarian and Civil Rights Activist, she was known for starting a private school for African-American students in Daytona Beach, FL. She also worked on the presidential campaign for Franklin D. Roosevelt in 1932. Bethune was close friends with President Roosevelt and his wife Eleanor, she was invited to join his Cabinet.

2013 - Hinchliffe Stadium became designated a National Historic Landmark. Located in Paterson, N.J. The Stadium served as the home field for the New York Black Yankees between 1933 and 1937, and again from 1939 to 1945. Hinchliffe is the sole surviving regular home field for a Negro League Baseball Team in the Mid-Atlantic Region. The stadium was named after former Paterson City Mayor, John V. Hinchliffe, who served during planning and construction of the stadium between 1929 and 1932.

On this Day in History...

March 17th

1863 - Alexander T. Augusta became the first African-American Surgeon in the U.S. Army during the Civil War, he also became the first African-American Hospital Administrator in U.S. history while serving in the Army. In 1868, Augusta was also the first African-American appointed to the faculty of Howard University and the first to any Medical College in the United States.

1870 - (HBCU) Benedict College was founded in Columbia, S.C., by Rhode Island native, Bathsheba Benedict. Mrs. Benedict along with another investor, the Baptist Home Mission, purchased an 80-acre plantation with a long-term goal of educating emancipated African-Americans in order to produce citizens who will become "powers for good in society."

1949 - William A. Hinton became the first African-American Professor at Harvard Medical School. As a world-renowned Bacteriologist, he developed the Hinton test for Syphilis and the Davis-Hinton tests for blood and spinal fluid. His daughter, Jane Hinton, became the first African-American woman to graduate from Veterinary school and to receive the Doctorate of Veterinary Medicine Degree.

2009 - Fire Station No. 30, located in Los Angeles, CA., was added to the National Register of Historic Places. The building is now the African-American Firefighter Museum (AAFFM). The AAFFM features vintage fire equipment and photos of pioneering African-American Firefighters in Los Angeles. Other displays include photos, artifacts and memorabilia of African-American firefighters, officers and historical women fire service professionals from around the country.

On this Day in History...

March 18th

1920 - Dr. Harold Ellis became the first African-American to obtain a Degree in Neurology. He then worked in Neurology at Harlem Hospital.

1983 - Actress, Dorothy Dandridge was inducted into the Hollywood Walk of Fame and awarded a star on Hollywood Boulevard. Dandridge was also the first African-American woman to be nominated for an Academy Award for Best Actress.

1985 - Julius Wesley Becton Jr., became the first African-American Director of the Federal Emergency Management Agency (FEMA).

1992 - Singer and Songwriter, Donna Summer was inducted into the Hollywood Walk of Fame and awarded a star on Hollywood Boulevard. Throughout her career, Summer has sold over 140 million records worldwide, making her one of the world's all time best-selling Artists.

2003 - Actor, Morgan Freeman was inducted into the Hollywood Walk of Fame and awarded a star on Hollywood Boulevard. Freeman is ranked as the 4th highest box office star with over $5 billion in total box office gross, an average of $75 million per film.

2018 - Pilot, Stephanie Johnson became the first African-American woman Captain for Delta Airlines. Twenty years earlier, Johnson was the first African-American woman pilot for Northwest Airlines. When Delta, merged with Northwest she was promoted to the rank of Captain. Johnson said she was inspired by the Tuskegee Airmen, the first African-American military aviators in the U.S. Army Air Corps.

On this Day in History...

March 19th

1872 - Rebecca J. Cole became the first African-American woman to establish a medical practice in the State of Pennsylvania. In 1867, she was the first African-American graduate of the Female Medical College of Pennsylvania and only the second African-American woman Physician in the United States.

1881 - Newly elected President James A. Garfield appointed Frederick Douglass as Recorder of Deeds for the District of Columbia. Douglas was the first African-American to hold this position, he held the post for five years.

1947 - Louis R. Lautier became the first African-American Journalist admitted to the Congressional Press Gallery. In 1955, Lautier was also the first African-American Journalist admitted to the White House Correspondents Association.

1973 - Dr. Clive Orville Callender established the only Transplant Center at a (HBCU) Medical School in the country when he founded the center at Howard University. As one of the Nation's foremost Transplant Surgeons, he was also the only top-rated African-American Transplant Surgeon in the country.

1989 - Audrey Forbes Manley became the first African-American appointed Principal Deputy Assistant Secretary to U.S. Health and Human Services, she was then appointed Deputy U.S. Surgeon General in 1994. Manley was also the first African-American woman appointed as Chief Resident at Cook County Children's Hospital in Chicago, IL.

On this Day in History...

March 20th

1943 - Two American Navy Destroyer Ships, the USS Mason and the Submarine Chaser, PC1264, were staffed entirely by African-American crews following a letter sent to President Roosevelt by the NAACP, demanding that African-Americans be used in roles other than mess-men in the U.S. Military. The momentum of the NAACP and the African-American community forced President Roosevelt to deal with the issue of segregation against African-Americans in the Armed Services during World War I.

1954 - Actress, Dorothy Dandridge became the first African-American woman to be nominated for the Academy Award for Best Actress for the motion picture "Carmen Jones."

1982 - The National Black Women's Health Project (NBWHP) held the first National Conference on African-American women's health issues. The NBWHP was founded under the leadership of Health Care Activist, Byllye Y. Avery. The organization aimed to mobilize African-American women to take charge of their lives and also improve their health. Avery also co-founded the Women's Health Center in Gainesville, FL., to provide an alternative birthing place for women in the City.

2017 - Lauren Simmons became both the youngest and only full-time woman Equity Trader at the New York Stock Exchange (NYSE), at the age of twenty-three. Simmons was the only woman trading on the floor of the New York Stock Exchange and she became the second African-American woman to sign the book that contained the constitution for the New York Stock Exchange.

On this Day in History...

March 21st

1946 - Kenneth S. Washington became the first African-American to sign a contract with a National Football League (NFL) Team. He attended the University of California, Los Angeles (UCLA), where he played both Baseball and Football. As a Baseball Player, Washington was teammates with Jackie Robinson. Washington was the signed by the Los Angeles Rams. He was inducted to the College Football Hall of Fame in 1956 and his number 13 Jersey was the first to be retired at UCLA.

1977 - Togo Dennis West Jr., became the the first African-American U.S. Navy General Counsel, he was also the second African-American to be Secretary of Veterans Affairs.

1994 - Actress and Comedian, Whoopi Goldberg hosted the 66th Annual Academy Awards in Los Angeles, she became the first African-American and the first solo woman ever to host the event. More than one billion people watched the Academy Awards that year. Goldberg made her film debut in "The Color Purple" (1985). She won an Academy Award for "Best Supporting Actress" in the film, "Ghost" in 1991, she became the second African-American Actress to win the award since Hattie McDaniel in 1939. Goldberg is also the only performer to win an Oscar (1991), Tony (2002), Emmy (2002), Grammy (1985) as well as the Mark Twain Prize for American Humor (2001), for which she was the first woman Honoree. Goldberg is one of fifteen individuals to ever achieve "EGOT Status." A winner of the the Emmy, Grammy, Oscar and Tony Awards.

On this Day in History...

March 22nd

1832 - Augustus Jackson became the first African-American Head Chef in the White House during the first quarter of the 19th century, he was known as the "Father of Ice Cream." Although he did not invent ice cream, he is often incorrectly given credit, he did create many popular ice cream recipes, making him one of the wealthiest people in Philadelphia, PA., during the time.

1891 - Minnie M. Geddings Cox became the first African-American Postmistress in the United States. Cox was appointed to serve in the town of Indianola, Mississippi. President Benjamin Harrison appointed her to the post, President William McKinley then reappointed her in 1897.

1933 - H. Naylor Fitzhugh became the first African-American to receive a Harvard MBA. He had a long career at Harvard and was known there as the "Dean of Black Business."

1971 - Walter S. McAfee, ranking Scientist at the Army Electronics Research and Development Command became the first African-American to attain the civil service rank of GS 16, while working for the U.S. Army. He was also involved in the first radar contact with the moon in 1946.

1977 - Joan Scott Wallace became the first African-American and the third woman to serve as Assistant Secretary for Administration in the Department of Agriculture. While in office, she designed programs to address the plight of African-American farmers. She also held national forums to inform African-American farmers of assistance programs that were available to them.

On this Day in History...

March 23rd

1898 - Marshall W. "Major" Taylor became the first African-American to win a major Bicycle Race. He won his first professional start, a half-mile handicap held at Madison Square Garden. Taylor was also the first African-American member of an integrated professional team. Toward the end of the year, he compiled 21 first-place victories, 13 second-place berths and 11 third-place showings. Taylor was known as the "Fastest Bicycle Rider in the World," until his 1910 retirement.

1937 - Adrienne Fidelin became the first African-American Model to appear in a mainstream fashion magazine when her photograph was published in Harper's Bazaar Magazine.

1963 - Air Force Captain and Korean War Pilot, Marlon Green, challenged the Airline Industry hiring policies and won a landmark judgment against Continental Airlines in the U.S. Supreme Court, which opened Interstate Commercial Airlines to African-American Pilots.

1982 - Lee Patrick Brown became the first African-American Chief of Police for the City of Houston, TX. His career included both University Teaching and Law Enforcement, beginning as Sheriff of Multnomah County, Oregon. In 1990, he also became Police Commissioner of New York City. In 1993, President Bill Clinton announced Brown's nomination as Director of the Office of National Drug Control Policy.

1995 - Shirley Ann Jackson became first African-American woman to Chair the Nuclear Regulatory Commission (NRC). She was in charge of regulating the safety of the country's 110 nuclear power plants.

On this Day in History...

March 24th

1870 - Susan McKinney Steward became the first African-American woman to graduate from a New York State Medical School. Steward undertook postgraduate work at the Long Island Medical School Hospital in 1888, she was the only woman in the entire college.

1970 - Legendary Actress and Sportscaster, Jayne Kennedy became the first African-American woman crowned "Miss Ohio." In 1978, she also became one of the first women to join the all-male contingency of television sports announcers.

1997 - Philadelphia 76ers "Point Guard" Allen Iverson became the first rookie in National Basketball Association (NBA) history to score 40 points or more in four consecutive games. Wilt Chamberlain had previously set the record of 40 or more points in three consecutive games during the 1959-60 season. In Iverson's next game after he broke the record, he again scored 40 points, raising the new benchmark to five consecutive games. His performance won him the "NBA Player of the Week" award, he was also awarded the NBA "Rookie of the Year" title.

2001 - Stephanie Ready became the first woman to Coach a Professional Men's Basketball Team (Charlotte Hornets). From 2001 to 2003, she was also an Assistant Coach for National Basketball Association (NBA) Minor League Men's Team, Greenville, Groove.

2002 - Denzel Washington became the second African-American Actor to receive an Academy Award for "Best Actor." In 1989, he also won an Academy Award for "Best Supporting Actor." Washington has the most Academy Award nominations for an African-American Actor, including six for "Best Actor" and two for "Best Supporting Actor."

On this Day in History...

March 25th

1806 - "Monkey" Simon became the first known African-American Jockey, he was known to be the best Jockey of his day. During the 1820's, horse racing became the most popular sport in the United States, a large number of the best trainers and Jockeys in the country were African-Americans. The most prestigious horse race in America began in 1875, "The Kentucky Derby" which is an annual event scheduled on the first Saturday in May. During its inaugural year, 13 out of the 15 Jockeys were African-American. Organized horse racing dates back to the 17th century in North America.

1965 - Dr. Martin Luther King, Jr., lead a 54 mile march from Selma to Montgomery, AL. The initial 3,300 marchers at the beginning, eventually grew to 50,000 when they reached the Alabama Capitol. Hundreds of Ministers, Priests, Rabbis and Social Activists joined the "Voting Rights March." After the march, President Lyndon B. Johnson proposed the "Voting Rights Act," the Act secured the right to vote for minorities throughout the country, especially in the South.

1996 - A. Leon Higginbotham, Jr., was awarded the NAACP Spingarn Medal. He was the first African-American United States District Judge for the Eastern District of Pennsylvania. He was later appointed to the United States Court of Appeals for the Third Circuit, for which he served as Chief Judge.

2017 - Jusan Hamilton became the first African-American Race Director in NASCAR history. Directors oversee everything that occurs in the car race, including penalties, crashes and cleanups.

On this Day in History...

March 26th

1897 - Augustus Nathaniel Lushington became the first African-American to earn a Doctor of Veterinary Medicine Degree from the University of Pennsylvania.

1937 - William H. Hastie was appointed Judge of the Federal District Court in the Virgin Islands by President Franklin D. Roosevelt, becoming the first African-American appointed to the Federal Bench. Hastie was also one of the first African-American members of Roosevelt's Administration. He was appointed the President's Race Relations Advisor. Later he was given the post of Assistant Solicitor for the Department of Interior. While working for the department, he wrote a Constitution for the Virgin Islands, an American territory.

1982 - Jazz Pianist, Organist, Bandleader and Composer, Count Basie was inducted into the Hollywood Walk of Fame and awarded a star.

1991 - Emanuel Cleaver II became the first African-American Mayor of Kansas City, MO. Prior to serving in public office, Cleaver founded a local chapter of the Southern Christian Leadership Conference (SCLC) in Kansas City, he was also Pastor of the St. James United Methodist Church where he built the congregation from 47 members to more than 2,000. In 2004, he was elected to represent Missouri's 5th Congressional District in the U.S. House of Representatives. In January 2010, he became Chair of the Congressional Black Caucus.

2001 - Jackson State University women's Golf Team became the first women's team from a Historically Black College and University (HBCU) to receive an invitation to the NCAA Regional Championship. They played in a twenty-one team NCAA East Regional in Chapel Hill, N.C.

On this Day in History...

March 27th

1909 - Gertrude Elizabeth Curtis McPherson became the first African-American woman to pass the New York State Board of Dentistry. She studied at the New York College of Dental and Oral Surgery and received the Doctor of Dental Surgery (DDS).

1962 - Samuel R. Delany became the first African-American to earn acclaim as a Science Fiction Writer. In 2002, he was inducted to the Science Fiction and Fantasy Hall of Fame.

1964 - Professional Golfer and Tennis Player, Althea Gibson became the first African-American woman to play on the Ladies Professional Golf Association (LPGA) Tour. She is best known for her achievements in Professional Tennis. She played in several Golf Tournaments from 1963 to 1967.

1985 - Actor and Singer, Billy Dee Williams was inducted into the Hollywood Walk of Fame and awarded a star on Hollywood Boulevard. Known as a TV, film and stage icon, particularly for his roles opposite Diana Ross in "Lady Sings the Blues" and "Mahogany" as well as "Lando Calrissian" in the Sci-fi epics "The Empire Strikes Back" and "Return of the Jedi."

1992 - Ron Simmons became the first African-American World Heavyweight Wrestling Champion, operating first as a Tag-Team member, he then became an individual Wrestler in 1988. Simmons was also a three-time All-American "Nose Tackle" at Florida State University.

On this Day in History...

March 28th

1865 - James Lewis became the first African-American to receive an appointment from the Federal Government as Inspector of Customs for the Port of New Orleans. When the Union troops occupied New Orleans in 1862, Lewis abandoned the Confederate ship on which he was serving as a steward, raised two companies of African-American soldiers and led the 1st Regiment of the Louisiana National Guard during the battle for Port Hudson. He was active in Reconstruction politics and received several Federal appointments.

1970 - Chris Dickerson became the first African-American winner of the Mr. America Contest. He earned fifteen bodybuilding titles in his career.

1999 - Carolyn Peck became the first African-American woman to Coach a Team to the women's NCAA National Championship. She coached the Purdue Boilermakers to a 62-45 win over Duke University and to its first NCAA Championship. Peck was also named Big Ten Conference Coach of the Year.

2012 - Los Angeles Lakers Star and NBA Legend, Earvin "Magic" Johnson became an Owner of the Los Angeles Dodgers Baseball Team in a $2 billion deal. He is also an Owner of the Los Angeles Sparks women's Professional Basketball Team. During his Professional Basketball career, Johnson played point guard for the Lakers for 13 seasons, appeared in 12 All-Star games, won 3 NBA MVP Awards and 5 NBA titles. When he retired from Basketball, he founded Magic Johnson Enterprises (MJE) and began investing in movie theaters, restaurants and fitness centers in low-income neighborhoods. MJE has also focused on bringing high-quality businesses to diverse communities.

On this Day in History...

March 29th

1879 - Frank Hart became the first African-American to set a United States record for marathon walking, he won the prestigious O'Leary Belt Competition and smashed the World Record, after covering 565 miles in six days of racing. He earned about $17,000 in prize money. As the race ended, he waved an American flag to thousands of cheering fans who packed Madison Square Garden. Another African-American, William Pegram of Boston finished second with 540 miles.

1926 - The United Golf Association (UGA) held its first National Tournament. The winners were Harry Jackson, of Washington, D.C., and Marie Thompson, Chicago, IL. Founded in the 1925, UGA was a group of African-American Professional Golfers who operated a separate series of Professional Golf Tournaments during the era of racial segregation in the United States.

2002 - Professional Poker Player, Phillip D. "Phil" Ivey became one of the world's best all-around poker players. He appeared in nine World Poker Tour final tables. Ivey was given the nickname, "The Phenom" after winning three World Series of Poker. In 2017, he was elected to the Poker Hall of Fame.

2004 - James "Bubba" Stewart became the first African-American Racer to dominate the sport of Motorcross, he earned the nickname "Fastest Man on The Planet." He earned eleven Motorcyclist Association National Titles and was named Rookie of the Year in 2002. In 2004, he won both the AMA 125 East Supercross Championship and the AMA 125 Motorcross National Championships. In 2008, he became the second Rider ever to complete a perfect Motorcross season.

On this Day in History...

March 30th

1946 - Ann Petry became the first African-American woman to write a Best-Selling Novel. After her book "The Street" was published, it quickly became a sensation and sold over one million copies, she was also one of the first women writers to address the problems that African-American women faced.

1981 - Charles Sampson became the first African-American Cowboy to win a World Rodeo Championship. The bull rider was awarded the World Title in the Winston Rodeo Series. For five consecutive years, (1981-85) Sampson qualified for the National Finals Rodeo, with a total of 10 appearances.

1996 - Jackson State University mens Golf Team became the first team from a Historically Black College and University (HBCU) to reach the Championship. Eddie Payton coached the team to a record 70 wins and 19 losses in the Southwestern Athletic Conference.

1999 - Lieutenant General, Walter E. Gaskin Sr., became the first African-American to Command the 22nd Marine Expeditionary Unit (MEU) at Camp Lejeune, North Carolina. In 2010, he became Deputy Chairman of NATO Military Committee in Brussels, Belgium.

2007 - As Owners of the D.C. United Soccer Team, Victor B. McFarlane and Brian K. Davis became the first African-American Owners in Major League Soccer. McFarland acknowledged that Soccer had become the number one sport in the world, but not so in the United States. He wanted to be a part of the change and make Soccer the sport that all children look to for recreation and entertainment.

On this Day in History...

March 31st

1870 - Thomas Mundy Peterson of New Jersey became the first African-American to vote in an election under the Fifteenth Amendment to the United States Constitution, granting voting rights to all citizens regardless of race.

1891 - Dr. Halle Johnson became the first African-American woman Doctor in the State of Alabama. Hired by Tuskegee Institute's Founder, Booker T. Washington, she was responsible for the health care of the school's 450 students and 30 faculty and staff. She also established a training school for nurses and founded the Lafayette Dispensary.

1932 - James Herman Banning became the first African-American Aviator to be granted a license by the U.S. Department of Commerce, he was also the first African-American Pilot to fly coast to coast across the United States.

1960 - Frank D. Reeves became the first African-American Special Assistant to the President, John F. Kennedy. He was also an Assistant NAACP Counsel and served on Thurgood Marshall's staff. Reeves was known for his great legal mind, he was a pioneer in civil rights cases, including Brown vs. Board of Education which led to school integration in 1954. Reeves was the representative for the NAACP Legal Defense and Educational Fund between 1946 and 1961.

1995 - Thomas "Hit Man" Hearns won the vacant Welterweight Title and became the first African-American to win Boxing Titles in five different weight classes. Throughout his career, Hearns was known as a devastating puncher, he was inducted into the International Boxing Hall of Fame in 2012.

On this Day in History...

April 1st

1868 - (HBCU) Hampton University was founded in Hampton VA., by General Samuel Armstrong. He was appointed in 1866 to Superintendent of the Freedmen's Bureau of the Ninth District of Virginia. Drawing upon his experiences with mission schools in Hawaii, he acquired funding from the American Missionary Association to establish a school, Hampton Normal and Agricultural Institute. The "Emancipation Oak" tree is a lasting symbol of the university's heritage and perseverance. The young oak served as the first classroom for newly freed men and women eager for an education. Mrs. Mary Peake conducted the first lessons taught under the oak located on the University's campus.

1880 - (HBCU) Southern University of New Orleans was founded in New Orleans LA. The school began its mission of providing post-secondary education for African-Americans with a total of twelve students and five faculty members. In 1890, the school's name officially changed to Southern University and was recognized as a land grant college. In 1914, the campus was moved to the State Capitol in Baton Rouge.

1943 - Graduates of the first all African-American Military Aviation Program created at the Tuskegee Institute headed to North Africa as the 99th Pursuit Squadron. Their commander, Captain Benjamin O. Davis Jr., later became the first African-American Military General. The Tuskegee Airmen saw combat against German and Italian troops, flew more than 3,000 missions and served as a great source of pride for many African-Americans back home in the United States. Davis was also first African-American to Command a Military Base.

On this Day in History...

April 2nd

1829 - George Moses Horton became the first African-American to publish a Collection of Poetry. "The Hope of Liberty," contained twenty-one poems, he anticipated proceeds from this volume would pay his way to the Country of Liberia.

1863 - Susie King Taylor became the first African-American Army Nurse in the United States, serving the First Regiment of the South Carolina, where her husband served for four years during the Civil War. Despite her service, like many African-American nurses, she was never paid for her work. As the author of "Reminiscences of My Life in Camp with the 33rd United States Colored Troops," she was the only African-American woman to publish a memoir of her wartime experiences.

1942 - The desperate need for factory labor to build war machines needed to win World War II lead to an unprecedented migration of African-Americans from the South, North and West. This migration transformed American politics, African-Americans increasingly put pressure on Congress to protect their civil rights throughout the Nation. Their activism laid much of the foundation for the Civil Rights Movement a decade later.

1956 - The Booker T. Washington National Monument was established in Franklin County, VA., it preserves the 207-acre tobacco farm where he was born. The site was listed on the National Register of Historic Places and designated a National Monument. Washington was one of the most prominent African-American leaders of the 18th and 19th centuries, he founded Tuskegee University in Alabama in 1881.

On this Day in History...

April 3rd

1865 - (HBCU) Virginia Union University was founded in Richmond, VA. The American Baptist Home Mission Society (ABHMS) founded the school shortly after Union troops took control of Richmond at the end of the American Civil War.

1888 - The True Reformers Bank of Richmond, also know as the Grand Fountain of the United Order of True Reformers Savings Bank became the first bank created, owned and operated by African-Americans. The bank was established in Virginia.

1902 - Justina L. Ford became the first African-American woman Licensed to Practice Medicine in the State of Colorado.

1984 - Georgetown University Head Basketball Coach, John Thompson became the first African-American Coach to win a NCAA Division I Championship. His team, led by Patrick Ewing, defeated Houston 84-75. Thompson was also elected "Coach of the Year" seven times. In 1988, he coached the U.S. Olympic Team that won a bronze medal and was the Assistant Coach of the 1976 gold medal team. He was inducted into the Naismith Memorial Basketball Hall of Fame in 1999.

1990 - Actress and Singer, Diahann Carroll was inducted into the Hollywood Walk of Fame and awarded a star on Hollywood Boulevard. Carroll appeared in some of the earliest major studio films to feature African-American casts such as "Carmen Jones." She also starred in "Julia," one of the first series on television to star an African-American woman in a non-stereotypical role. Carol played the role of Dominique Deveraux on the popular prime time Soap Opera, Dynasty.

On this Day in History...

April 4th

1953 - The first chapter of Phi Beta Kappa at a (HBCU) was established at Fisk University. The chapter at Howard University was formed four days later. The only other HBCU's with a Phi Beta Kappa chapter were Morehouse and Spelman colleges. Founded in 1775, Phi Beta Kappa is the most prestigious Honorary Society for undergraduate achievement in the humanities.

1962 - "Big O," Oscar Robinson became the only player in NBA history to average a "Triple-Double" for an entire season. Robinson averaged 30.8 points, 12.5 rebounds and 11.4 assists per game.

1967 - Dr. Martin Luther King, Jr., delivered the speech, "Beyond Vietnam, A Time to Break Silence" at a meeting of Clergy and Laity concerned at Riverside Church, New York City. The speech was his first public criticism of the Vietnam War.

1977 - Terence A. Todman became the first African-American named Assistant Secretary of State for Latin America.

1993 - Cherie Greer became the first African-American and the youngest player ever named to a Women's World Cup Team, they won the title that year. Greer was named to her second World Cup Team in 1997 and led the U.S. Women's Team to its 3rd straight World Cup title.

2017 - Frederick Douglass became the second African-American to be prominently featured on a U.S. coin. The quarter he was featured on was released into circulation representing the District of Columbia.

On this Day in History...

April 5th

1826 - Ira Frederick Aldridge became the first African-American Actor to attain international fame, he was one of the leading Shakespearean Actors of the 19th century.

1884 - James Conway Farley became the first African-American to gain recognition as a Photographer. He was a photo technician for G.W. Davis Photography Gallery, where he was able to set up the scenes for his photos and develop them. In 1895, Farley opened his own studio, the Jefferson Fine Arts Gallery, where he specialized in transferring the pictures he made of individuals and groups into greeting cards. The Valentine Museum in Richmond, VA., had one of his photographs on display as late as 1982. Of his many photographs, only one remains that can be attributed to him.

1973 - Doris A. Davis became the first African-American woman Mayor of a Metropolitan City in the U.S., Compton, CA.

2000 - C. Vivian Stringer became the first African-American woman College Basketball Coach in Division I history to record 600 victories. Stringer was also the first woman's Head Coach to advance to the Final Four from two different colleges. She coached the women's team at Cheyney State in 1982, and women's team at the University of Iowa in 1983.

2008 - Karen Bass became the first African-American woman elected Speaker of the California State Assembly. Her post was recognized as the second most powerful position in the State's Government.

On this Day in History...

April 6th

1903 - (HBCU) Albany State University was founded in Albany, Georgia. by Joseph Winthrop Holley, a native of South Carolina. Holly was the son of former slaves and he was inspired by the writings of W.E.B. Du Bois. He wanted to improve the conditions for the South's African-American population by offering industrial and religious education. The school was named Albany Bible and Manual Training Institute, initially the goal was to offer primary and secondary education and to train teachers.

1906 - William Sidney Pittman became the first African-American Architect to receive a federal contract. Pittman designed several notable buildings, such as the Zion Baptist Church and the nearby Deanwood Chess House in the Deanwood neighborhood of Washington, DC. He was the son-in-law of Booker T. Washington.

1971 - James E. Williams Sr., became the first African-American elected as Mayor of East St. Louis, MO.

1985 - August Wilson became the first African-American to have two concurrent plays on Broadway. His play Fences opened at the forty-sixth Street Theatre on Broadway, it depicted the personal and economic problems of African-American families. The play grossed $11 million in one year and broke the record of earnings for nonmusical plays. In 1987, Wilson won a Pulitzer Prize and a Tony Award for the play. While Fences was still running on Broadway, Wilson's Joe Turner's Come and Gone opened at the Ethel Barrymore Theater.

On this Day in History...

April 7th

1867 - (HBCU) Johnson C. Smith University was founded in Charlotte, N.C. Rev. S.C. Alexander and the Rev. W. L. Miller wanted to establish an institution in this section of the South. During a meeting of the Catawba Presbytery in the old Charlotte Presbyterian Church, the movement for the school was formally inaugurated, which by charter was named The Freedmen's College of North Carolina, the two ministers were elected as teachers.

1940 - Booker T. Washington became the first African-American commemorated on the U.S. Postal Stamp, born a slave on a Virginia farm, Washington rose to become one of the most influential African-American intellectuals of the late 19th Century. In 1881, he founded Tuskegee Institute, a Historically Black College and University (HBCU) in Alabama that was devoted to training teachers. Washington was also behind the formation of the National Negro Business League. He later served as an adviser to President's Theodore Roosevelt and William Howard Taft.

1986 - Jazz Musician, Singer and Songwriter, Billie Holiday was inducted into the Hollywood Walk of Fame and awarded a star on Hollywood Boulevard. Considered to be the greatest Jazz vocalist of all time, Holiday changed the art of American Pop vocals forever.

2008 - As a Colonel in the Maryland National Guard, Allyson Solomon was promoted to Brigadier General and the Air Guard's Assistant Adjunct General. Solomon became the first African-American to hold that post, with her promotion she lead over 1,500 Air Guard members in the State.

On this Day in History...

April 8th

1974 - Baseball Legend, Hank Aaron hit career "home run" number 715 and broke the long-standing record held by Babe Ruth. Aaron's record-breaking 715th "home run" came in the fourth inning of the Braves home opener against the Los Angeles Dodgers, with over 53,000 fans in attendance at Atlanta-Fulton County Stadium, Aaron hit a pitch and the ball went sailing over the fence in left center field. After Aaron rounded the bases and reached home plate, he was lifted up and congratulated by his teammates. He then shook his father's hand and hugged his mother. In 1992, Aaron was inducted into the National Baseball Hall of Fame, he was also awarded the Presidential Medal of Freedom in 2002.

1976 - Octavia Butler became the first African-American woman Science Fiction Writer to be published. She was a multiple recipient of both the Hugo and Nebula Awards, in 1995 she became the first Science Fiction Writer to receive a MacArthur Fellowship.

1991 - Willie W. Herenton was elected as the first African-American Mayor of Memphis, TN. Herenton began his teaching career in the elementary schools of the Memphis City School System, he became the first African-American Superintendent of the system in 1979.

1999 - David Stephens beat out nearly one hundred applicants to become the first African-American Jaguar Dealer in the United States. After a $1 million loan from Ford Motor Company, he renovated a former Jaguar dealership and established Stephens Automotive Group's Millennium Motor Cars in Plano, TX. Stephens repaid the loan in five months. In his first year of operation the company sold over 1000 cars, with $48 million in sales.

On this Day in History...

April 9th

1916 - Lucy Madden Smith founded the All Nations Pentecostal Church in Chicago, IL., she became the first woman in the City to transform the congregation into an established church. Known as "Elder Smith," she was the first to broadcast her Sunday night services over radio station WSBC; later station WIND aired her services on Sundays and Wednesdays. Smith was the first African-American religious leader to broadcast services on the air. In 1933, she became a pioneer in Gospel radio, exposing her ministry to wider audiences. She was the first in the City to mix Gospel programming with appeals for the poor.

1947 - The first known Freedom Ride occurred when the Congress of Racial Equality (CORE) sent twenty-three African-American and Caucasian riders through the South. This was the first challenge to segregation on Interstate Buses.

1950 - Cleveland Robinson became the first African-American Officer of the American Federation of Labor and Congress of Industrial Organizations, (AFL-CIO) he led 30,000 members who worked in small shops and department stores in New York City. He was a close ally of Dr. Martin Luther King Jr., and a member of the Southern Christian Leadership Conference's board. Robinson was also a prominent figure in the 1963 March on Washington, serving as Chairman for the Historic Event.

1999 - Second-Degree "Black Belt," Lauren Blanks became the youngest and the only "Black Belt" in the American Taekwondo Association (ATA) to win a World Title in three consecutive tournament years, (1999, 2000, 2001) by age eleven, Blanks won over 100 trophies.

On this Day in History...

April 10th

1852 - The African Zion Baptist Church was founded in Malden, W.V. The church was a central part of the African-American community in West Virginia for much of the 20th century. In 1865, Booker T. Washington became a member at the age of nine. In 1964, the church was added to the National Register of Historic Places, it is the oldest African-American church in the State of West Virginia.

1865 - (HBCU) Bowie State University was founded in Baltimore, MD. In 1910, the State of Maryland decided to relocate the school to the City of Bowie, purchasing a 187-acres of land.

1941 - Oscar W. Holmes became the first African-American Air Traffic Controller, he was assigned to the New York Airway Traffic Control Center as Assistant Controller.

1992 - "Boyz II Men" became the first African-American Singing Group to have a record at the top of Billboard's Hot 100 chart for twelve consecutive weeks. Their single "End of the Road" held first place and became the longest-running Pop single shattering all previous records. Their debut album, "Cooleyhighharmony," went quadruple platinum.

1993 - Fred Whitfield became the first African-American to win the World Title in Calf Roping. By the year 2000 Whitfield had won four World Calf Roping Titles, he was also the first African-American Rodeo Performer to earn more than $100 million. In 2000, he became the first African-American to win the Professional Rodeo Cowboys Association's (PRCA) World Champion All-Around Cowboy Title.

On this Day in History...

April 11th

1853 - While working at a restaurant in Saratoga Springs, New York, Chef, George Crum invented one of the world's most popular snack foods "Potato Chips." His creation was conceived when a patron sent back the restaurant's popular french fried potatoes dish, complaining that the potatoes were cut too thick. An annoyed Crum, sliced a new batch of potatoes as thin as he possibly could and fried them until they were completely hard and crunchy, he then added a generous amount of salt to them. He was surprised to find out the patron actually enjoyed the new dish he invented, at that moment "Potato Chips" were born.

1881 - (HBCU) Spelman College, the first College for African-American women in the United States is founded by Sophia B. Packard and Harriet E. Giles.

1929 - The Harlem Broadcasting Corporation was established and became the first African-American radio venture of its kind, operating its own radio studios at Lenox Avenue on 125th Street in Harlem, N.Y. The company leased time on local radio outlet WRNY.

1968 - The Fair Housing Act was signed by President Lyndon B. Johnson. This new law provided equal housing opportunities regardless of race, religion or national origin. Johnson also signed the Civil Rights Act and Voting Rights Act into law a few years earlier.

1983 - Actor, Louis Gossett Jr., became the first African-American Actor to win an Academy Award for "Best Supporting Actor" for the film, "An Officer and a Gentleman."

On this Day in History...

April 12th

1861 - During the first day of the Civil War, there were approximately 200,000 African-American soldiers that served in the Union Armed Forces.

1888 - Edward Park Duplex was elected Mayor of Wheatland, California. He became the first African-American Mayor elected to a predominantly Caucasian town in the United States.

1916 - Ella P. Stewart became the first African-American woman graduate of the University of Pittsburgh School of Pharmacy, she was also the first African-American woman to pass the Pennsylvania State Board of Pharmacy.

1983 - Harold Washington was elected as the first African-American Mayor of Chicago, IL. As Mayor, he reduced the City's budget deficit and placed more minorities in visible positions. He also hired the City's first African-American Chief of Police. Washington was also a member of the U.S. House of Representatives from January, 1981 until beginning his tenure as Chicago Mayor, representing the Illinois 1st District.

1996 - Track and Field Star, Michael Johnson, who won four Olympic gold medals and eight World Championships gold medals, appeared on the breakfast cereal box "Wheaties." He held the World and Olympic records in the 200 meter and 400 meter as well as the World Record in the indoor 400 meter races.

On this Day in History...

April 13th

1964 - Actor, Sidney Poitier became the first African-American man to win an Academy Award for "Best Actor" as well as the Golden Globe Award for "Best Actor" for his role in "Lilies of the Field." Among his various honors, Queen Elizabeth II knighted him in 1968. He also became the first African-American to win a Lifetime Achievement Award at the Academy Award ceremony in 1992.

1969 - As a seventeen year-old Senior in High School, Ruth C. White became the youngest woman and the first African-American to win a National Fencing Championship. She held four National Titles. In 1972, she was a member of the U.S. Olympic Team in Munich, Germany.

1982 - Mildred Glenn became President of the New World National Bank in Pennsylvania, she became the first African-American woman Bank President in the State. New World National Bank became the only minority Bank in the State.

1990 - Television Sportscaster, Robin Roberts became the first on-air African-American Anchorwoman for ESPN. In 1996, she was named new host of ABC's Wide World of Sports, the first African-American woman to hold that position. Roberts was also the first African-American woman to host a network televised NFL pre-game show. In 2014, she won the Walter Cronkite Award for Excellence in Journalism. In 2016, Roberts was inducted into the Sports Broadcasting Hall of Fame.

2001 - William Burrus become the first African-American elected President of a major national union, "The American Postal Workers Union." He was also appointed to the AFL-CIO Executive Council.

On this Day in History...

April 14th

1905 - Rodeo Cowboy, Wild West Show Performer and Actor, Bill Pickett invented the technique of "Bulldogging," the skill of grabbing cattle by the horns and wrestling them to the ground. The name Bill Pickett soon became synonymous with successful rodeos. He toured the country performing his bulldogging act.

1949 - Frank G. Yerby became the the first African-American to write a series of bestselling novels. His first novel "The Foxes of Harrow" was an instant success and best seller. He became known also as one of the popular novelists who based his tales in the Old South.

1962 - Nelson Jack Edwards became the first African-American member of the United Auto Workers (UAW) International Executive Board. In 1970, he also became the first African-American Vice President of that union.

1983 - Alice Walker became the first African-American woman Writer to win a Pulitzer Prize for a work of Fiction. Her novel "The Color Purple" also won the American Book Award for Fiction and established Walker as a major American Writer. In 1985, her novel was made into an Oscar-Nominated film, starring Whoopi Goldberg and Oprah Winfrey.

1995 - Jacquelyn L. Williams-Bridgers became the first woman and African-American Inspector General of the State Department.

2007 - Comedian, Dave Chappelle set an endurance record of 6 hours and 12 minutes with his stand-up comedy show, he performed at the Laugh Factory Comedy Club in Los Angeles, CA.

On this Day in History...

April 15th

1947 - Jackie Robinson became the first African-American to play Major League Baseball, as he debuted with the Brooklyn Dodgers as a "Third-Baseman." Robinson played his first game against the Boston Braves at Ebbetts Field in Brooklyn, he was also named Rookie of the Year the same year. Robinson stood up for equal rights even before he did so in Baseball. He was arrested and court-martialed during training in the Army for refusing to move to the back of a segregated bus. He was eventually acquitted of the charges and received an honorable discharge. He then started his Professional Baseball career.

1977 - Inventor, Gerald Lawson patented the world's first Home Video Gaming System that used interchangeable cartridges. Lawson pioneered the Home Video Game Industry, he created The Fairchild Channel F. Video Entertainment Computer. This device was the world's first ROM based cartridge video game console system with interchangeable cartridges. This new technology allowed video gaming companies to sell individual games separately from the console itself, which is a business model that remains the cornerstone of the Video Game Industry today.

1985 - Considered to be among the finest Boxing matches in history, known as the "The Fight" between Undisputed Middleweight Champion, "Marvelous" Marvin Hagler and challenger Thomas "Hitman" Hearns. The opening three minutes was one of the most exciting first rounds ever in Boxing history, the two fighters went "toe to toe" the entire first round. The action in the second round was a continuation of the first, neither boxer backed down. Hagler won the fight by a third round knockout in a battle known as "The Eight Minutes of Fury," due to its constant action and violent back-and-forth exchanges.

On this Day in History...

April 16th

1889 - The Mutual Bank and Trust Company of Chattanooga, TN., was founded, it was the first African-Americans owned Bank in the State..

1960 - One hundred fifty African-American and Caucasian students gathered together at Shaw University in Raleigh, N.C to form the Student Nonviolent Coordinating Committee (SNCC). This committee was one of the major civil rights movement organizations of the 1960's. It emerged from the first wave of student sit-ins and was heavily involved in the Voter Education Project, which was federally endorsed by the Kennedy Administration.

1969 - Clarence M. Mitchell, Jr., was awarded the NAACP Spingarn Medal. As the Regional Director of the Washington Bureau of the NAACP, he waged a tireless campaign on Capitol Hill, helping to secure passage of Civil Rights Legislation in the 1950s and 1960s, including the the Civil Rights Act of 1964, the Voting Rights Act of 1965 and the Fair Housing Act of 1968.

1971 - Singer, Isaac Hayes became the first African-American Composer awarded with an Academy Award. The award was for the "Best Song from a Motion Picture," titled "Shaft." His recording of "Shaft," the song for which he is best known, reached number one on the Pop Charts also earned him a Grammy award the same year.

1996 - Gymnast, Dominique Dawes, who was a ten year member of the U.S. National Gymnastics Team, the 1994 U.S. All-Around Senior National Champion and three-time Olympian, appeared on the breakfast cereal box "Wheaties."

On this Day in History...

April 17th

1818 - Thomas Day became the first African-American Furniture and Cabinet Maker in the South. He operated one of North Carolina's largest furniture enterprises, they created sofas, chairs, chests, tables and bedsteads from walnut, mahogany and oak. His work was represented in homes of distinguished families throughout the State. Day was recognized as one of the finest craftsman of his day. His workshop, "The Yellow Tavern," is a National Historical Landmark.

1866 - Bridget "Biddy" Mason became the first African-American woman to own property in Los Angeles, CA. Mason also organized first A.M.E. Church, the oldest African-American church in the City.

1964 - Joseph Jacob "Jake" Simmons Jr., broke the color barrier in the Oil Industry, he became the first African-American in the world to represent a Major Oil Company abroad. Phillips Petroleum hired Simmons as Corporate Ambassador for its permanent office in Lagos, Nigeria. Simmons also brokered oil leases for African-American farmers in Oklahoma and Texas, helping to prevent big oil companies from exploiting them.

2000 - Aviator, Gustavus "Gus" McLeod took off in a 1939 Boeing Stearman open-cockpit biplane and flew a 3,500-mile odyssey over the North Pole. He became the first person to fly over the pole in such an aircraft. His achievement was included in the Congressional Record. When McLeod took the historic trip, a film crew from the National Geographic Society trailed him in a chase plane. The National Geographic Society provided partial funding for McLeod's trip.

On this Day in History...

April 18th

1922 - The first African-American Heavyweight Champion of the World, Jack Johnson received a U.S Patent for his invention of the "Wrench." Johnson is also credited for coining the term "Wrench."

1944 - Doris E. Spears became the first African-American woman Deputy Sheriff in the United States. She worked for the Los Angeles Sheriff's Department, the largest Sheriff's Department in the World.

1966 - Bill Russell became the first African-American Head Coach in the National Basketball Association (NBA). He was named Head Coach of the Boston Celtics. As a player, Russell was the centerpiece of the Boston Celtics Dynasty, his team won eleven NBA Championships, including an unprecedented eight Championships in a row.

1993 - Clifton R. Wharton Jr., became the first African-American named United States Deputy Secretary of State.

1995 - Detroit Entrepreneur, Don H. Barden was approved to operate a Casino Riverboat in Gary, IN. His company was selected over nineteen other companies that applied for a license from the Gaming Commission. Barden, served as Chairman, President and Chief Executive Officer of Barden Companies, Inc. When his company acquired the Fitzgeralds Las Vegas Casino, he became the first African-American Casino Owner in Las Vegas. For thirty years, Barden had successfully developed, owned and operated many business enterprises in various industries including, broadcasting, casino gaming, international trade and real estate development and cable television.

On this Day in History...

April 19th

1821 - Samuel E. Cornish established the first African-American Presbyterian Church in New York City, it was the second in the country. A notable Abolitionist, Cornish was also coeditor along with John B. Russworm, of the first African-American newspaper, Freedom's Journal, in 1827.

1929 - Louis L. Redding broke the color barrier of the Delaware Bar Association, he become the first African-American Attorney in the State. After graduating from Harvard University's Law School, he had a private practice in Wilmington and became involved in several Landmark Civil Rights decisions that resulted in the desegregation of public schools throughout the nation.

1983 - Thomas J. Mann Jr., became the first African-American State Senator for the State of Iowa. He was also Executive Director of the Iowa Civil Rights Commission.

1990 - Walter E. Massey became the first African-American to head the National Science Foundation. Throughout his career, he was also served as President of Morehouse College for 10 years, Managing Director of Argonne National Laboratory and Chairman of Bank of America.

2007 - Girl Genius, Brittney Exline, then fifteen years old, became the youngest African-American woman ever accepted to an Ivy League School, the University of Pennsylvania. When Exline was fifteen months old, she completing 100 piece jigsaw puzzles. In High School, she was fluent in Spanish, French, Japanese, Russian, Arabic and German.

On this Day in History...

April 20th

1929 - Jane Ellen McAllister became the first African-American woman in the United States to receive a Doctorate in Education. She received her degree from Teachers College of Columbia University in New York.

1935 - John L. Wilson became the only African-American appointed to a team of seven Architects to design the Harlem River Houses in New York City. He was also the first African-American student to attend Columbia University's School of Architecture in 1923.

1967 - James E. Dearing became the first African-American Special Agent for the Georgia Bureau of Investigation (GBI), he was also one of the first African-American Officers in the Savannah Police Department. Dearing later became Chief of Police and Director of Safety at Georgia State University in Atlanta, GA. He strengthened the police force at Georgia State, moving it from a security force to a full-fledged police force.

1990 - Singer, Songwriter, Dancer and Actress, Janet Jackson was inducted into the Hollywood Walk of Fame and awarded a star on Hollywood Boulevard. As the youngest child of the talented Jackson Family, she has sold over 100 million records worldwide. Jackson is one of the best-selling Artists in the history of Contemporary Music.

1993 - President Bill Clinton appointed Jesse Brown as the first African-American United States Secretary of Veterans Affairs. Brown was a Veteran of the United States Marine Corps.

On this Day in History...

April 21st

1868 - Oscar Dunn became the first elected African-American Lieutenant Governor for the State of Louisiana.

1896 - Inventor, Charles Brooks received a U.S. Patent for his invention of the improved Self Propelled Street Sweeper.

1898 - The Spanish-American War began, sixteen Regiments of African-American volunteers were recruited. There were a total of five African-Americans who won Congressional Medals of Honor during the war.

1918 - Gertrude E. Durden Rush became the first African-American woman Attorney in the State of Iowa. In 1925, she was also one of the founding members of the National Bar Association (NBA). The National Bar Association is the Nation's oldest and largest national network of predominantly African-American Attorneys and Judges, it represents the interests of approximately 70,000 Lawyers, Judges, Law Professors and Law Students.

2010 - Jazz Vocalist, Jimmy Scott was awarded the Lifetime Achievement Award from the Jazz Foundation of America. Growing up, Scott never experienced puberty, the result of Kallmann's Syndrome, a hereditary hormonal deficiency, leaving him with a high, undeveloped voice. He first rose to prominence as "Little Jimmy Scott" in the Lionel Hampton Band as Lead Singer, he became famous for his high countertenor voice and his sensitivity on ballads and love songs. Scott also performed at the inaugurations of Presidents Eisenhower (1953) and Clinton (1993). On both occasions, he sang "Why Was I Born."

On this Day in History...

April 22nd

1809 - St. Philip's Episcopal Church was founded in the Harlem, New York City, it is the oldest African-American Episcopal Parish in New York City. St. Philips has been the spiritual home for tens of thousands of African-American New Yorkers for over two centuries, it paved the way for Harlem to become the center of African-American political and cultural life in New York City and arguably for the entire Nation. The church was designated as a New York City Landmark in 1993 and added to the National Register of Historic Places in 2008.

1864 - Dr. Rebecca Davis Lee became the first African-American woman Awarded a Medical Degree in the United States after studying at New England Female Medical College.

1871 - Daniel Alexander Murray became the first African-American to hold a Professional Position at the Library of Congress. Murray was proficient in several languages and acquired great research skills. In 1881, he was advanced to an Assistant Librarian, he was asked to prepare an exhibit on African-American achievements for the 1900 Paris Exposition.

1959 - Mahala A. Dickerson was admitted to the State Bar, she later became the first African-American Attorney in the State of Alaska. Growing up in Alabama, Dickerson had a lifelong friendship with civil rights Hero Rosa Parks.

1990 - George Haley became the first African-American to Chair the United States Postal Rate Commission. President Bill Clinton also appointed Haley to serve as the U.S. Ambassador to the Republic of Gambia.

On this Day in History...

April 23rd

1918 - While serving as an Officer of the Machine Gun Company with the 369th Infantry Regiment in Europe, James Reese Europe became the first African-American Officer to lead troops into combat during World War I. He was also the first to lead a raid on enemy lines.

1969 - The Ford Foundation donated $1 million to Morgan State University, Howard University and Yale University to help prepare faculty members to begin teaching courses in African-American Studies.

1995 - Sea Captain, Michael Augustine Healy became the first African-American to have a U.S. Coast Guard Vessel named in his honor. Due to his fearless exploits including prowling the Arctic, he was nicknamed "Hell-Roaring" Mike Healy.

1997 - Doo-Wop, Jazz, Soul and R&B group, "The Four Tops" were inducted into the Hollywood Walk of Fame and awarded a star on Hollywood Boulevard. The Lead Singer Levi Stubbs, Abdul "Duke" Fakir, Renaldo "Obie" Benson and Lawrence Payton performed together for over four decades without a single change in personnel.

2007 - Barbara Hillary became the first African-American woman on record to reach both the North and South Poles. Hillary was also the oldest person to ever set foot on the North Pole, at the age of seventy-six. Three years later, she made history once again, becoming the oldest person to set foot on the South Pole, at the age of seventy-nine.

On this Day in History...

April 24th

1939 - Inventor, Frederick McKinley Jones patented Refrigerated Trucks, his creation revolutionized shipping and grocery businesses worldwide. He also has over 60 patents to his name, the majority pertain to refrigeration technologies. Jones was inducted into the National Inventors Hall of Fame in 2007.

1944 - Frederick D. Patterson founded the United Negro College Fund. His goal was to coordinate the fundraising efforts of 41 private, accredited four-year schools. Chartered in New York, it was the first attempt by private African-American Colleges to establish a cooperative fundraising organization. Known today as the College Fund/UNCF, its efforts still contribute significantly to the survival of African-American higher education.

1949 - Singer and Actress, Juanita Hall became the first African-American to win a Tony Award for her performance as "Bloody Mary" in the 1949 Broadway production of "South Pacific."

1984 - Leander "Frank" McCall Jr., became the first African-American Police Officer at the Fishkill Police Department in Fishkill, N.Y. His career as an Officer resulted in many high profile arrest and high speed pursuits, he was responsible for capturing some of New York's most wanted fugitives. He became well known by his colleagues in the law enforcement community in the cities of Fishkill and Poughkeepsie, N.Y. In 1987, he started his own security firm "Big Mac Security." His company quickly built a reputation for ensuring the safety and personal protection for all clients. Along with his law enforcement background, his company Big Mac Security provided protection for local businesses, sporting arenas, concert venues and A list celebrities.

On this Day in History…

April 25th

1790 - Dr. James Durham became recognized as the first African-American Physician in the United States. Born into slavery, he purchased his freedom by the age of twenty. Encouraged to go into Medicine, Durham began working as a Nurse, he was hired by Dr. Benjamin Rush, the "Father of American Medicine." A few years later, Durham moved to New Orleans, LA., and had a flourishing practice. He treated patients with Diphtheria and was instrumental in helping to contain the Yellow Fever epidemic that ravaged New Orleans in 1796.

1873 - (HBCU) The University of Arkansas at Pine Bluff was founded. The primary objective was to provide skills and educate African-American Students to become Teachers for States with African-American schools.

1968 - Known as "The Jackson Five," Tito, Jermaine, Marlon, Jackie and Michael received their first big break at Harlem's Apollo Theater, they caught the attention of Motown Records and its President, Berry Gordy. In 1969, they made their debut album, "Diana Ross Presents the Jackson Five."

1999 - Broadine M. Brown became the first African-American named as Management Chief at the U.S. Marshal Service, a Federal Law Enforcement Agency within the U.S. Department of Justice.

2001 - The San Diego Padres "Left-Fielder," Rickey Henderson broke the Major League all-time "Walks" record. Nicknamed "The Man of Steal," he is widely regarded as one of Baseball's greatest leadoff hitters and baserunners. Henderson also holds the Major League records for career stolen bases, runs, unintentional walks and leadoff home runs.

On this Day in History...

April 26th

1876 - Edward Alexander Bouchet became the first African-American to earn a Doctorate in the United States. He received a Ph.D. in Physics from Yale University. Dr. Bouchet taught Chemistry and Physics for 26 years at the Institute for Colored Youth in Philadelphia, PA. He was also on the faculty of Bishop College in Marshall, TX.

1892 - Inventor, Sarah Boone became the second African-American woman to receive a U.S. Patent, she invented the "Improved Ironing Board.

1975 - Jeanne Sinkford became the first woman to ever to become Dean of a Dental School in the United States.

1976 - Clara Leach Ender became the first African-American woman and Nurse to graduate with a Masters Degree the United States Army Command and General Staff College.

2006 - Violet Palmer became the first African-American woman to serve as Referee in a National Basketball Association (NBA) game. The only other woman Official in the league at this time was Dee Kanter, together they were the first two women Officials in any men's Professional Sports League.

2007 - Major General, Joseph C. Carter became the first African-American Commander of the Massachusetts Army National Guard (MANG). He was sworn into office by Governor Deval Patrick (Massachusetts first African-American Governor). Carter became the Governor's Senior Military Advisor overseeing MANG preparedness. He also held the post as Chief of Police for Massachusetts Bay Transportation Authority Transit Police Department.

On this Day in History...

April 27th

1878 - Composer and Minstrel Entertainer, James Bland became the first African-American to compose a song that became an Official State Song. "Carry Me Back to Old Virginny," was adopted by the State of Virginia, although few knew that it was by an African-American composer. Bland wrote approximately seven hundred songs in his career, including "Oh, Dem Golden Slippers" and "In the Evening by the Moonlight." He attended Howard University Law School but gave up his Law Studies to join the Entertainment World.

1931 - Jane M. Bolin became the first African-American woman to graduate from the Yale University Law School. At the age of thirty-one, she became the first African-American woman Judge in the United States. She was appointed as a Family Court Judge in New York City.

1969 - Georgia M. Davis Powers became the first African-American and the first woman elected to the Kentucky State Senate. She served as a member of the State Senate for twenty-one years.

1995 - Bessie Coleman was commemorated on the U.S. postage stamp. In 1922, she became was the first African-American woman to earn her Pilots License. Due to both racial and gender discrimination, Aviation schools in the United States denied her entry. She taught herself French and moved to France, earning her license from France's Caudron Brother's School of Aviation in just seven months. She specialized in stunt flying and parachuting, earning a living barnstorming and performing aerial tricks. She remains a pioneer of women in the field of Aviation.

On this Day in History...

April 28th

1949 - Howard University's School of Architecture became the first (HBCU) Architecture School to receive accreditation. By 1990, accredited programs in either Architectural Engineering or Professional Architecture also existed at Hampton University, Tuskegee University, Florida A&M University, Southern University Baton Rouge, Morgan State University and Prairie View A&M University.

1979 - Singer, Songwriter, Musician and Composer, Ray Charles became the first person of any race to perform before the Georgia Assembly. Throughout his career, he made a number of hit records, including "Georgia on My Mind," which set new sales records in 1959 and became the State Song for his home State of Georgia. Charles developed the concept of Soul, Merging Gospel, Rhythm and Blues as well as Popular music into a musical entity.

1981 - "Linebacker" Lawrence Taylor was drafted from the University of North Carolina (UNC) to the New York Giants in the National Football League (NFL). He is considered one of the greatest players ever to play the game. Taylor has also been ranked as the greatest defensive player in league history.

1993 - The African-American Museum of Iowa was founded by a small group of members of the Mt. Zion Missionary Baptist Church in Cedar Rapids. The church provided meeting space and money to launch the organization.

On this Day in History...

April 29th

1854 - Originally established as The Ashmun Institute, Lincoln University received its charter from the Commonwealth of Pennsylvania, making it the Nation's first degree-granting Historically Black College and University (HBCU).

1859 - Thomas Greene Bethune "Blind Tom" also known as Thomas Wiggins, became the first African-American Musical Prodigy and Piano Player to win national fame. He was also the first African-American Artist known to have performed at the White House. Then about ten years-old, he played the piano for President James Buchanan. He had numerous original compositions published and a successful performing career throughout the United States. During the 19th century, he was one of the best-known American Performing Pianists. Although he lived and died before Autism was described as a mental condition, he is now regarded as an Autistic Savant.

1949 - Alonzo G. Moron became the first African-American President of Hampton University, this event was extremely significant to the African-American community in Virginia. Moron influenced the civil rights movement as he worked to upgrade Hampton Institute from a Trade School to a College.

1986 - Duke Ellington was commemorated on the U.S. postage stamp. Ellington was a Composer, Pianist and Bandleader of a Jazz Orchestra. A major figure in the History of Jazz Music, his career spanned more than fifty years, during which time he composed thousands of songs for the stage, screen and contemporary songbook.

On this Day in History...

April 30th

1959 - Motion Picture "Imitation of Life" was released. This groundbreaking film addressed issues of race, class and gender. Imitation of Life is the second film adaptation of Fannie Hurst's novel of the same name. Actress, Juanita Moore received an Academy Award nomination for her performance as Annie Johnson, an African-American single mother who has a daughter, Sarah Jane, who inherited her father's fair skin and can pass for Caucasian. The popular film did well at the box office clearing $6.4 million. In 2015, the United States Library of Congress selected Imitation of Life for preservation in the National Film Registry, finding it "culturally, historically, or aesthetically significant."

1979 - John D. Glover became the first African-American Federal Bureau of Investigations Field Office Chief, he headed the FBI's operations in Milwaukee, WI. In 1986, Glover became the highest-ranking African-American in the Bureau, he was an Executive Assistant Director in Charge of Administration.

1993 - Myrick Bismarck became the first African-American to serve as Consul General in Durban, South Africa. In 1996, he was appointed as U.S Ambassador to the Country of Lesotho. Bismarck was inducted into the U.S. Army's Hall of Fame at Fort Benning's Officers Candidate School. He also represented the United States at the swearing in of South Africa's first Democratic Parliament, led by Nelson Mandela.

1997 - President Bill Clinton appointed Alexis M. Herman as the first African-American Secretary of the Department of Labor. Prior to serving as Secretary, she was Assistant to the President and Director of the White House Office of Public Engagement.

On this Day in History...

May 1st

1922 - Mary Morris Burnett Talbert became the first African-American woman to receive the NAACP Spingarn Medal, for her efforts to preserve the home of Frederick Douglass in Anacostia, VA. In 1922, the home was dedicated as the Frederick Douglass Museum. In 1920, Talbert also became the first African-American delegate to be seated at the International Council of Women.

1937 - Boxer, Henry "Hammering Hank" Armstrong became the only person to hold three Championships and three World Titles at once. During a ten-month period between 1937 and 1938, he won the Featherweight, Welterweight and Lightweight Titles. In 1937, he won 27 fights, in which 26 were by knockout.

1950 - Gwendolyn Brooks became the first African-American to win a Pulitzer Prize. Her book of poetry "Annie Allen" won the award for the "Best Book of Poetry" in the United States.

1975 - Paul Laurence Dunbar was commemorated on the U.S Postage stamp. He was a Poet, Novelist and Playwright of the late 19th and early 20th centuries. Dunbar was one the first influential African-American Poets in American literature. He enjoyed his greatest popularity following the publication of dialectic verse in collections such as Majors and Minors and Lyrics of Lowly Life.

1980 - Norma H. Johnson was named Chief Federal Judge for the District of Columbia, making her the first African-American woman to lead the Federal Court in the Nation's Capital.

On this Day in History...

May 2nd

1950 - President Harry S. Truman appointed Edith S. Sampson as the first African-American woman Delegate to the United Nations. Sampson continued her term under the Eisenhower Administration until 1953. Sampson was also the first African-American woman Judge in the State of Illinois elected to the Municipal Court.

1970 - The African-American Museum of Nassau County was founded. The 6,000 sq. ft. facility is operated by the Museum Services Division of the Nassau County Department of Recreation, Parks and Support Services, it is one of the only African-American museum in New York City. The museum hosts a number of events including Black History Month and Kwanzaa celebrations and commemorations of the lives of important figures including Dr. Martin Luther King, Jr., and Malcolm X among others.

1982 - Reginald W. Gibson became the first African-American to sit on the Bench of the the U.S. Court of Federal Claims.

1989 - Roscoe M. Moore Jr., became the first Chief Veterinary Officer for the U.S. Public Health Service (USPHS). A Federal Uniformed Service that is one of the seven Uniformed Services of the United States.

1994 - Garromme P. Franklin became the first African-American Regional Administrator for the Federal Aviation Administration (FAA). As a twenty-five year Veteran of the FAA, she was named as the Head of the Eight States, with 6,750 employees.

On this Day in History...

May 3rd

1845 - Macon B. Allen became the first African-American in the United States Licensed to Practice Law, he passed the Massachusetts Bar Exam. He then opened the first African-American Law Office in the country. In 1848, Allen set his sights even higher and passed another rigorous exam to become Justice of the Peace, making him the first African-American to hold a Judiciary Position. One year later he was elected Judge to Probate Court for Charleston County, S.C.

1920 - Tulsa, Oklahoma became one of the most prominent concentrations of African-American businesses in the United States, it was popularly known as America's "Black Wall Street." A neighborhood in Tulsa named Greenwood, featured over 600 businesses including, 2 Movie Theaters, 21 Churches, 30 Grocery Stores, 21 Restaurants, 6 Private Planes, Hospitals, Banks, Schools, Libraries, a Post Office and Bus System. All of these business were owned by African-Americans.

1953 - The African-American Museum in Cleveland was founded by Icabod Flewellen, it became the first Independent African-American Museum to open in the United States.

1969 - Lillian Lincoln Lambert became the first African-American woman to earn an MBA Degree from Harvard Business School. While there her mentor was H. Naylor Fitzhugh, the first African-American ever to receive a Harvard MBA in 1933. While at Harvard, she established an African-American student union. In 1976, she founded a janitorial services company, Centennial One Inc., she was Chief Executive Officer and President. In 2001, she sold her company for $20 million. During the mid-1970s, Lambert also taught at Bowie State University.

On this Day in History...

May 4th

1875 - (HBCU) Alabama A&M University was founded by a former slave, William Hooper Councill and opened as the "Huntsville Normal School" in downtown Huntsville.

1959 - Count Basie became the first African-American man to win a Grammy Award. Basie was also the first African-American from the United States to have a band give a command performance before Queen Elisabeth. He led his Jazz Orchestra continuously for nearly fifty years.

1959 - Jazz Singer who was often referred to as the "First Lady of Song" and "Queen of Jazz," Ella Fitzgerald became the first African-American woman to win a Grammy Award. She developed her famous Skat singing style while on a tour with Dizzy Gillespie. Fitzgerald became one of the most celebrated Singers of the 20th century. During her career she recorded more than 250 albums and won 13 Grammys. She also won the Kennedy Center Honor, the National Medal of the Arts and the American Black Achievement Award.

1961 - Congress of Racial Equality (CORE) began Freedom Rides from Washington, D.C. to New Orleans, LA., in order to desegregate southern bus terminals after the Supreme Court decisions Morgan vs. Virginia (1946) and Boynton vs. Virginia (1960), which ruled that segregated public buses were unconstitutional. "Freedom Rides," were also organized by the Student Nonviolent Coordinating Committee (SNCC). The Freedom Rides followed dramatic sit-ins against segregated lunch counters conducted by students and youth throughout the South. They also participated in Boycotts of retail establishments that maintained segregated facilities.

On this Day in History...

May 5th

1929 - Inventor, David Crosthwait was commissioned to design the Heating and Cooling system for Rockefeller Center and Radio City Music Hall in New York City. He has 119 patents to his name, which include 39 in the United States and 80 internationally. All of his inventions are related to heating, cooling and temperature regulating technology. He designed the HVAC (Heating Ventilation Air Conditioning) system. He also invented Central Air Conditioning.

1957 - John Kitzmiller became the first African-American to win the "Best Actor" Award at the Cannes Film Festival for the film, "Valley of Peace." The film was also selected for screening as part of the Cannes Classics section at the 2016 Cannes Film Festival.

1969 - Boston Celtics star and NBA Legend, Bill Russell won his eleventh NBA Championship during his thirteen year career. He was the centerpiece of the Boston Celtics Dynasty. Russell holds the record for the most Championships won by an Athlete in a North American Sports League. He helped the Celtics win an unprecedented eight Championships in a row. Russell is widely considered one of the best players in NBA history. He was inducted into the Naismith Memorial Basketball Hall of Fame and the National Collegiate Basketball Hall of Fame.

1993 - Josiah Henson became the first African-American commemorated on the postage stamp for the Country of Canada. In 1830, Henson fled to Canada with his family, where he became involved in the Underground Railroad, leading nearly 200 slaves to freedom. Henson was also a Methodist Preacher, he went on lecture tours and spoke as an Abolitionist throughout Britain and Canada.

On this Day in History...

May 6th

1893 - President Grover Cleveland appointed Charles Henry James Taylor as the first African-American Minister Resident and Consul-General to the Country of Bolivia.

1982 - Singer, Songwriter and Actress, Diana Ross was inducted into the Hollywood Walk of Fame and awarded a star on Hollywood Boulevard. Ross was the Lead Singer of the Group "The Supremes," on Motown Records. They became one of the most successful singing groups in history.

1984 - Jesse Jackson became first African-American to win a Delegate Awarding U.S. Presidential Primary/Caucus. He is the second African-American (after Shirley Chisholm) to mount a nationwide campaign for President of the United States.

1995 - Ron Kirk was elected as the first African-American Mayor of Dallas, TX. Later in his career after his tenure as Mayor, Kirk served as U.S. Trade Representative for President Barack Obama's Administration. As trade representative, Kirk was the President's Principal Trade Advisor, Negotiator and Spokesperson. He was also responsible for the development of U.S. Trade Policy and the oversight of existing trade treaties such as the North American Free Trade Agreement (NAFTA).

2006 - Sophia Danenberg became the first African-American to climb to the Summit of Mount Everest. Withstanding bad weather during her climb, Danenberg suffered from bronchitis, a stuffed nose, frostbite on her cheeks and a clogged oxygen mask. She reached the summit thirteen days later.

On this Day in History...

May 7th

1878 - Inventor, Joseph Winters patented the folding Fire Escape Ladder that attaches to fire engines. In 1882, he also invented the improved Fire Escape Ladder that connects to buildings.

1921 - Dr. Sadie T. Mossell became the first African-American woman to receive a Ph.D. in Economics in the United States and the first woman to receive a Law Degree from the University of Pennsylvania Law School. Dr. Mossell was also the first African-American woman to practice law in the State of Pennsylvania as well as the first National President of Delta Sigma Theta Sorority. In 1946, she was appointed to the President's Committee on Civil Rights, established by President Harry S. Truman.

1942 - The first African-American combat unit to face the Japanese during World War II was the 24th Infantry Regiment. The Regiment encountered the Japanese at the New Georgia Islands, two days before the battle of Coral Sea.

1952 - Journalist and Political Activist, Charlotta A. Bass became the first African-American woman to run for Vice President of the United States. She was the nominee of the Progressive Party.

2002 - "Shortstop" Ozzie Smith, who played in Major League Baseball (MLB) for the San Diego Padres and St. Louis Cardinals appeared on the breakfast cereal box "Wheaties." Smith set Major League records for career assists and double plays by a shortstop. He also won the National League Gold Glove Award for play at shortstop for thirteen consecutive seasons.

On this Day in History...

May 8th

1823 - Alexander L. Twilight became first African-American College graduate in the United States, he attended Randolph Academy and graduated from Middlebury College in Middlebury, Vermont. The City of Middlebury later named a building in his honor. After college, he went on to become a Vermont State Legislator.

1862 - Entrepreneur and Businessman, Robert R. Church became the first African-American millionaire in the South, he built a reputation for great wealth and influence in the business community. He founded Solvent Savings Bank, the first bank owned and operated by African-Americans in Memphis, TN. He extended credit to African-Americans so they could buy homes and develop businesses. Church was also the largest land owner in the State of Tennessee.

1952 - Floyd Bixler McKissick became the first African-American to graduate from the University of North Carolina Law School. He later served as Youth Counsel for the NAACP and worked with the Congress of Racial Equality (CORE). In 1955, he started his own Law Firm, specializing in Civil Rights Cases. McKissick also served as Legal Counsel for CORE, he was its National Chairman 1963, he then became its National Director in 1966.

1983 - Singer, Actress and Civil Rights Activist, Lena Horne was awarded the NAACP Spingarn Medal, for her efforts as a humanitarian and a living symbol of excellence. Horne also played a major role at the March on Washington in August 1963.

On this Day in History...

May 9th

1899 - Inventor, John Albert Burr patented the "Improved Rotary Blade Lawn Mower." Burr held over 30 patents for lawn care and agricultural inventions, unlike many inventors who unfortunately never witnessed their designs become commercialized, he enjoyed the fruits of his success by receiving royalties for many of his inventions.

1970 - Gail Fisher became the first African-American Actress to receive an Emmy Award and a Golden Globe Award. She won both awards for her portrayal of Secretary Peggy Fair on the CBS television show "Mannix." Fisher also won an NAACP Image Award in 1969.

1990 - Marcelite J. Harris became the first African-American woman Brigadier General in the U.S. Air Force. In 1995, she also became the first African-American woman Major General.

2005 - Maryland Lawmakers approved a bill that renamed Baltimore/ Washington International Airport (BWI) after Thurgood Marshall, the Nation's first African-American Supreme Court Justice and a native of Baltimore, MD.

2008 - Comedian, Chris Rock became the first Comedian to play the O2 Arena in London, England. He also broke a Guinness World Record for the largest audience for a comedy show, performing his Stand-up Comedy Act before 15,900 fans.

2009 - Dr. Mary Hopkins became the first African-American woman to earn a Ph.D. Degree in Mathematics from Florida Atlantic University.

On this Day in History...

May 10th

1853 - Elizabeth T. Greenfield became the Nation's first African-American Concert Singer, she was also the first African-American woman to give a command performance before royalty when she appeared before Queen Victoria of England. Greenfield was often called "The Black Swan" due to her sweet tones and wide vocal compass. She toured the United States and Canada extensively during her career and became the best known African-American concert Artist of her time.

1949 - James R. Gladden became the first African-American Certified in Orthopedic Surgery in the United States.

1984 - The Afro-American Historical and Cultural Society Museum was founded. Located is on the upper floor of the Greenville Branch of the Jersey City, N.J. Public Library, its collection is dedicated to the African-American experience. The museum has galleries for Lectures, Special Exhibits and a Permanent Collection of Books, Newspapers, Documents, Photographs and Memorabilia regarding African-American History. Their collection also includes information about the Underground Railroad, the civil rights movement, the NAACP in New Jersey, Historic African-American churches and Genealogical Records.

1997 - Professional Tennis Player, Arthur Ashe, who won three Grand Slam Titles, appeared on the breakfast cereal box "Wheaties." He was also ranked as the world's number one Tennis Player.

On this Day in History...

May 11th

1869 - George Lewis Ruffin became the first African-American to graduate from Harvard University Law School. After his graduation, he became the first African-American to practice law in Boston. He went on to become Judge of the District Court of Charlestown, MA.

1902 - Joe Gans became the first African-American Boxer to win a World Lightweight Title, defeating Frank Erne. In 1954, he was elected to the International Boxing Hall of Fame.

1965 - Dr. Martin Luther King Jr., appointed Civil Rights Leader Hosea Williams as President of the SCLC (Southern Christian Leadership Conference) Summer Community Organization and Political Education. Williams was a trusted member of Dr. Kings inner circle and played a leadership role in the march to Montgomery, AL., this highly publicized event ultimately prompted President Lyndon Johnson to sign the Voting Rights Act. In 1971, Williams founded a non-profit foundation, "Hosea Feed the Hungry and Homeless," widely known in Atlanta for providing hot meals, haircuts, clothing and other services for less fortunate people on Thanksgiving, Christmas, Martin Luther King, Jr., Day and Easter Sunday each year.

2018 - LaToya Cantrell became the first African-American woman Mayor of New Orleans, LA. She was previously a member of the New Orleans City Council. During her time in office, she led the passage of an ordinance that prohibited smoking in bars, casinos and most public spaces in New Orleans, she also took part in an initiative to make the City more diverse.

On this Day in History...

May 12th

1855 - Mifflin W. Gibbs became Owner and Editor of the "Mirror of the Times," California's first newspaper owned by African-Americans. In 1873, Gibbs was also elected as a City Judge, the first African-American Judge elected in the United States. In 1897, President William McKinley appointed Gibbs as an American Consul to the Country of Madagascar.

1918 - Reporter and Government Official, Ralph Waldo Tyler became the first and only African-American official war correspondent during World War I. In 1907, upon the advice of Booker T. Washington, Tyler was appointed by President Theodore Roosevelt to fill the post of Auditor of the Department of the U.S. Navy.

1940 - Della Raney became the first African-American Nurse commissioned as a Lieutenant in the Army Nurse Corps during World War II. As a Lieutenant serving at Tuskegee Army Airfield in Alabama, she also became the first African-American appointed as Chief Nurse. Raney later served as Chief Nurse at Fort Huachuca, Arizona, she was later promoted to Captain in 1945. After the war, she was assigned to head the Nursing staff at the Station Hospital at Camp Beale, California.

1955 - Major League "Pitcher," Samuel "Toothpick Sam" Jones became the first African-American to pitch a no-hitter, his Chicago Cubs defeated the Pittsburgh Pirates 4-0. He was the first pitcher to have a no-hit game in forty years. During his career, Jones led the National League in strikeouts and walks three times in 1955, 1956 and 1958.

1972 - Known as "Hammering Hank, Major League "Outfielder," Hank Aaron became the first player hit 30 or more home runs in 14 seasons.

On this Day in History...

May 13th

1891 - Isaac Murphy became the first Jockey of any race to win the Kentucky Derby three times, he was considered one of the greatest race riders in American history, winning 44 percent of all the races he rode. Murphy won his first in 1884, second in 1890 and third in 1891, which made him the first Jockey to capture Derby titles two years in a row. In 1884, he became the only Jockey to win the Derby, the Kentucky Oaks and the Clark Stakes in the same Churchill Downs meeting. In 1955, Murphy was the first Jockey voted into the Jockey Hall of Fame at the National Museum of Racing in Saratoga Springs, New York.

1969 - James Charles Evers became the first African-American Mayor of Fayette, Mississippi, he was also the first African-American candidate for Governor in the State of Mississippi. He was the brother of the Civil Rights Activist Medgar Evers.

1987 - The first National Black Catholic Congress (NBCC) since 1894 met in Washington, D.C., it was comprised of member organizations that represented African-American Roman Catholics who work with National Roman Catholic Organizations. The Bishops elect one of its members to serve as President of the NBCC's Board of Trustees, two other members are elected to serve as trustees. Catholic Journalist and Civil Rights Leader, Daniel Rudd founded the Congress in 1894.

2007 - Tennis Coach, Traci Green became the first African-American woman to head a coaching staff for a Harvard University sport. Green was a former University of Florida Tennis Champion, she was mentored by Tennis Legend, Arthur Ashe. She also coached women's Tennis at Temple University.

On this Day in History...

May 14th

1880 - First Sergeant, George Jordan of the 9th Cavalry, commander of the Buffalo Soldiers won a Medal of Honor for leading a successful defense of Tularosa, New Mexico Territory. The Buffalo Soldiers originally were members of the 10th Cavalry Regiment of the United States Army. Their nickname came from Native Americans, who believed their brave and fierce fighting matched the buffalo. Eleven Buffalo soldiers earned the Congressional Medal of Honor in combat against Utes, Apaches and Comanches.

1955 - Clotilde D. Bowen was commissioned in the U.S. Army with the Rank of Captain, she became the first African-American woman Medical Officer in the Army, her medical specialty was Neuropsychiatry. Bowen was also the first African-American woman promoted to Colonel. During the Vietnam War, she was awarded the Bronze Star and the Legion of Merit. In recognition of her service, she was also awarded the Meritorious Service Medal in 1974.

1988 - The Arna Bontemps African-American Museum and Cultural Arts Center was founded by the Arna Bontemps Foundation. The organization was formed through the Division of Community Affairs and the City of Alexandria, LA. The museum is the restored childhood home of Arna Bontemps, a Poet, Author, Anthologist and Librarian who was considered the leading authority of the Harlem Renaissance. The period (sometimes referred to as the "New Negro" movement) when young African-American writers went to Harlem to share the African-American experience through their writing.

On this Day in History...

May 15th

1891 - (HBCU) Delaware State University was founded in Dover, DE. The School was established by the Delaware General Assembly under the provisions of the Morrill Act of 1890, by which land-grant Colleges for African-Americans came into existence in States maintaining separate educational facilities.

1917 - Tally Holmes of Washington, D.C. and Lucy Diggs Slowe of Baltimore, MD., won the men's and women's singles, respectively, to become the first African-American players to win the American Tennis Association Championships.

1923 - Howard Thurman graduated from Morehouse College as Valedictorian, after graduation, he was ordained a Baptist Minister in 1925. He then became the first African-American Dean at Boston University, then later Dean of Rankin Chapel at Howard University. Thurman traveled broadly, heading Christian missions and meeting with world figures like Mahatma Gandhi. When Thurman asked Gandhi what message should take back to America, Gandhi replied "I regret not having made nonviolence more visible worldwide," and suggested some African-American man would succeed where he had failed. Prior to the civil rights movement, Dr. Martin Luther King, Jr., read from Thurman's book "Jesus and the Disinherited." This book that laid much of the philosophical foundation for a nonviolent civil rights movement. According to Thurman, fear, deception and hatred prohibits a peaceful end to racial bigotry.

1996 - James Green became the first African-American Head Basketball Coach at the University of Southern Mississippi.

On this Day in History...

May 16th

1899 - Inventor, Andrew Beard patented the Automatic Coupler for Railroad Cars. He also patented the Rotary Steam Engine in 1891. Beard held several other patents for farming tools and he was inducted into the National Inventors Hall of Fame in 2006.

1942 - President Franklin D. Roosevelt signed the Act that created the Women's Auxiliary Army Corps (WAAC). The voluntary unit consisted of both African-American and Caucasian recruits. Charity Adams Earley completed basic training in the WAAC and became the first African-American woman commissioned in that organization. When she retired from the corps after the end of World War II, she was the highest-ranking African-American Officer in the service.

1978 - Founded in 1838, Bethel Baptist Institutional Church was added to the National Register of Historic Places, it is the oldest African-American Baptist Church in the State of Florida.

1997 - Patricia "Patti" G. Smith became the first African-American woman to head the Commercial Space Transportation section of the Federal Aviation Administration (FAA). Under her administration, the FAA licensed the Mojave Air and Space Port, the first commercial spaceport in the United States.

2010 - Katie Washington became Notre Dame University's first African-American Valedictorian in its one hundred sixty-one year history. Washington presented the valedictory address during commencement exercises at the school's stadium.

On this Day in History...

May 17th

1875 - Oliver Lewis, a Jockey in Thoroughbred Horse Racing won the the first ever Kentucky Derby race on the winning horse, Aristides. In 2010, the Newtown Pike Extension in Lexington, KY., was named the Oliver Lewis Way in his honor.

1954 - Thurgood Marshall succeeded in having the Supreme Court declare segregated public schools unconstitutional in the landmark case, Brown vs. Board of Education. Marshall argued many more court cases after this victory in support of civil rights. His passion for ensuring the rights of all citizens regardless of race caught the attention of President John F. Kennedy, who appointed him to the U.S. Court of Appeals. In 1965, President Lyndon B. Johnson appointed him to the post of Solicitor General (this person argues cases on behalf of the U.S. Government before the Supreme Court, it is the third highest office in the Justice Department). In 1967, President Johnson appointed Marshall to the U.S. Supreme Court.

1954 - The site of two Topeka, KS., schools, Monroe Elementary School and Sumner Elementary School, both played a significant role in the landmark U.S. Supreme Court decision, Brown vs. Board of Education. Both schools were listed as National Historic Landmarks.

1988 - Ophthalmologist and Laser Scientist, Dr. Patricia Bath invented and patented the Laserphaco Probe, a medical tool that is used by doctors during eye surgery to correct cataracts. Her laser device has helped restore and improve vision for millions of people worldwide.

On this Day in History...

May 18th

1969 - Singer and Dancer, Sammy Davis Jr., became the first African-American Entertainer to sleep in the White House as a guest. He was known as America's "Ambassador of Goodwill." Davis began his career at age three, performing with his father, Sam Sr. and his uncle, Will Mastin. The Singer, Dancer and Actor appeared on almost every variety show and comedy series on network television between 1956 and 1980.

1971 - Shirley Ann Jackson became the first African-American woman to earn a Doctorate at the Massachusetts Institute of Technology (MIT). She is also the second African-American woman in the United States to earn a Doctorate in Physics.

1994 - Al Mauldin became the first African-American to direct the White House Military Office, which is a sub unit of the Executive Office of the President. His position included coordinating the President's travels and providing necessary security.

2008 - Benjamin Todd Jealous became the youngest President and Chief Executive Officer of the National Association for the Advancement of Colored People (NAACP). The Oxford University-educated Activist was thirty-five years old at the time of his appointment. The NAACP broke with its tradition of picking politicians and ministers to lead. Jealous was a former News Executive, having served as Executive Director of the National Newspaper Publishers Association, which encompasses about 200 African-American newspapers. Jealous was also the Democratic nominee for Governor of Maryland in the 2018 Gubernatorial election.

On this Day in History...

May 19th

1917 - Leo Pinckney became the first African-American drafted into World War I.

1927 - Actress, Josephine Baker became the first African-American to star in an international motion picture, "La Sirène des tropiques."

1935 - American Beach was founded, it was the only beach in the State of Florida that welcomed African-Americans and offered safe, secure overnight accommodations during segregation. The beach was founded by the Afro-American Life Insurance Company, (AALIC) which was established in 1901 to provide the Jacksonville African-American community with life insurance. The firm's Afro-American Pension Bureau purchased a 33-acre piece of property at the beach as an investment but also to provide it as a resort area for African-American Floridians who had been excluded from other beaches. They envisioned a resort that would signify success, self-sufficiency and respectability for middle-class African-American families from Atlanta and Savannah, GA. The original section of the beach property was added to the U.S. National Register of Historic Places.

1969 - William C. Handy was commemorated on the U.S. postage stamp. Handy was an African-American composer and musician, he was known as the "Father of the Blues."

2018 - Film and Television Actress, Meghan Markle became the first African-American in modern history to become a member of the British Royal Family upon her marriage to Prince Harry. Following their wedding, Markle became known as the Duchess of Sussex.

On this Day in History...

May 20th

1876 - William Francis Yardley became the first African-American to run for Governor for the State of Tennessee, he was also one of the first African-American Attorney in Tennessee. Yardley was a Fireman, a Justice of the Peace, an Insurance Agent and an Alderman for the Fifth Ward of Knoxville.

1965 - Milton L. Olive III became the first African-American Medal of Honor winner in the Vietnam War. First Class Private Olive was a member of the 3rd Platoon of Company B, 2nd Battalion (Airborne), 503rd Infantry on duty in Vietnam.

1992 - Actor, Louis Gossett Jr., was inducted into the Hollywood Walk of Fame and awarded a star on Hollywood Boulevard. Gossett has starred in numerous film and television productions, his acting career spans of five decades.

1996 - Composer, George Theophilus Walker was awarded the Pulitzer Prize in music for his composition Lilacs (for voice and orchestra), making him the first African-American to win the award in the area of music.

1996 - Comedian and Actor, Richard Pryor was inducted into the Hollywood Walk of Fame and awarded a star on Hollywood Boulevard. Pryor reached a broad audience with his storytelling style, he is widely regarded as one of the greatest and most influential stand-up comedians of all time.

2002 - Civil Rights Attorney, Fred Gray Sr. became the first African-American President of the Alabama State Bar Association.

On this Day in History...

May 21st

1923 - Atlanta University Center Historic District began as a consortium of Historically Black Colleges and Universities (HBCU's), which included the Clark Atlanta University, Spelman College, Morehouse College and the Morehouse School of Medicine. Students were able to cross-register at the other institutions in order to attain a broader collegiate experience. These institutions played an important role in the Civil Rights Movement of the 1950's and 1960's.

1969 - Tina S. Green became the first African-American Head Coach in women's Collegiate Lacrosse, she is also the co-founder of the Black Women in Sport Foundation. Green established Temple University as a premiere lacrosse program from 1975 through 1992, leading the Owls to three National Championships and eleven consecutive Final Four appearances. Green had her best season in 1988, she carried the Owls to a 19-0 record, capped off with a huge win over Penn State for the NCAA crown.

1982 - Roscoe Robinson, Jr., became the first African-American to be a Four-Star General in the U.S. Army, he was also the first African-American Representative on the NATO Military Committee. He served at posts in the United States and abroad, including assignments as Commanding General of the U.S. Army in Japan and as Commander of a Battalion of the 1st Cavalry Division during the Vietnam conflict. Robinson was considered a war hero, his decorations include the Distinguished Flying Cross and the Master Parachutist Badge. He remained active after his retirement by serving on several corporate boards.

On this Day in History...

May 22nd

1831 - William L. Garrison published the first issue of "The Liberator," an Abolitionist Newspaper.

1912 - Dr. Lydia Ashburne Evans became the first African-American woman to graduate from Howard University Medical School, she was also the first African-American woman licensed to Practice General Medicine in the State of Virginia.

1950 - Juanita E. Jackson Mitchell became the first African-American woman to graduate from the University of Maryland Law School, she was also the first African-American woman to Practice Law in the State of Maryland.

1954 - Jewel Limar Prestage became the first African-American woman to receive a Doctorate in Political Science. She later became Dean and Professor of Political Science in the Benjamin Banneker Honor College at Prairie View Agricultural and Mechanical College in Texas.

2002 - The town of Quindaro, in what is now Kansas City, KS., was placed on the National Register of Historic Places. This town was an important station on the Underground Railroad, with slaves escaping from Platte County and hiding with local farmers before traveling to Nebraska for freedom.

2018 - Georgia Democrats selected Stacey Abrams as the first African-American woman to be a major party nominee for Governor in the United States. Abrams also served as a minority leader of the Georgia House of Representatives from 2011 to 2017.

On this Day in History...

May 23rd

1911 - A group of African-Americans built a small chapel, one of the first for the town of Las Cruces, N.M. Their church, Phillips Chapel Colored Methodist Episcopal (now Christian Methodist Episcopal) CME Church has been placed on the New Mexico State Register of Cultural Properties, it was also listed with the National Register of Historic Places. The church was named after Rev. Charles H. Phillips, first Bishop of the Colored Methodist Episcopal Church in America. Since its beginning, the Chapel has been a focal point and gathering place for the African-American community of Las Cruces, it has served as a center for worship, weddings, christenings and social outings.

1966 - "Beale Street Historic District" in Memphis, TN., was declared a National Historic Landmark, this street is the birthplace of a style of music called "Blues." In the early 1900s, Beale Street was filled with many clubs, restaurants and shops, many of them owned by African-Americans. In 1889, NAACP co-founder Ida B. Wells was a co-Owner and Editor of an anti-segregationist newspaper called "Free Speech" which was based on Beale Street. The Beale Street Baptist Church, the oldest surviving African-American church in the State of Tennessee also played an important role in the early Civil Rights Movement in Memphis.

1968 - Huel Washington became the first African-American "Davis Cup" Umpire, he officiated in the United States vs. Mexico match at the Berkeley Tennis Club. The Davis Cup is the Premier International Team Event in men's Tennis, it is run by the International Tennis Federation and is contested annually between teams from competing countries in a knock-out format.

On this Day in History...

May 24th

1916 - The Lincoln Motion Picture Company became the first movie company organized by African-American Filmmakers. Established in Omaha, NE., the company relocated to Los Angeles the following year. The State of California formally incorporated the company and issued 25,000 shares of common stock. The company released 5 films, "The Realization of a Negro's Ambition," (1916) "Trooper of Company K," (1917) "The Law of Nature," (1917) "A Man's Duty" (1919) and "By Right of Birth." (1921)

1953 - The Niagara Falls Underground Railroad Heritage Center was founded. This Heritage site commemorates and preserves the people, places and stories connected to the Underground Railroad found within the City of Niagara Falls. As a program of the National Park Service, it is located in the former 1863 U.S. Custom House attached to the new Niagara Falls Amtrak Station.

1987 - The first National Black Arts Festival in the United States was held in Atlanta, GA., Michael L. Lomax founded the world-class celebration. The mission was to engage, cultivate and educate diverse audiences about African culture and provide opportunities for Artistic and Creative Expression.

1997 - Running Back, Tony Dorsett, who played professionally in the National Football League (NFL) for the Dallas Cowboys and Denver Broncos, appeared on the breakfast cereal box "Wheaties." Dorsett was the NFL Offensive Rookie of the Year and played for eleven seasons.

On this Day in History…

May 25th

1817 - Thomas Freeman became the first African-American man to own property in Livingston Parish, LA. His home was on the Historic Carter Plantation, it was listed on the National Register of Historic Places.

1952 - Frank E. Petersen Jr., became the first African-American Marine Pilot and the first to win U.S. Marine Corps wings. He was designated a Navy Aviator and received additional flight training at several training facilities. In 1979, he became the first African-American General in the Marines, he was also named the first African-American commander of the Quantico, Virginia facility, a major Marine Base. In 2010, President Barack Obama appointed Petersen to the Board of Visitors to the United States Naval Academy.

1956 - Lila Fenwick became the first African-American woman to graduate from the Harvard Law School. The school was one of the first University Law Schools in the country to admit African-American Students, but one of the last to admit women.

1981 - Jennie R. Patrick became the first African-American woman to earn a Doctor of Science Degree in Chemical Engineering from Massachusetts Institute of Technology (MIT). In 1980, she also recognized and was the recipient of the Chemical Engineers Outstanding Women in Science Award.

2010 - Steve Benjamin became the first African-American Mayor of Columbia, S.C. As an Attorney and Lobbyist, he was also former head of the State Department of Probation, Pardon, and Parole.

On this Day in History...

May 26th

1961 - Mercer Cook became the first African-American Ambassador to the Country of Nigeria. He was also the first African-American Ambassador to the Country of Gambia and the second African-American Ambassador to the Country of Niger.

1978 - Dr. Faye Wattleton became both the youngest person and the first African-American President of the Planned Parenthood Federation of America. Wattleton was also the first African-American woman honored by the Congressional Black Caucus. She was cited for her work on women's reproductive rights issues. Wattleton has received over a dozen Honorary Doctorate Degrees and was inducted into the National Women's Hall of Fame in 1993.

1987 - Karen C. Keith became the first woman of any race to coach Men's and Women's Track and Field Teams at a Major Institution, Boston College. During her first year, she became Division I Region Coach of the Year.

1994 - Irene Trowell-Harris became the first African-American woman Brigadier General, making her the highest-ranking African-American in the National Guard. She was also the first woman, first member of a minority group and first nurse to head a Medical Clinic in the National Guard. Prior to her promotion, she was served as Nursing Assistant to the Director of the Directorate of Nursing, Office of the Inspector General, Office of the Air Force Surgeon General at Bolling Air Force Base in Washington, D.C. She also held an appointment with the Department of Veterans Affairs, serving as Director of the Patient Care Inspection and Evaluation Division.

On this Day in History...

May 27th

1869 - Robert B. Elliott became the first African-American Commanding General of the South Carolina National Guard. Elliott also served as a member of the United States House of Representatives from South Carolina, serving from 1871 to 1874. In 1879, he was appointed as a Customs Inspector for the Treasury Department in Charleston, South Carolina.

1956 - Ann Gregory became the first African-American to play in an integrated Women's Amateur Golf Championship. Golf legend and Wimbledon Champion, Arthur Ashe called Gregory the best African-American woman golfer of the 20th century.

1963 - Leslie N. Shaw became the first African-American Postmaster to head a Postal Unit of a Major City. Shaw was appointed Postmaster of Los Angeles, CA., the third largest postal operation in the world. He supervised over 10,000 employees and handled more than $84 million in stamps and services. Shaw began his career in the Post Office as a Janitor.

1969 - Moneta Sleet, Jr., of Ebony Magazine became the first African-American to win a Pulitzer Prize for "Feature Photography" for his photograph of Coretta Scott King. Sleet is the first African-American man to win award for journalism.

2009 - The Tampa Bay Buccaneers hired thirty-two year-old Raheem Morris as its new Head Coach, he became the youngest Head Coach in National Football League (NFL) history.

On this Day in History...

May 28th

1890 - Dr. Ida Gray Nelson Rollins became the first African-American woman Dentist in the United States. She earned a Doctor of Dental Surgery Degree from the University of Michigan.

1944 - Surgeon and Medical Researcher, Charles Drew was awarded the NAACP Spingarn Medal. He was chosen for his outstanding work in blood plasma research, which led to establishment of the blood bank.

1962 - Activist and Leader in the Civil Rights Movement, Horace Julian Bond helped to establish the Student Nonviolent Coordinating Committee (SNCC). Bond was elected to four terms in the Georgia House of Representatives and later to six terms in the Georgia State Senate, serving a combined twenty years in both legislative chambers. From 1998 to 2010, he was Chairman of the National Association for the Advancement of Colored People (NAACP) and the first President of the Southern Poverty Law Center.

1992 - Anthony J. Polk became the first African-American to hold at Senior Management post at the American Red Cross, he was Director of Transformation Operations.

2001 - Aprille Ericsson-Jackson became the first African-American woman to receive a Doctorate from NASA's Goddard Space Flight Center. Jackson received her Bachelor's Degree from the Massachusetts Institute of Technology (MIT) in Aeronautical/Astronautical Engineering, she was also the first African-American woman to receive a Doctorate in Mechanical Engineering from Howard University.

On this Day in History...

May 29th

1851 - Abolitionist and Woman's Rights Activist, Sojourner Truth addressed the first Black Women's Rights Convention in Akron, OH. Her famous speech titled "Ain't I a Woman?" was a landmark moment in Feminist and Abolitionist history. Originally bearing the name Isabella Baumfree, Truth was born into slavery, she escaped in 1826. She claimed the Lord gave her the name Sojourner Truth, as he had called upon her to "travel up and down the land declaring the truth to people." Truth was the guest of President Lincoln at the White House on several occasions and was one of the voices that influenced Lincoln to recruit African-American soldiers for the Union Army during the Civil War. She was a powerful and impassioned speaker whose legacy of Feminism and Racial Equality still resonates today.

1862 - Mary Jane Patterson became the first African-American woman to earn a Bachelor's Degree in the United States, she attended Oberlin College in Ohio.

1985 - Sherian G. Cadoria became the first African-American woman to earn the rank of Brigadier General in the U.S. Army as well as the first to command a Male Battalion. Cadoria was also the first African-American woman Director of Manpower and Personnel for the Joint Chiefs of Staff, she served as one of four women Army Generals.

1997 - Wynton Marsalis became first Jazz Musician to win a Pulitzer Prize. He was honored for his epic Jazz Opera, "Blood on the Fields." Marsalis has been awarded nine Grammy Awards in both genres of Classical and Jazz music. He has also performed the National Anthem at Super Bowl XX in 1986.

On this Day in History...

May 30th

1817 - Jarena Lee became the first woman to preach in the African Methodist Episcopal (AME) Church. After hearing the church's founder Richard Allen preach, she felt it was her calling. Although she was not formally licensed to speak by the church, Lee began an extraordinary career as an Evangelist.

1965 - Samuel D. Wright became the first Chairperson of the Black and Puerto Rican Caucus. He headed the Caucus in both the State House and Senate.

1968 - Dr. Paul S. Green became the first African-American Captain in the U.S. Navy Medical Corps.

1975 - Elaine Brown moved up in ranks and became Chairperson of the Black Panther Party, making her the highest ranking woman in the party. Brown was the first African-American woman to hold the post and second in command only to Huey P. Newton, who founded the party.

1984 - Claude H. Organ Jr., became the first African-American Surgeon to Chair the American Board of Surgery. He taught at Creighton University School of Medicine in Omaha, NE.

1995 - Regina M. Benjamin became the first African-American woman named to the American Medical Association's Board of Trustees. In 2009, President Barack Obama nominated Benjamin as Surgeon General of the United States and as a Medical Director in the regular corps of the Public Health Service. She assumed office and became 18th person as well as the 2nd African-American woman to hold that post.

On this Day in History...

May 31st

1970 - Melvin H. Evans became the first popularly elected Governor of the Virgin Islands, a U.S. territory on the eastern Caribbean. In 1969, President Richard M. Nixon appointed him Governor, but it was not until August 1968 that Congress passed the Virgin Islands Elective Governor Act, giving residents the right to elect their Governor. He was also the first African-American Vice Chairman of the Southern Governors Conference.

1975 - Dr. Mary McLeod Bethune's Washington, D.C. townhouse became a National Historic Site. Bethune lived on the third floor of the home while the National Council of Negro Women (NCNW) occupied the first and second floors, it was their the first headquarters. The floor plan of the home remains unchanged from the days when Bethune lived there, most of the furnishings are originals. Bethune and the NCNW spearheaded strategies and developed programs that advanced the interests of African-American women.

1992 - Martin Stephan and Art Prince became the first African-Americans to sail in the America's Cup, match races between two sailing yachts.

1994 - Rhea L. Graham became the first African-American nominated as a Director of the United States Bureau of Mines. Graham was also a Senior Geologist with a private engineering firm in Albuquerque, NM.

2000 - Darrell L. Davis became the first African-American to be named Laboratory Director for the Drug Enforcement Administration's Office of Forensic Sciences.

On this Day in History...

June 1st

1972 - Singer, Johnny Mathis was inducted into the Hollywood Walk of Fame and awarded a star on Hollywood Boulevard. According to The Guinness Book of World Records, Mathis sold over 360 million records worldwide making him one of the biggest selling Artist of the 20th century.

1976 - The United States Naval Academy at Annapolis admitted women for the first time. Janie L. Mines became the first African-American women Cadet to enter. Mines graduated in 1980.

1984 - Gwendolyn C. Baker became the first African-American woman to be named National Executive Director for the YWCA.

1990 - The Buffalo Soldiers Memorial Park was added on the grounds of Historic Fort Leavenworth, KS. The park is dedicated to the Buffalo Soldiers who served throughout the West from 1866 through World War I.

1993 - Elaine R. Jones became the first woman to head the Legal Defense Fund (LDF), a nonprofit organization that fights discrimination and civil rights violations.

1997 - Ann D. Jordan became the first African-American woman to serve in the command role as Chair for the Inauguration of a U.S. President. She prepared for the second term inauguration of President Bill Clinton and spearheaded the theme of diversity, utilizing minorities and women in each activity that was planned.

On this Day in History...

June 2nd

1950 - George A. Owens became the first African-American to graduate from the Columbia University Business School. He held several administrative posts at Tougaloo University before becoming President from 1965 to 1984. Owens was named Interim President of LeMoyne College in Memphis in 1986.

1956 - Vincent Cullers and his wife Marian founded the Vince Cullers Group, it was recognized as the first full-service Advertising Agency in the United States owned and operated by African-Americans.

1972 - The first Major Automobile Dealership owned by African-Americans opened in the Bronx, N.Y., when Richard D. "Dick" Gidron opened "Dick Gidron Cadillac." Prior to opening the dealership, Gidron worked as General Manager of Cadillac Motors in Chicago, IL. He later opened a second Automobile Dealership, "Dick Gidron Ford," also located in the Bronx.

1983 - George H. Raveling became the first African-American Head Basketball Coach at the University of Iowa. The following year, he was an Assistant Coach for the 1984 Olympic Mens Basketball Team.

2001 - Phillip L. Clay was named Chancellor at Massachusetts Institute of Technology (MIT), making him the highest-ranking African-American Administrator in the institution's 136-year history. He became the second in command at the school. He was also Assistant Director of the MIT-Harvard Joint Center for Urban Studies and headed the Urban Studies and Planning Department.

On this Day in History...

June 3rd

1909 - Dr. Charles Victor Roman became the first Editor of the Journal of the National Medical Association. He was also the first African-American Physician in the United States to receive training in both Ophthalmology and Otolaryngology. Roman was the fifth president of the National Medical Association.

1959 - Ruth Jean Bowen became the first African-American woman to establish a successful Booking and Talent Agency in New York City. Her firm, "Queen Booking Corporation," has represented such Artists as Ray Charles, Sammy Davis Jr., Lola Falana, Aretha Franklin, Marvin Gaye, Gladys Knight, Smokey Robinson, Patti LaBelle and the Staples Singers. Bowen stared the company with an initial $500 investment and within ten years owned the largest agency in the world owned by African-Americans.

1975 - Virginia E. Hamilton became the first African-American to receive the "Newbery Medal," the American Library Association's most prestigious award in American Children's Books. Her novel, "M.C. Higgins, the Great" also won her the National Book Award in 1975.

1990 - Cora Billings became the first African-American Nun to head a parish in the United States. In 1999, she became Diocesan Director for African-American Catholics.

1997 - Professional Golf and Tennis Player, Althea Gibson, won eleven Grand Slam Tournaments, including six Doubles Titles, appeared on the breakfast cereal box "Wheaties." Gibson is known as one of the greatest Tennis Players who ever lived.

On this Day in History...

June 4th

1911 - Roscoe Conklin Giles became the first African-American admitted to Cornell University Medical School.

1922 - Clilan B. Powell became the first African-American Roentgenologist in New York City. As a X-Ray Specialist, he opened the first laboratory for x-ray Diagnosis and Treatment in an African-American community. He served on many government commissions and operated a finance company, insurance company as well as the New York Amsterdam News. Powell was educated at Virginia State University and Howard University College of Medicine.

1964 - Margaret F. Bailey became the first African-America Colonel in the Army Nurse Corps. She enlisted in the Army in 1944 and served in bases in the United States and abroad in France, Germany, and Japan.

1973 - Rosalie A. Reed became the first woman Veterinarian employed by a major American Zoo. Reed worked at the Los Angeles Zoo, the third largest in the Nation. Her responsibilities included maintaining healthy animals, performing surgery, determining the animals dietary needs and quarantining new arrivals. She also aided in the rehabilitation of a California condor at the site.

1981 - Charles P. Chapman became the first African-American Swimmer to cross the English Channel. In 1988, he earned a World Record by circumnavigating the Island of Manhattan, he swam 28.5 miles in 9 hours, 25 minutes. In 1997, he swam from Alcatraz Island to Aquatic Park in San Francisco using the butterfly swimming style.

On this Day in History...

June 5th

1894 - Inventor, George Murray patented the Fertilizer Distributor, Cotton Chopper and the Seed Furrow Opener, he also patented several other farming tools. Murray was a former slave who later became an Inventor as well as a United States Congressman, representing the State of South Carolina. He was the only African-American Congressman to hold a seat in the (53rd and 54th) Congresses. He focused his efforts on protecting the rights African-American citizens, he was also a member of the House Committee of Education.

1971 - Robert M. Duncan became the first African-American appointed to the United States Court of Appeals for the Armed Forces (CAAF). Duncan was also the first African-American elected to judicial office in Franklin County, Ohio and the first to serve on the Ohio Supreme Court.

1973 - Cardiss Collins became the first African-American woman to represent the Midwest in Congress. She was elected to in an Illinois special election and served in the United States House of Representatives from 1973 to 1997.

1977 - Margaret Santiago became the first African-American Registrar of the Smithsonian's National Museum of Natural History.

1979 - Major League "Outfielder," Dave Parker became the first Professional Athlete to earn an average of one million dollars per year when he signed a five-year, five-million dollar contract with the Pittsburgh Pirates.

On this Day in History...

June 6th

1900 - The last will and testament of Frederick Douglass was executed after his passing, his widow Helen received his home "Cedar Hill," a 20-room colonial mansion where Douglass lived for the last thirteen years of his life. She invited members of the National League of Colored Women to Cedar Hill to raise support for establishing it as a Historic Site. Congress chartered the Frederick Douglass Memorial and Historical Association (FDMHA), a non-profit group formed by Helen Douglass with the mission "to preserve to posterity the memory of the life and character of the late Frederick Douglass" and "to collect, collate, and preserve an historical record of the anti-slavery movement" at Cedar Hill. The National Site is located in Washington D.C.

1979 - The First Congregational Church of Detroit was listed on the National Register of Historic Places. The church served an important role as the last stop in a long journey for slaves taking the underground railroad into Canada. The church was also designated a Michigan State Historic Site in 1974.

2004 - Actress, Phylicia Rashad became the first African-American to win a Tony Award for "Best Lead Actress" in the Broadway Play "A Raisin in the Sun."

2006 - Alysa Stanton became the first African-American woman in the United States to be ordained as a Rabbi. She began work as a Rabbi at Congregation Bayt Shalom, a small synagogue in Greenville, N.C. Stanton converted to Judaism at the age of twenty-four.

On this Day in History...

June 7th

1863 - Known for her work as Conductor on the Underground Railroad, Harriet Tubman also led Union Troops in a raid along the Combahee River, becoming the only woman during the Civil War to plan and carry out an armed expedition against enemy forces.

1892 - Inventor, George T. Sampson patented the "Improved Clothes Dryer." This device utilized heated air that was drawn from a stove and blown through clothing that was tumbled around in a circle. The hot air evaporated the water in the damp fabrics and accelerated the drying process. He also invented a Sled Propeller in 1885, which is the predecessor to the Snow Mobile.

1971 - Cleo W. Blackburn became the first African-American Director of the United States Chamber of Commerce. Blackburn was also an Educator who was President of Jarvis Christian College in Hawkins, TX., from 1953 to 1964.

1997 - "Defensive Tackle" "Mean" Joe Greene, who played for the Pittsburgh Steelers of the National Football League (NFL) appeared on the breakfast cereal box "Wheaties." Greene is widely considered one of the greatest defensive linemen to play in the NFL.

2001 - The Baton Rouge African-American Museum was founded by Sadie Roberts-Josephis. Located in Baton Rouge, LA., it is the only museum dedicated to African and African-American history in the State of Louisiana. The museum celebrates Juneteenth, Black History Month and American history all year round.

On this Day in History...

June 8th

1823 - "The Drama of King Shotaway" became the first African-American Play that was produced in the United States. The play was written by Henry Brown and produced by the African Company, it dealt with the insurrection of the Caravs on Saint Vincent and featured Actor and Singer, James Hewlett.

1966 - Radio-Talk Show Host Petey Greene was hired by Dewey Hughes to work as a Disc Jockey at AM Radio Station WOL/1450 to host his own show. He aired in the Washington Metropolitan Area throughout the late 1960's and early 1970's. He rallied against poverty and racism on his show and on the streets during the height of his popularity. Greene had a six-year run from 1976 to 1982 on WDCA/20 and his show won two Emmy Awards. He was invited as a guest to the White House by President Jimmy Carter to honor visiting Yugoslavian President Josip Broz Tito. The film, "Talk to Me" starring Actor, Don Cheadle, opened in 2007, tells the Petey Greene Story.

2001 - Boxers, Laila Ali and Jacqui Frazier-Lyde fought at the Tuning Stone Casino in Verona, New York. This was the first pay-per-view Boxing match between two African-American women. The two fighters were the daughters of Boxing Legends, Muhammad Ali and Joe Frazier. Ali had a Professional Record of 24-0 and held the WBC, WIBA and IBA female Super Middleweight Titles, she also held the IWBF Light Heavyweight Title. Ali defeated Frazier-Lyde in a majority decision.

2018 - Mareena Robinson Snowden became the first African-American woman to earn a Ph.D. in Nuclear Engineering from Massachusetts Institute of Technology (MIT).

On this Day in History...

June 9th

1836 - Elijah Abel became the first African-American to become an Elder (Priest) in the Mormon Church, during the time the Mormons were Headquartered in Nauvoo, Illinois. Abel converted in 1832 and later relocated with the church to help establish their new Headquarters in Salt Lake City, Utah.

1960 - Charles Edward Anderson became the first African-American to receive a Doctorate in Meteorology from Massachusetts Institute of Technology. During World War II, he was a Captain in the U.S. Air Force as well as a Weather Officer for the Tuskegee Airmen in Tuskegee, AL.

1969 - Actress, Della Reese became the first African-American woman to host a Television Variety Show, "The Della Reese Show." The show aired five days a week for the 1969-70 season. Reese also became the first woman of any race to host The Tonight Show. She was recognized in 1994 with a star on the Hollywood Walk of Fame.

1982 - Samuel Fredrick Lambert became the first African-American President of the National Association of Power Engineers.

1997 - Harvey Johnson Jr., became the first African-American Mayor of Jackson, MS. His professional career includes the founding of the Mississippi Institute of Small Towns, a non-profit agency developed to assist small towns with minority leadership with housing, community development and infrastructure needs. In 2009, Johnson was elected once again, becoming a three term Mayor.

On this Day in History...

June 10th

1854 - James A. Healy became first African-American in the United States to be ordained as a Priest in the Catholic Church. In 1875, he also became the first African-American ordained as a Bishop in the Catholic Church.

1973 - Vernice Ferguson became the first African-American Nurse to become Chief of the Nursing Department at the National Institutes of Health in Washington, D.C.

1977 - Louisa Harris became the first African-American woman ever drafted by a National Basketball Association (NBA) Team. She refused the offers from the New Orleans Jazz and the Milwaukee Bucks. Harris is considered to be one of the pioneers of women's Basketball. She played for Delta State University and won three consecutive National Championships. She also represented the United States National Team and won the silver medal in the 1976 Olympic Games.

1982 - John Chaney became the first African-American Basketball Coach at Temple University in Philadelphia, PA. Chaney won a total of 741 career games. He took Temple to the NCAA Tournament a total of seventeen times.

2007 - "Center," Bill Russell, who played thirteen seasons in the National Basketball Association (NBA) for the Boston Celtics appeared on the breakfast cereal box "Wheaties." Russell was the centerpiece of the Boston Celtics Dynasty, his team won eleven NBA Championships, including an unprecedented eight Championships in a row. He is widely considered one of the best players in NBA history.

On this Day in History...

June 11th

1879 - Josephine Silone Yates became the first African-American certified to teach public school in the State of Rhode Island. In 1877, she was also the first African-American to graduate from Rogers High School in Newport, Rhode Island. Booker T. Washington offered Yates a position of Lady Principal at Tuskegee Institute, she refused the offer. Yates later became the President of the National Association of Colored Women.

1936 - Charles W. Anderson became the first African-American Legislator in the State of Kentucky. He championed the cause of civil rights in Kentucky and greatly improved African-Americans access to a quality education during his six terms as a Legislator.

1955 - Elston Gene "Ellie" Howard became the first African-American Player for the New York Yankees. When he became the starting "Catcher" for the Yankees, his immediate predecessor was the legendary Yogi Berra. Howard played with the Yankees for thirteen seasons and appeared in ten World Series.

1992 - Leroy T. Walker became the first African-American to hold the four-year post of President of the United States Olympic Committee. The retired coach, who in 1976 was Head Coach of the United States Track and Field Team at the Olympic Games in Montreal. He is a member of several Halls of Fame, including the U.S. Olympics Hall of Fame.

1998 - Oates Archery became the first African-American Sheriff in the State of Indiana.

On this Day in History...

June 12th

1876 - A monument of Richard Allen was dedicated in Philadelphia's Fremont Park. Allen founded the African Methodist Episcopal Church (AME), the first Independent African-American denomination in the United States.

1934 - Ralph H. Metcalfe broke three World Records while training for the Olympics, 100 meters, 200 meters, and 220 yards. He was the first man to win the NCAA doubles three times, the next year he became the only sprinter to win five times in a single event. In 1934-35 he was called the "World's Fastest Human." He and Jesse Owens were the first African-Americans to win a gold medal for the 400 X 100-meter relay, which they ran in Berlin Olympics in 1936.

1976 - Aerospace Psychophysiologist, Patricia S. Cowings became the first African-American woman Scientist to be trained as an Astronaut by NASA. Although she was an alternate for a space flight in 1979, she did not travel to space. She is most well known for her studies in the physiology of astronauts in outer space, as well as helping find cures for astronaut's motion sickness.

1981 - Grant Fuhr became the first African-American player drafted into the National Hockey League (NHL). He was picked in the first round and became the "Goaltender" also known as "Goalie" for the Edmonton Oilers. Fuhr became the most celebrated player in the League. He led his team to five Stanley Cup victories in 1984, 1985, 1987, 1988 and 1990. In 1988, he was awarded the Venzina Trophy, presented to the best Goaltender in the league.

On this Day in History...

June 13th

1945 - Horace Mann Bond became the first African-American President of Lincoln University, Pennsylvania, he was also the father of Civil Rights Leader, Julian Bond. He was an influential leader at several Historically Black Colleges and Universities (HBCU's). In 1939, Bond was appointed as the President of Fort Valley State University in Georgia.

1953 - James Del Rio became the first African-American Licensed Mortgage Banker in the United States, he established one of the first mortgage companies in the country that was owned an operated by African-Americans. Del Rio was a successful Real Estate Broker in Detroit, MI. He later served in the Michigan Legislature until 1973, he then became a Detroit Recorder's Court Judge.

1957 - George E. Norford became the first African-American Producer of Network Television programs at National Broadcasting Company (NBC).

1974 - Moses Malone became the first player ever drafted directly from High School to play Professional Basketball in the National Basketball Association (NBA). Over his twenty-one year career, Malone was a three-time NBA Most Valuable Player (MVP) and one of the game's greatest rebounders and scorers. He was inducted into the Basketball Hall of Fame in 2001. Bill Willoughby and Darryl Dawkins were also drafted directly from High School to play Basketball in the NBA the following year after Malone was drafted.

2018 - London Breen became the first African-American Mayor of San Francisco, CA.

On this Day in History...

June 14th

1921 - Georgiana Simpson, Sadie T. Mossell and Eva Beatrice Dykes became the first three African-American women in the United States to earn Ph.Ds. Simpson earned a Ph.D. in German Philology at the University of Chicago. Mossell earned a Ph.D. in Economics from the University of Pennsylvania, she went on to become the first African-American woman to earn a Law Degree there and the first to practice law in the State of Pennsylvania. Dykes earned a Ph.D from Radcliff College, she then joined the faculty of Oakwood University in Huntsville, AL., where she taught for more than fifty years.

1992 - Delano E. Lewis became the first African-American President of National Public Radio (NPR), a network that provides news, information and cultural programs to several hundred radio stations, with a total audience of more than fourteen million. U.S. President Bill Clinton named Lewis the U.S. Ambassador to South Africa, a post in which he served from 1999 to 2001.

2003 - George Foreman was inducted into the International Boxing Hall of Fame. Foreman had an Amateur Boxing record of 27 wins with no losses and won the gold medal in the Heavyweight Division at the 1968 Mexico City Olympic Games. In 1973, he won the World Heavyweight Championship, defeating Joe Frazier. He retired from the ring in 1977 and became an ordained Christian Minister. Ten years later he announced a comeback. In 1994, at age of forty-five, Foreman regained the Heavyweight Championship by knocking out twenty-seven year-old Michael Moorer to win the unified WBA, IBF and lineal titles. Foreman retired from the ring a second time with a 76-5 (68 KOs) record.

On this Day in History...

June 15th

1877 - Henry Ossian Flipper became the first African-American to graduate from the United States Military Academy at West Point, N.Y., earning a commission as a Second Lieutenant in the US Army. In 1878, he joined the 10th Calvary, making up what became known as the "Buffalo Soldiers." He served in Oklahoma and Texas.

1921 - Calvary Baptist Church was founded in Oklahoma City, Oklahoma. Constructed by African-American Architect and church member Russell B. Bingham. In the early 20th century the church served as the religious and social center of Oklahoma City's African-American community, it is also the site where Oklahoma students organized "sit-ins" at segregated lunch counters in 1957. The church was added to the National Register in 1978. Dr. Martin Luther King Jr., also preached at this church during its reformation period.

1951 - Mildred F. Jefferson became the first African-American woman to graduate from Harvard University's Medical School, she later became President of the National Right to Life Committee.

1953 - Albert Edward Manley became the first African-American President of Spelman College. An advocate for equality and education, he believed women were as capable of leadership as men and emphasized the achievement of excellence in all aspects of life. He was also a guest lecturer at Harvard University from 1970 through 1975.

1975 - Actor and Singer, Adam Wade became the first African-American Game Show Host, he hosted of the 1975 CBS game show, "Musical Chairs."

On this Day in History...

June 16th

1990 - Muhammad Ali was inducted into the International Boxing Hall of Fame. Ali is regarded as one of the greatest Heavyweight Boxers of the 20th century, he remains the only boxer in history to win the Heavyweight Championship Title three times. At the age of twenty-two, he won the WBA, WBC and lineal Heavyweight Titles from Sonny Liston in a major upset. Known as "The Greatest of All Times," he was involved in several historic Boxing matches. Notable among these were the first Liston fight, the "Fight of the Century," "Super Fight II" and the "Thrilla in Manila," against his rival Joe Frazier. He was also involved in the "The Rumble in the Jungle," against George Foreman.

1990 - Joe Frazier was inducted into the International Boxing Hall of Fame. Nicknamed "Smokin Joe" he reigned as the undisputed Heavyweight Champion from 1970 to 1973. As an amateur, he won a gold medal at the 1964 Summer Olympics Games in in Tokyo. Frazier was known for his sheer strength, durability, formidable punching power and relentless pressure fighting style.

1990 - "Sugar" Ray Robinson Jr., was inducted into the International Boxing Hall of Fame. Widely considered the greatest pound-for-pound Boxer of all time, his performances in the Welterweight and Middleweight divisions prompted a "pound for pound" ranking, where fighters were compared regardless of weight. Robinson had a professional record of 175-19 with 106 knockouts.

2000 - Actor, Samuel L. Jackson was inducted into the Hollywood Walk of Fame and awarded a star on Hollywood Boulevard. Jackson's films have generated more than $7.4 billion worldwide at the box office, making him the highest-grossing Actor in history.

On this Day in History...

June 17th

1992 - Six-foot-eight, 882-pound Sumo Wrestler, Mixed Martial Arts (MMA) competitor Emanuel "Manny" Yarbrough became the first African-American to win numerous Sumo Championships. In 1995, he won first place in the Judo World Championship competition, he also won the Dutch Open in 1999. One of Yarborough's Football teammates at Morgan State University in Maryland introduced him to Sumo Wrestling, he became an All-American Wrestler while in college. Since college, he traveled abroad extensively to participate in Sumo Competitions and demonstrations.

1994 - Beach Volleyball Pioneer, Dain Blanton became the first African-American to participate in the Association of Volleyball Professionals Tour. In 1997, he became the first African-American to win a major tournament in that sport, the Hermosa Beach AVP Grand Slam. His victory paid $300,000, the largest payoff in Professional Beach Volleyball history. Blanton and his teammate, Eric Fonoimoana, also won gold medals at the Sydney Olympics in 2000.

1999 - Ray Rhodes became the first African-American Head Coach for the Green Bay Packers. After Rhodes appointment, the Packers became the first NFL franchise to have three African-American men in the top three coaching positions, including Offensive Coordinator, Sherman Lewis and Defensive Coordinator, Emmitt Thomas.

2018 - Dr. Patrice Harris became the first African-American woman elected President of the American Medical Association (AMA). First elected to the AMA Board of Trustees in 2011, Dr. Harris has also held the Executive Offices of AMA Board Secretary and AMA Board Chair.

On this Day in History…

June 18th

1945 - The Mason Temple, Church of God in Christ was founded in Memphis, TN. This church served as a focal point of civil rights activities in Memphis during the 1950s and 1960s. The Temple was also the largest church building owned by a predominantly African-American Christian denomination in the United States. Dr. Martin Luther King, Jr., delivered his prophetic "Mountaintop" speech at this church on the eve of his assassination.

1956 - Charles Everett Dumas won a gold medal for the High Jump at the Olympics in Melbourne with an Olympic record leap of 6 feet 11 ¼ inches, he was also the first man to break the 7-foot barrier at the Olympic finals trial at the Los Angeles Coliseum.

1991 - Wellington Webb became the first African-American Mayor of Denver, CO. In 1977, Webb was selected by President Jimmy Carter to serve as Regional Director of the U.S. Department of Health, Education and Welfare.

2005 - Norries Wilson became the first African-American Head Football Coach for an Ivy League School, Columbia University. He led the school to its winningest season, the best record of any first-year coach in the school's history. He is also the first Football Coach at Columbia to lead the school to victories over Princeton in consecutive seasons.

2018 - A Richmond, VA., school honoring a confederate general was renamed "Barack Obama Elementary School." President Obama's name was chosen from a total of seven finalists. Students, parents, staff and community members all submitted ideas for the school's new name.

On this Day in History...

June 19th

1865 - Enslaved African-Americans in the State of Texas finally received news of their emancipation. From that point, an American Holiday was formed commemorating the announcement, it was called "Juneteenth," also known as Juneteenth Independence Day or Freedom Day. Each year, Juneteenth celebrations are observed in various cities all across the United States. Traditions include public readings of the Emancipation Proclamation, singing traditional songs such as "Lift Every Voice and Sing" and reading of works by noted African-American writers such as Ralph Ellison and Maya Angelou.

1895 - Historian and Civil Rights Leader, (William Edward Burghardt) W.E.B. Du Bois became the first African-American to earn a Ph.D. from Harvard University. He is perhaps best known for his work in being one of the founders of the National Association for the Advancement of Colored People (NAACP) in 1909 and helping it to become the country's single most influential organization for African-Americans.

1985 - Sharon P. Dixon became the first African-American Treasurer of the Democratic National Committee.

2018 - Talk Show Host, Actress and Philanthropist, Oprah Winfrey became the first African-American woman Entrepreneur to appear on the Bloomberg Billionaires Index, the list ranks the world's 500 richest people, Winfrey stood as the 494th richest person in the world. Her business endeavors included the ownership of "The Oprah Winfrey Show," which ran for twenty-five years and her cable network Oprah Winfrey Network (OWN) and a partnership with Apple Inc, which she produced original content and programming for the tech company.

On this Day in History...

June 20th

1960 - Renowned Singer and Actor, Harry Belafonte became the first African-American performer to win an Emmy Award. He was dubbed as the "King of Calypso" for popularizing the Caribbean musical style with an international audience in the 1950's. His "Calypso," was the first album in history to sell more than one million copies. Belafonte was also an early supporter of the Civil Rights Movement and one of Dr. Martin Luther King, Jr.'s confidants. Throughout his career, he has been an advocate for political and humanitarian causes, such as the anti-apartheid movement and USA for Africa. Since 1987, he has been a UNICEF Goodwill Ambassador.

1960 - Floyd Patterson became the first Boxer to win the Heavyweight Championship twice. He first won the Championship in 1956 at the age of twenty-one. As an Amateur, he won a gold medal in the middleweight division during the 1952 Olympics in Helsinki, Finland. He became the first African-American Olympic Medallist to win a World Title.

1994 - Lori M. McNeil defeated five-time Wimbledon Champion and number one ranked, Steffi Graf in the first round of the Ladies Singles. Until then, no reigning woman champion had lost in the first round to an unseeded opponent, making McNeil the first woman to accomplish this feat, it was McNeil's second straight victory over Graf.

2003 - Singer, Songwriter and Record Producer, Lionel Richie was inducted into the Hollywood Walk of Fame and awarded a star on Hollywood Boulevard. In the 1970's, Richie was a founding member of R&B group "The Commodores" before finding success as a solo Artist with his self-titled debut album.

On this Day in History…

June 21st

1912 - Theodore "Ted" Cable became the first African-American to win an Intercollegiate Weight Championship. He was the Hammer-Throw Champion of Harvard University.

1935 - Ora Washington became the first African-American woman to win seven consecutive titles in the American Tennis Association. She used her blazing pace to upset many American Tennis Association top-seeded stars. She was undefeated as a professional for twelve consecutive years.

1979 - Amalya L. Kearse became the first African-American woman Justice in the Second Circuit Court. President Jimmy Carter appointed her to the U.S. Court of Appeals in New York City (Thurgood Marshall was the first African-American in that post.). Kearse also became the first African-American woman Partner in a Wall Street Law Firm, Hughes, Hubbard, and Reed.

1990 - Musician, Songwriter, Singer and Actor, Little Richard (Richard Penniman) was inducted into the Hollywood Walk of Fame and awarded a star on Hollywood Boulevard. He is known as the "Architect of Rock & Roll" and an influential figure in Popular music for more than seven decades.

2001 - Professional Basketball Player and Businessman, Earvin "Magic" Johnson was inducted into the Hollywood Walk of Fame and awarded a star on Hollywood Boulevard. As a "Point Guard." Johnson played for the Los Angeles Lakers for thirteen seasons and won five National Basketball Association (NBA) Championships.

On this Day in History...

June 22nd

1958 - The Sivart Mortgage Company was founded as the first African-American Mortgage Banking firm, the firm was established by Dempsey J. Travis, a Chicago Businessman. The company was the first African-American owned firm approved by the Federal Housing Administration and the Veterans Administration.

1964 - Simon Shanks became the first African-American Patrolman in the State of Mississippi, working for the Laurel Police Department, he was later promoted to Captain.

1965 - The Freedom National Bank became the first chartered bank that was owned and operated by and African-Americans in Harlem, N.Y.

1986 - Vickie Miles LaGrange became the first African-American woman elected to the Oklahoma State Senate.

1993 - Boxer, Joe Louis was commemorated on the U.S. postage stamp. He reigned as World Heavyweight Champion from 1937 until 1949, he is regarded as one of the sport's all-time greats. Louis was considered the first true African-American national hero in the United States when he defeated a Nazi Germany fighter named Max Schmeling in 1938 at Yankee Stadium in front of 70,000 fans. Louis knocked out Schmeling in the first round. The fight symbolized the struggle between Democracy and Fascism.

2005 - Jeanine Menze became the first African-American woman to serve as a United States Coast Guard Aviator. She was assigned to fly a C-130 Hercules aircraft out of Air Station Barbers Point in Hawaii.

On this Day in History...

June 23rd

1927 - Journalist, Floyd Joseph Calvin became the first African-American to host a radio talk show. The show broadcasted on WGBS, it was the first show of its kind sponsored by an African-American newspaper, "The Pittsburg Courier."

1939 - Wynston Brown became the first President of the National Negro Bowling Association, organized in Detroit, MI. The organization later dropped the word "Negro" from its title and included Caucasian members as well.

1947 - Frazier L. Thompson became the first African-American to graduate from the University of Notre Dame. In 1997, the university named an award in his honor. The first recipient of the award was Percy A. Pierre, a graduate of the institution and member of its Board of Trustees.

1966 - Merle J. Smith became the first African-American graduate of the Coast Guard Academy.

1975 - Professional Tennis Player, Arthur Ashe became the first African-American man to win the Singles Title at Wimbledon, the US Open and the Australian Open. He was also ranked as the worlds number one Tennis Player. Ashe was posthumously awarded the Presidential Medal of Freedom by the President Bill Clinton in 1993.

1981 - Jewel Plummer Cobb became the first African-American President of California State University at Fullerton. She was also the first African-American to head a Major Public University on the West Coast.

On this Day in History...

June 24th

1907 - Educator, Writer and Historian, Alain Locke became the first African-American to win a Rhodes Scholarship to study at Oxford University in England. Known as the Dean of the African-American Literary Movement, Locke graduated with honors from Harvard University. A Scholar who focused on the achievements of African-Americans, Locke published the book, "The New Negro," which made him a nationally known figure. He encouraged the work of African-American writers during the Harlem Renaissance.

1936 - Educator, Civil Rights Leader, Government Official and Advisor to Presidents, Dr. Mary McLeod Bethune became the first African-American woman to head a federal office. President Franklin D. Roosevelt appointed Bethune to serve as Director of the Division of Minority Affairs of the New Deal's National Youth Administration (NYA). The NYA was founded in 1935 to provide job-training for unemployed youths and part-time work for students.

1971 - The firm of Daniels and Bell became the first African-American owned brokerage firm to become a member of the New York Stock Exchange. The firm was founded by Willie L. Daniels and Travis Bell Jr.

1975 - Lee Elder became the first African-American Golfer to compete in the Masters Tournament in Augusta, GA. He was also the first African-American to compete against Caucasians in South Africa, at the South African PGA Open.

1995 - Gene C. McKinney became the first African-American Sergeant Major of the United States Army.

On this Day in History...

June 25th

1827 - "Freedoms Journal" became the first newspaper owned and operated by African-Americans, it was founded in New York City by Rev. Peter Williams, Jr.

1886 - Peter "The Black Prince" Jackson became the first African-American to win a National Boxing Crown, the Australian Heavyweight Title. In 1892, he knocked out Frank Slavin to gain the British Empire Heavyweight Title.

1984 - Singer, Songwriter, Musician, Record Producer and Filmmaker, "Prince" Rogers Nelson released his sixth studio album, "Purple Rain" which is also the soundtrack to the 1984 film of the same name. The album was certified 13-times platinum, it has sold over 25 million copies worldwide, making it the third-best-selling soundtrack album of all time. In 2012, the album was added to the Library of Congress National Recording Registry list of sound recordings.

1996 - Franklin Delano Raines became the first African-American Director of the Office of Management and Budget (OMB), which is the largest office within the Executive Office of the President of the United States. The Office of Management and Budget's most prominent function is to produce the President's Budget.

2008 - Soul and Gospel Singer, Candi Staton was inducted into the Christian Music Hall of Fame. Over the course of her fifty-year career, Staton scored hits in every decade, her style ranged from Gospel, R&B, Disco to Electronic Dance Music. Along the way, she garnered four Grammy nominations and won over generations of fans with her powerhouse voice and timeless songs.

On this Day in History...

June 26th

1968 - Coretta Scott King established the Atlanta-based Dr. Martin Luther King Jr., Center for Nonviolent Social Change as a living memorial to her husband's life and dream. Situated in the Freedom Hall complex encircling Dr. King's tomb, The King Center is located inside of a 23-acre national historic park which includes his birth home, which hosts over one million visitors a year. As founding President, Chair and Chief Executive Officer, she dedicated herself to providing local, national and international programs that have trained tens of thousands of people in Dr. King's philosophy and methods.

1995 - Terry Edmonds became the first African-American Presidential Speechwriter, he was also the first African-American Director of Speechwriting to work in the White House for the President of the United States.

1996 - Comedian, Actor and Singer, Eddie Murphy was inducted into the Hollywood Walk of Fame and awarded a star on Hollywood Boulevard. Throughout his career, Murphy has been ranked as one of the greatest stand-up comedians of all time. As an Actor, his films have grossed over $3.8 billion in the United States and $6.6 billion worldwide. In 2015, Murphy was awarded the Mark Twain Prize for American Humor by the John F. Kennedy Center for the Performing Arts.

2018 - Kiko Davis became the the only African-American woman in the Nation to own a bank. She is the majority stockholder of Detroit-based First Independence Bank, one of the top 10 largest banks in the United States owned and operated by African-Americans.

On this Day in History...

June 27th

1877 - George Washington Henderson became the first African-American elected into Phi Beta Kappa, the oldest collegiate Academic Honor Society in the country.

1951 - Inventor, Bessie Blount Griffin patented the "Feeding Tube" while working with injured World War II Veterans. She also invented the Portable Receptacle Support and the Disposable Emesis Basin (the kidney shaped basins used in hospitals for medical waste).

1974 - Reverend Alice M. Henderson became the first African-American woman commissioned as a Captain in the Army Chaplains Corps.

1977 - Founded in 1866, Burns United Methodist Church (UMC) Church was added to the National Register of Historic Places, it is the oldest African-American Church in the State of Iowa.

1995 - Singer, Songwriter and Actress, Gladys Knight was inducted into the Hollywood Walk of Fame and awarded a star on Hollywood Boulevard. Knight is a seven-time Grammy Award winner who is best known for the hits she recorded during the 1960s, 1970s and 1980s, for both the Motown and Buddah Records labels.

2001 - Kwame Brown became the first High School Senior ever selected as first overall pick in the National Basketball Association (NBA) Draft. Basketball Legend, Michael Jordan; who was Owner and President of Basketball Operations of the Washington Wizards, picked the nineteen year-old in the draft. Brown was drafted out of Glynn Academy, a High School in Brunswick, GA.

On this Day in History...

June 28th

1887 - Sam Bass became the first African-American Mayor of Mound Bayou, Mississippi, a town incorporated by African-Americans.

1936 - Track and Field Star, Jesse Owens, who wowed the crowds by winning four gold medals at the 1936 Summer Olympics in Berlin, Germany, became the first ever African-American Athlete to appear on the breakfast cereal box "Wheaties." He made a second appearance in 2003.

1976 - Mary Hall became the first woman of any race to selected as a S.W.A.T (Special Weapons and Tactics) Team Member of the Atlanta Police Department. She was twenty-two years old at the time.

1991 - Barbara Brandon became the first African-American woman to publish a nationally syndicated comic strip. "Where I'm Coming From" appeared first in the Detroit Free Press, it was later acquired by Universal Press Syndicate

2002 - "Outfielder," Hank Aaron, who hit career "home run" number 715 and broke the long-standing record, appeared on the breakfast cereal box "Wheaties." Aaron played Major League Baseball (MLB) for twenty-one seasons. During his career, Aaron hit thirty or more home runs in a season at least fifteen times.

2003 - Bunche Hall opened on the campus of University of California at Los Angeles (UCLA). The building honors Ralph J. Bunche, the Diplomat who won the Nobel Peace Prize in 1950 for his efforts to end the 1948 Arab-Israeli conflict. Bunche was a 1927 graduate of UCLA.

On this Day in History...

June 29th

1908 - Birmingham, AL., became the home of the first African-American owned and operated Architectural Firm in the State when Wallace Augustus Rayfield opened his office in the City. He collaborated with contractor Thomas C. Windham and together they changed the architectural face of Birmingham.

1929 - Sherman "Jocko" Maxwell became the first African-American Sportscaster for WNJR radio station in Newark, NJ. His career lasted four decades.

1942 - Homer Garrott became California's first African-American Highway Patrol Officer. For thirteen years, he remained the only African-American on the police force working motorcycle duty. Throughout his career, Garrott was also a Deputy Public Defender, Juvenile Court Referee and a Los Angeles Municipal Court Commissioner until he was appointed to the Compton Municipal Court.

1967 - Entrepreneur and Educator, William H. Ross III became Maryland's first African-American Stockbroker. He was one of fifty African-American registered representatives in the United States.

1987 - Henry Cade became the first African-American President of the National Association of Boards of Pharmacy. Cade was also Public Affairs and Professional Relations Manager for the Walgreen Company in Deerfield, IL.

1991 - Roland Burris became the first African-American Attorney General for the State of Illinois.

On this Day in History...

June 30th

1967 - The U.S. Air Force selected the first African-American Astronaut, Major Robert Lawrence, to train for a highly secretive mission to spy on the Soviet Union from space. Lawrence, an accomplished Jet Pilot with a Doctorate in Physical Chemistry, was selected for the Manned Orbiting Laboratory (MOL) program the day after he graduate from the U.S. Air Force Test Pilot school. Publicly, the goal of the joint Air Force and National Reconnaissance Office project was to study whether crewed spaceflight could be useful for the military. Behind the scenes, however, MOL's real goal was to keep an eye on the Soviet Union from low polar orbit. From a series of small orbiting stations, two-man crews composed entirely of Air Force Officers, spent 30 days at a time photographing Soviet operations around the world. Polar orbits can take advantage that the Earth rotating beneath the orbital path, giving satellites a chance to view the entire planet once a day.

1997 - The first person in the United States to undergo Experimental Laser Heart Surgery was Dorothy Walker. Cardiothoracic Surgeon, Dr. Keith Howard performed the surgery at Northwestern Memorial Hospital. The procedure is less painful and requires a shorter recovery time than previous methods.

2001 - "Center-Fielder," Kirby Puckett, who played his entire twelve-year Major League Baseball (MLB) career for the Minnesota Twins, appeared on the breakfast cereal box "Wheaties." Puckett is the Twins all-time leader in career hits, runs, and total bases. At the time of his retirement, his .318 career batting average was the highest by any right-handed American League Batter.

On this Day in History...

July 1st

1904 - George C. Poage became first African-American to represent the United States in the Olympic Games, he participated in the 1904 Summer Olympics in St. Louis. He earned bronze medals in both the 220-yard and 440-yard hurdles.

1976 - The African-American Museum in Philadelphia (AAMP) was founded. Noted as the first museum funded and built by a municipality to help preserve, interpret and exhibit the heritage of African-Americans. The AAMP is located in historic Philadelphia, a few blocks away from the Liberty Bell.

1999 - Warrick L. Carter became the first African-American President of Columbia College in Chicago, IL. He took office as head of the Independent Graduate Liberal Arts College. Throughout his career, Carter was also Director of Entertainment Arts for Walt Disney Entertainment.

2013 - Susan Rice became the 24th United States National Security Advisor. Throughout her career, Rice also served as U.S. Ambassador to the United Nations and Assistant Secretary of State for African Affairs during President Bill Clinton's second term.

2018 - Dr. Lily D. McNair become Tuskegee University's 8th President after being unanimously selected by its Board of Trustees. She also served as the first woman President in the institution's 136-year history. As a Clinical Psychologist by training, Dr. McNair's higher education career includes other academic, research and executive appointments at Spelman College, University of Georgia, the State University of New York at New Paltz, and Vassar College.

On this Day in History...

July 2nd

1829 - "The Oblate Sisters of Providence," the first Religious Institute for African-American Roman Catholic Nuns was founded by Mother, Mary Elizabeth Lange and Rev. James Nicholas Joubert in Baltimore, MD., for the education of girls of African descent. This was the first successful Roman Catholic sisterhood in the world established by African-American women. The Oblate Sisters were free women of who sought to provide Baltimore's African-American population with education.

1940 - Elizabeth Catlett became the first person to receive a Masters of Fine Arts Degree in Sculpture from the University of Iowa. She went on to become an Internationally Celebrated Artist who was known for her figurative sculpture and prints. She was also a Cultural Nationalist and Civil Rights Activist.

1964 - The Civil Rights Act was signed into law by President Lyndon B. Johnson. The law ended segregation in public places and banned employment discrimination on the basis of race, color, religion, sex or national origin, it is considered one of the crowning legislative achievements of the Civil Rights Movement. The legislation had been proposed by President John F. Kennedy in June 1963, but opposed by filibuster in the Senate. Thereafter, President Lyndon B. Johnson pushed the bill forward.

1968 - Hannah Diggs Atkins became the first African-American woman member of the Oklahoma House of Representatives. She was later appointed as Secretary of State of Oklahoma and Secretary of Social Services. Atkins was the highest ranked woman in Oklahoma State Government until she retired in 1991.

On this Day in History...

July 3rd

1935 - Eunice Hunton Carter became the first African-American District Attorney in New York City, she held the post for ten years. Carter was also the only African-American to serve on the staff of Thomas E. Dewey (47th Governor of New York).

1941 - Robert B. Howard Jr., became the first African-American Firefighter in Buffalo N.Y., he later became Commissioner of the Department in 1966. Throughout his career, Howard was elected to the Board of Directors of the National Fire Protection Association (NFPA). He was also named Field Service Representative in 1974.

1944 - James E. Johnson became the first African-American Warrant Officer in the United States Marine Corp.

1977 - Chemist, Henry Aaron Hill became the first African-American President of the American Chemical Association.

2011 - Alvin Brown became the first African-American Mayor of Jacksonville, FL. Earlier in his career, he served as an Advisor to Andrew Cuomo, the Secretary of Housing and Urban Development, and to President Bill Clinton. He also served as the Deputy Administrator for Community Development in the Clinton Administration.

2018 - Referees, Danielle Scott and Angelica Suffren made National Basketball Association (NBA) history when they became the first two women to Referee a Professional Basketball game together. They officiated an NBA Summer League game between the Los Angeles Lakers and the Miami Heat.

On this Day in History...

July 4th

1881 - (HBCU) Tuskegee University was founded in Tuskegee, AL. The University was founded by Lewis Adams and Booker T. Washington. Washington was then a twenty-five year-old Teacher at Hampton Institute in Virginia, he became Tuskegee's first President. He developed a network of wealthy American Philanthropists who donated to the school, such as Andrew Carnegie and John D. Rockefeller.

1930 - Wallace D. Fard, also known as Wallace Fard Muhammad, founded the Nation of Islam in Detroit, MI. He taught a form of Islam to members of the City's African-American population. Four years later Elijah Muhammad assumed control of the movement and moved the headquarters to Chicago, IL. During Elijah Muhammad's leadership, the most notable departure of senior leadership was Malcolm X. In 1977, Louis Farrakhan was appointed as the new National Representative and Leader of the Nation of Islam.

1996 - Professional Baseball Player, Jackie Robinson, who was the first African-American to play in Major League Baseball (MLB) appeared on the breakfast cereal box "Wheaties." Robinson had an exceptional ten year MLB career. He was the recipient of the inaugural MLB Rookie of the Year Award in 1947, he was an All-Star for six consecutive seasons and winner the National League Most Valuable Player (MVP) Award in 1949.

2003 - Dennis Archer became the first African-American appointed President of the American Bar Association. Archer also served on the Michigan Supreme Court and as Mayor of Detroit, MI.

On this Day in History...

July 5th

1908 - Track and Field Athlete, John B. Taylor became the first African-American to win an Olympic gold medal. He was a member of the men's Medley Relay Team at the Olympics in London, England.

1947 - Larry Doby became the second African-American Baseball Player to join the Major Leagues, a few months after Jackie Robinson's Major League debut. The Cleveland Indians signed Doby and he became the first African-American player in the American League. In 1948, Doby also became the first African-American to hit a "home run" in the World Series, he hit the winning "home run" in Game 4.

1952 - Charles Moore Jr., became the first African-American to win the 400-meter hurdles at the 1952 Summer Olympics in Helsinki, Finland. He won the gold medal with a time of 50.8 seconds.

1966 - "Black Panther" became the first African Fictional Superhero to appear in comic books published by Marvel Comics. The character first appeared in the Fantastic Four #52 edition. Black Panther's real name is T'Challa, King and Protector of the fictional African Nation of Wakanda. Black Panther is the first superhero of African descent in mainstream comics, debuting years before other African-American superheroes such as Marvel characters, The Falcon (1969), Luke Cage (1972) and Blade (1973).

1998 - Susan D. Davis became the first African-American Federal Magistrate for the State of New Jersey, as well as the State's youngest Judge on the Federal Bench. She was the second woman to become U.S. Magistrate and one of eleven Magistrates in the District.

On this Day in History...

July 6th

1971 - Inventor, Dr. Henry T. Sampson co-invented the "Gamma-Electric Cell," a direct-conversion energy device that converts the energy generated from gamma rays into electricity. His revolutionary invention made it possible for cell phone technology to exist. There are currently more active mobile devices in the world than there are people. Due to Dr. Sampson's invention, there are an estimated seventy-five billion cell phone calls made each day worldwide.

1996 - Basketball Player, Sheryl Swoopes became the first Sportswoman to release her own signature line of athletic footwear; Nike introduced "Air Swoopes" for women. Director, Spike Lee directed a high-profile commercial for Swoopes, who made numerous personal appearances across the country to promote the shoe line.

1998 - Jesse Owens was commemorated on the U.S. postage stamp. Known as "The Buckeye Bullet," Owens began his athletic career in High School when he won three Track and Field events at the 1933 National Interscholastic Championships. Two years later while competing for Ohio State University, he equaled one World Record and broke three others before qualifying and competing in the 1936 Olympics.

2008 - Journalist, Brie Wright founded STYLE Media Group, a multimedia lifestyle company activating editorial content, premium events and interactive social platforms to bring brands and consumers together. In her role as Publisher and Editor-in-Chief at STYLE Magazine, she works with her team to bring the best of fashion and style in the Carolinas to readers around the globe. Her publication continues to build a reputation that delivers both style and substance.

On this Day in History...

July 7th

1805 - William "Bill" Richmond became the first American to become a prominent Boxer in England. He was the first African-American to seek a living as a boxer and achieve a substantial measure of success.

1961 - Dr. Kenneth Bancroft Clark became the first African-American President of the American Psychological Association. His achievements as a distinguished Psychologist were recognized and he was awarded the NAACP Spingarn Medal.

1964 - Edward Melvin Porter became the first African-American elected to the Oklahoma Senate. He was also the Co-owner and Publisher of "Black Voices Magazine."

1973 - John Hope Franklin became the first African-American President of Phi Beta Kappa. He held office until 1976 and presided over the two-hundredth anniversary celebration of this honorary society for humanities. He was also the first African-American President of the Southern Historical Association as well as the American Historical Association.

1984 - Track and Field Athlete, Carl Lewis, who won nine Olympic gold medals and ten World Championships medals appeared on the breakfast cereal box "Wheaties." He made a second appearance in 2004. He is one of only three Olympic Athletes who won a gold medal in the same individual event in four consecutive Olympic Games.

On this Day in History...

July 8th

1904 - John R. Mitchell Jr., became the first African-American member of the American Bankers Association. A native of Virginia, he served on the Richmond City Council from 1888 to 1896. He also founded the Mechanics Savings Bank in 1902.

1924 - William D. Hubbard became the first African-American in Olympic history to win an individual gold medal when he won the broad jump by leaping 24 feet 5 ½ inches at the 1924 Summer games in Paris.

1940 - The National Negro Newspapers Association was founded. The co-founders were Frank L. Stanley Sr., and Carter Walker Wesley. In 1956, the association was renamed the National Newspaper Publishers Association (NNPA). In the early 21st century, the NNPA was composed of two-hundred newspapers that were owned operated by African-Americans in the United States and Virgin Islands.

1972 - Dr. Willie Hobbs Moore became the first African-American woman to receive a Doctorate in Physics, she received a total of three Degrees from the University of Michigan. Much of her research has been published in scientific journals. She held engineering positions at Bendix Aerospace, Barnes Engineering Company and Sensor Dynamics Inc. She later became an Executive with Ford Motor Company, working with the warranty department of automobile assembly.

1976 - Vinnette Justine Carroll became the first African-American woman to direct a Broadway Musical, "Your Arms Too Short to Box with God," the play was also commissioned for the Spoleto Festival in Italy.

On this Day in History...

July 9th

1950 - Peter Marshall Murray became the first African-American to serve in the American Medical Society's House of Delegates. He established a private practice in Washington, D.C., and was the Medical Inspector for the District of Columbia Public Schools. In 1920, Murray moved to New York City, he became the first African-American to serve on the New York City Board of Hospitals.

1960 - Marion S. Barry Jr., became the first National Chairman of the Student Nonviolent Coordinating Committee (SNCC). Barry later become the Mayor of Washington, D.C., in 1979.

1982 - Colonel William Lofton, Jr., became the first African-American named a fellow of the American Occupational Therapy Association. Lofton was Director of Occupational Therapy at Fitzsimons Army Medical Center in Aurora, CO.

1999 - Amber Boykins and her mother, Billie Boykins, became the only mother-daughter combination to serve in the Missouri House of Representatives. Elected in 1998, Amber Boykins was the youngest African-American woman legislator in the history of the Missouri House of Representatives. From 1978 to 1982, Billie Boykins served in the house, at the time she was the youngest African-American woman legislator.

2014 - Michelle J. Howard became the first African-American woman to be a Four-Star Admiral in the United States Navy. Howard was also the first African-American woman to command a U.S. Navy Ship, "The USS Rushmore."

On this Day in History...

July 10th

1925 - George H. Woodson became the first African-American President of the National Bar Association, the Nation's oldest and largest national network of predominantly African-American Attorneys and Judges.

1943 - Following the Pearl Harbor bombing in 1941, the number of African-American soldiers in the U.S. military increased. The U.S. Army activated 4000 soldiers of the 93rd Infantry at Fort Huachuca, Arizona, the first all African-American division formed during World War II. They became the largest concentration of African-American military personnel in the history of the nation.

1966 - James Colston became the first African-American to head a College in New York State when he was appointed President of Bronx Community College. He also served as President of Knoxville College in Tennessee in 1951.

1989 - Chicago Business Partners, Bertram Lee and Peter Bynoe became the first African-American Owners of a NBA Team, they purchased the Denver Nuggets for $65 million.

1992 - Juliann Bluitt became the first woman of any race elected President of the Chicago Dental Society. During the time of her selection, Bluitt was an Associate Dean of the Northwestern University School of Dentistry.

1999 - Briana Scurry became the only African-American Starter for the Champion U.S. women's Soccer Team. She also became the first "Goalie" of any race or gender to play in 100 International Games.

On this Day in History...

July 11th

1911 - Inventor and Railroad Worker, Elijah McCoy patented an Automatic Lubricator for Train Engines, all of his inventions have enabled trains to run faster and more efficiently. McCoy has nearly 60 more patents to his name, he was inducted into the National Inventors Hall of Fame in 2001.

1939 - Mary T. Washington became the first African-American woman in the United States to be named a Certified Public Accountant. She graduated from Northwestern University.

1955 - The National Association of Radio Announcers (NARA) became the first African-American Disc Jockey Trade Organization, it was organized and run by a group that became known as the "Original Thirteen."

1961 - Cecil F. Poole became the first African-American Federal Attorney in the continental United States. Poole was appointed to the San Francisco, CA. office. In 1976, he also became a U.S. District Judge.

1974 - Paul Gibson became the first African-American Deputy Mayor of New York City, he was in charge of City planning. Throughout his career, Gibson also served as Vice President of American Airlines.

2016 - Olympic Gold Medalist, Gabrielle "Gabby" Douglas was recognized by Barbie as a "Shero" honoree, she was honored with her very own Barbie doll. The Barbie Collection defines a "Shero" as a hero who inspire young girls by breaking boundaries and expanding possibilities for women everywhere.

On this Day in History...

July 12th

1971 - Cheryl White became the first African-American woman Jockey, she was also the first woman to win five thoroughbred races in one day at a major track. Early in her career, White was one of only three African-American Jockeys in the country. In 1991, after passing the California Horse Racing Board's Steward examination, White began serving as a Racing Official at California tracks.

1993 - Anthony A. Williams became the first African-American Chief Financial Officer for the U.S. Department of Agriculture, managing funds for 29 agencies throughout the United States and abroad. In 1998, he was also elected Mayor of Washington, D.C.

2012 - Edward S. "Ed" Temple became the first Track and Field Coach inducted into the U.S. Olympic Hall of Fame, he coached the Olympic Track Teams in 1960 and 1964. Temple was also Head Track and Field Coach for the Tennessee State University "Tigerbelles." He coached Track Legend, Wilma Rudolph, who claimed the goal medal in women's 100 meters at the 1960 Summer Games in Rome. Forty members of his team won twenty-three Olympic medals, including thirteen gold, six silver and four bronze.

2018 - Regina Scott became the first African-American woman Deputy Chief for the Los Angeles Police Department (LAPD). During her tenure with the department, Scott held a variety of positions including, Police Officer, Field Training Officer, Senior Lead Officer and Sergeant. She has also held positions in all advance pay grades of the Detective and Lieutenant ranks.

On this Day in History...

July 13th

1897 - Lutie A. Lytle became the first African-American woman to graduate from a Law School in the South, she received her Law Degree from Central Tennessee College. Throughout her career, she practiced law in Kansas and New York. In 1898, she joined the faculty of her Alma Mater, Central Tennessee College of Law, becoming the first woman Professor at the chartered Law School.

1955 - Willa Beatrice Player became the first African-American woman President of a four-year fully accredited Liberal Arts College, she was appointed at Bennett College for Women in Greensboro, N.C. During the Civil Rights Movement in the South, she supported Bennett Students who took part in the lengthy sit-ins started by the "Greensboro Four" to achieve integration of lunch counters in downtown stores.

1959 - Septima Poinsette Clark developed the Literacy and Citizenship Workshops that played an important role in the drive for Voting Rights and Civil Rights for African-Americans in the Civil Rights Movement. Clark was known to many as the "Grandmother" of the Civil Rights Movement, President Jimmy Carter honored her with a Living Legacy Award in 1979. Dr. Martin Luther King, Jr., commonly referred to Clark as "The Mother of the Movement." Clark's argument for her position in the civil rights movement was one that claimed, "knowledge could empower marginalized groups in ways that formal legal equality couldn't."

1975 - Gloria D. Randle Scott became the first African-American National President of the Girl Scouts of America.

On this Day in History...

July 14th

1885 - Sarah E. Goode is the first African-American woman to receive a U.S. Patent. She invented the "Folding Cabinet Bed," which is the predecessor of the Murphy Bed.

1943 - The George Washington Carver National Monument was founded, it was the first national monument dedicated to an African-American and first to a Non-President. President Franklin D. Roosevelt ordered the dedication of the monument located near the childhood home of Carver in Diamond Grove, MO. His childhood home site consists of 240-acre park, nature trail, museum and an interactive exhibit area for students. In 1966, it was listed on the National Register of Historic Places.

1967 - Percy A. Pierre became the first African-American to receive a Doctorate in Electrical Engineering. Howard University appointed him as Dean of the School of Engineering in 1971. Pierre later become Assistant Secretary for Research, Development and Regulation for the U.S. Department of the Army.

2001 - Vernice "Fly Girl" Armor became the first African-American woman Combat Pilot, she ranked No. 1 in her class. During her career, Armor worked for the Metro Nashville, TN., Police Department, starting as a Patrol Officer, she was later appointed as the department's first African-American woman Motorcycle Officer. In 1998, she also worked as for the Tempe, AZ., Police Department and became their first woman African-American Officer. Armor served in the U.S. Marine Corps from 1998 to 2007. While stationed at Camp Pendleton, she played women's Professional Football in San Diego, CA.

On this Day in History...

July 15th

1959 - Inventor, Otis Boykin patented a "Wire Precision Resistor" that would later be used in radios, televisions and computers. His most noteworthy invention was a control unit that would be later used for pacemakers. Boykin has 26 patents to his name and he was inducted into the National Inventors Hall of Fame in 2014.

1961 - William FitzGerald (Nathan Boya) became the first African-American Daredevil to go over Niagara Falls in a steel six foot diameter rubber ball.

1976 - Texas Congresswoman, Barbara Charline Jordan became the first African-American woman to deliver the keynote address at the Democratic National Convention in New York City.

2001 - Mary Bounds became the first woman and second African-American appointed as Chief of Police for the City of Cleveland, OH.

2009 - Charles F. Bolden Jr., became the first African-American to lead the NASA Space Program. Bolden was nominated by President Barack Obama and confirmed by the U.S. Senate as the 12th Administrator of the National Aeronautics and Space Administration. Bolden has overseen the safe transition from 30 years of space shuttle missions to a new era of exploration. He has led the agency in developing a Space Launch System Rocket and Orion Spacecraft that will carry Astronauts to deep space destinations such as Mars. He established a new Space Technology Mission to develop cutting-edge technologies for the missions of tomorrow. Bolden has also participated in the deployment of NASA's Hubble Space Telescope and also commanded space shuttles Atlantis and Discovery.

On this Day in History...

July 16th

1988 - Jackie Joyner-Kersey became the first U.S. woman to earned gold medals in both the heptathlon and the "Long Jump" at the Summer Olympic Games in Seoul, Korea. She also became the first woman ever to repeat as an Olympic Heptathlon Champion in 1992 when she won the two-day, seven-event marathon. She has been called the "World's Fastest Woman" and the "Greatest Female Athlete." At the time of her retirement, she had won six Olympic medals, the most at the time by any woman in the history of Track and Field.

1988 - Known affectionately by her fans as "Flo-Jo," Florence Delorez Griffith-Joyner was the first American woman to win four medals in Track and Field at a single Olympics, in Seoul, Korea. She won gold in the 100 and 200-meter dashes, the 400-meter relay, as well as a silver in the 1600-meter relay. "Flo-Jo" revolutionized women's Sprinting with her searing speed and flamboyant fashion sense, she was also the sister-in-law to Jackie Joyner-Kersey.

1996 - Considered as the "Godfather" of sports talk radio, Art Rust Jr., retired after fifty years of being a successful sports broadcaster in New York City. He was one of the first African-American Sportscasters, he interviewed sports icons such as Hank Aaron, Joe DiMaggio, "Sugar" Ray Robinson Jr., Muhammad Ali, Jessie Owens and Althea Gibson. Rust was a pioneering figure in radio sports talk shows as well as a sports historian.

1998 - Lillian Fishburne became the first African-American woman to hold the rank of Rear Admiral (RDML) in the United States Navy. She was appointed to the rank by President Bill Clinton.

On this Day in History...

July 17th

1933 - Albert E. Forsythe and Charles Alfred Anderson became the first African-American Pilots to make a round-trip transcontinental flight. They left Atlantic City in their Fairchild 24 plane called "The Pride of Atlantic City," and arrived safely in Los Angeles eleven days later completing their round trip on July 28.

1977 - Marilyn French Hubbard founded the National Association of Black Women Entrepreneurs, she was the first President. Hubbard was also the official Court Reporter for the Wayne County Court from 1969 to 1976 in Detroit MI.

1984 - Judge, Ann Claire Williams became the first African-American woman nominated to the Federal Bench in Chicago, IL. Prior to her appointment to the U.S. District Court, Williams was an Attorney and Adjunct Professor at Northwestern University.

1997 - Marie V. McDemmond became the first African-American woman to serve as the head of a Four-Year College in Virginia, Norfolk State University. She is also the first African-American woman President of the Southern Association of College and University Business Officers.

2001 - Dr. Algenia Freeman became the first African-American woman President of Livingston College in Salisbury, N.C. During a forty-year career in higher education, Dr. Freeman also served as President of Martin University as well as Wilberforce University.

On this Day in History...

July 18th

1863 - Sergeant, William Harvey Carney of Company C, 54th Massachusetts Infantry became the first African-American in the Civil War to earn the Medal of Honor.

1932 - Louise Stokes and Tydie Pickett became the first African-American women selected for Olympic competition, they qualified in the 100-meter race for the 1932 summer games held in Los Angeles.

1935 - Roger Arliner Young became the first African-American to receive a Doctorate in Zoology. While working at the Marine Biological Laboratory in Massachusetts, she conducted research and published her first article in "Science," making her the first African-American woman in her field to conduct research and publish her findings professionally.

1983 - William Watley became the first African-American National Chairman of the National Workshop of Christian Unity. Watley was ordained in the African Methodist Episcopal (AME) Church.

2001 - Lieutenant, Shelly Frank became the first African-American woman member of the U.S. Navy's Search-and-Rescue Team. In her role, she could jump from a helicopter and save lives.

2007 - Pioneering Firefighter, Floyd Madison became the first African-American to oversee New York State's Office of Fire Prevention and Control. New York Governor Eliot Spitzer appointed Madison to the post. Madison was also the first African-American Fire Chief for the City of Rochester N.Y., from 1995 to 2007.

On this Day in History...

July 19th

1898 - Robert Penn became the only African-American Seaman during the Spanish-American War to receive the Naval Medal of Honor. The USS Iowa was anchored off Santiago, Cuba, when an explosion occurred in the boiler room. Penn saved a coal handler, single-handedly averting another explosion that could have destroyed the Iowa and taken the lives of many crewmen.

1937 - Anna Julian became the first African-American to receive a Doctorate in Sociology, she graduated from the University of Pennsylvania. Julian was also the first African-American at the University awarded Phi Beta Kappa Honors.

1984 - Tyrone E. Medley became the first African-American Judge in the State of Utah, he served on the Fifth Circuit Court.

1992 - Leslie Seymore became the first woman Chair of the National Black Police Association. She also served on the Philadelphia police force since 1973.

1996 - In one of the most iconic moments in Olympic History, Heavyweight Champion, Muhammad Ali lit the Olympic cauldron during the Opening Ceremonies of the Centennial Olympic Games in Atlanta, GA.

2001 - James L. Dunlap was named Special Agent in charge of the U.S. Secret Service, Detroit Field Office, he became the first African-American to head the Secret Service in Michigan.

On this Day in History...

July 20th

1937 - Dr. Rose Butler Browne became the first African-American woman to earn a Doctorate Degree from Harvard University's Graduate School of Education. Dr. Browne taught for many years at Virginia State University and North Carolina College. She was devoted to improving education for minority children.

1962 - Herman Jerome Russell became the first African-American member of the Atlanta Chamber of Commerce. Russell was a land developer and builder in the Atlanta area, he served on many business civil and religious boards. In 1981, he became the second African-American President of the Chamber.

1967 - Renee Powell became the first African-American woman to join the Ladies Professional Golf Association (LPGA) Tour.

1979 - Mary Runge became the first African-American and the first woman President of the American Pharmaceutical Association. She was a Pharmacist in Oakland, CA.

1986 - "Running Back," Walter Payton, who played for the Chicago Bears of the National Football League (NFL) for thirteen seasons, appeared on the breakfast cereal box "Wheaties." He made a second appearance in 2000. Hall of fame NFL Player and Coach, Mike Ditka described Payton as the greatest Football Player he had ever seen.

2015 - Bishop, Michael Curry became the first African-American in the United States elected as Presiding Bishop of the Episcopal Church.

On this Day in History...

July 21st

1942 - Geologist and Geographer, Marguerite Thomas Williams became the first African-American in the United States to earn a Doctorate in Geology, from Catholic University of America. In 1930, she received a Master's Degree from Columbia University.

1992 - "Running Back," Barry Sanders, who played for the Detroit Lions of the National Football League (NFL) appeared on the breakfast cereal box "Wheaties." He made a second appearance in 1999. He joined the Lions in 1989 and made an immediate impact, winning the NFL's Rookie of the Year award. He averaged over 1,500 rushing yards per season and 100 yards per game. In 1997, he became the third player to rush for over 2,000 yards in a season and was named the NFL Most Valuable Player.

1998 - Carolyn D. Jordan became the first African-American Executive Director of the National Credit Union Administration, an Independent Federal Agency that supervises and insures 97 percent of the 12,000 federally-insured credit unions.

2001 - President of France, Jacques Chirac named Composer, Quincy Jones Commander of the French Legion of Honor during a ceremony at the Elysee Palace in Paris. Jones became the first musician born in the United States to achieve this status.

2008 - LaShunda Rundles became the first African-American woman to win a World Championship in Public Speaking. She delivered a speech called "Speak" at the Toastmasters International Speech Contest.

On this Day in History...

July 22nd

1949 - The first two African-American women to receive Doctorate Degrees in Mathematics were Marjorie Lee Brown from the University of Michigan and Evelyn Boyd Granville from Yale University. Granville taught at Fisk University, then moved to Washington where she was a Mathematician at the National Bureau of Standards. She later held a position with IBM and contracted for the U.S. Space Program, first for NASA's Project Vanguard and then for Project Mercury. Brown worked at North Carolina Central University, where she was Professor and Chair of the Department of Mathematics.

1967 - Helen Claytor became the first African-American President of the National Young Women's Christian Association (YWCA). From 1946 to 1973, she was a member of the National YWCA Board of Directors. Claytor was also a member of the YWCA World Council.

1969 - Clarence A. Ellis became the first African-American to receive a Doctorate in Computer Science. After graduation, he worked on Supercomputers for Bell Telephone Laboratories. Ellis has taught at Stanford University, the University of Texas, Massachusetts Institute of Technology, Stevens Institute of Technology and held an overseas teaching fellowship in Taiwan.

1977 - Donna L. Mosley became the first African-American to complete in the U.S. Gymnastics Federation Junior Olympics, at thirteen years old.

1999 - Carolyn B. Lewis became the first African-American to Chair the American Hospital Association's (AHA) Board of Trustees. The AHA is the country's largest hospital and health system association.

On this Day in History...

July 23rd

1936 - The Dunbar House, the final residence of Poet and Novelist, Paul Laurence Dunbar, became the first State Memorial to honor an African-American. The house, located at 219 Paul Lawrence Dunbar Street in Dayton, Ohio, contains many of Dunbar's personal and literary Artifacts. After the memorial was dedicated, it was then under the care of the Ohio Historical Society.

1974 - Richard Caesar became the first African-American President of the San Francisco Dental Society.

1989 - Ralph Cothran became the first African-American Chief of Police in Chattanooga, TN. Cothran graduated from Cleveland State College and the FBI National Academy.

1990 - Donna M. Cheek became the first African-American member of the U.S. Equestrian Team. In the same year, she was the first and only Equestrian to be inducted into the Women's Sports Hall of Fame.

1995 - Bernadette Locke-Mattox became the first African-American Head Coach of the women's Basketball Team at the University of Kentucky.

2000 - Negro Leagues "Center-Fielder," Norman "Turkey" Stearnes was inducted to the National Baseball Hall of Fame.

2001 - Carolynn Reid-Wallace became the first woman President of Fisk University. Her experiences at Fisk include six years of service on the institution's Board of Trustees. She is also the second Fisk graduate and the first woman to ascend to the presidency.

On this Day in History...

July 24th

1836 - The Second Baptist Church was established by thirteen former slaves, this was the first African-American Congregation in the State of Michigan. The church was only miles away from the freedom that the Canadian border offered to escaped slaves, the church became a stop on the Underground Railroad. The church was designated a Michigan State Historic Site in 1974 and listed on the National Register of Historic Places in 1975.

1913 - James Garfield Beck was hired by the Knoxville Post Office, he became the first African-American Postal Clerk in the State of Tennessee.

1971 - Isaiah Edward Robinson, Jr., became the first African-American President of the New York City Board of Education. Robinson graduated from the Tuskegee Institute Flight School in 1945, he was one of the original Tuskegee Airmen (DOTA).

1976 - Regarded as one of the greatest boxers of all time, "Sugar" Ray Leonard won the gold medal at the Olympic Games in Montreal, Quebec, Canada. Leonard was part of "The Fabulous Four," a group of boxers who all fought each other throughout the 1980's, consisting of himself, Roberto Durán, Thomas "Hitman" Hearns and "Marvelous" Marvin Hagler. Leonard was the first boxer to earn more than $100 million in purses, he was also named "Boxer of the Decade" in the 1980's.

1994 - Gregory M. Sleet became the first African-American U.S. Attorney for the State of Delaware.

On this Day in History...

July 25th

1937 - Dwight Oliver Holmes became the first African-American President of Morgan State College (now Morgan State University), where he guided the transition of the school from Methodist control to state control. Holmes is also known for his book Evolution of the Negro College, published in 1934. Through his career and his writings, he significantly influenced African-American higher education.

1956 - Professional Golfer and Tennis Player, Althea Gibson became the first African-American to win a major Tennis Title when she won the women's singles in the French Open. The following two years she won both Wimbledon and the U.S. Open. Gibson was voted "Female Athlete of the Year" by the Associated Press in both years. She won eleven Grand Slam tournaments, including six doubles titles. She was also inducted into the International Tennis Hall of Fame and the International Women's Sports Hall of Fame. Gibson is known as one of the Greatest Tennis Players who ever lived.

1978 - The APEX Museum (African-American Panoramic Experience) was founded in 1978 by Dan Moore, it is located on Auburn Avenue in the "Sweet Auburn" Historic District of Atlanta, GA.

2002 - Ida Louise Jackson was honored at the University of California at Berkeley campus with "The Ida Louise Jackson Graduate House," a graduate student residence hall. Jackson graduated from High School in Vicksburg, Mississippi, at the age of twelve. She then enrolled at Berkeley earning a Bachelor's Degree in 1922 and a Master's Degree in Education in 1924. For most of her professional career, she was a Teacher in the Oakland Public School System.

On this Day in History...

July 26th

1865 - Dr. Patrick Francis Healey became the first African-American to receive a Ph.D Degree, he was also the first African-American President of Georgetown University. As President, he was known for expanding the school following the American Civil War. Healy Hall was constructed during his tenure and is named in his honor, it was designated as a National Historic Landmark in the late 20th century.

1910 - George Herriman became the first African-American to achieve fame as a Syndicated Cartoonist. He created a strip called "Krazy Kat" which was extremely popular, especially among intellectuals.

1948 - President Harry S. Truman issued Executive Order 9981. This order abolished racial discrimination in the United States Armed Forces and led to the end of segregation in the services.

1987 - Negro Leagues "Third-Baseman," Ray Dandridge was inducted to the National Baseball Hall of Fame.

1987 - Chicago Cubs "Left-Fielder," Billy Williams was inducted to the National Baseball Hall of Fame. As a clutch performer, Williams was one of the most respected hitters of his day.

1998 - Negro Leagues "Pitcher," Bullet Rogan was inducted to the National Baseball Hall of Fame. Rogan's early Baseball career took place in the U.S. Army, where he played for a team in the 25th Infantry. After joining the Kansas City Monarchs, he was the top Pitcher and one of the best hitters on a team that won three pennants from 1923 to 1925.

On this Day in History...

July 27th

1951 - United States Army Soldier, William H. Thompson became a recipient of the military's highest decoration, the Medal of Honor, for his actions in the Korean War.

1977 - Samuel L. Williams became the first African-American President of the Los Angeles Bar Association. In 1981, he also became the first African-American President of the State Bar of California. Having a passion working as a Los Angeles Attorney, Williams turned down an offer of an appointment to the State Supreme Court.

1992 - Dominique Dawes and Elizabeth Anna Okino became the first two African-American women Gymnasts to compete on a United States Olympic team during the games in Barcelona, Spain in 1992. Dawes won a bronze medal at the games, she also won two silver medals at the World Gymnastics Championships Competition held in Birmingham, England in 1993. Dawes was a member of the "Magnificent 7" women gymnastics team during the 1996 Olympic games in Atlanta, GA., their team won the gold medal.

2004 - Then Illinois State Senator and future President of the United States, Barack Obama delivered the Keynote Address at the Democratic National Convention. He was a rising star within the National Democratic Party, speculation began about a Presidential future which led to the reissue of his memoir, "Dreams from My Father." His keynote address was well received, which further elevated his status within the Democratic Party and led to his reissued memoir becoming a bestseller.

On this Day in History...

July 28th

1917 -   Ten thousand African-Americans led by W.E.B Du Bois and James Weldon Johnson, marched down New York City's 5th Avenue in an NAACP organized protest against lynchings, race riots and the denial of rights. This was the first major civil rights demonstration of the 20th Century.

1959 -   Chicago Cubs "First-Baseman," Ernie Banks, became the first National League player to win the Most Valuable Player (MVP) Award two years in a row. Also known as "Mr. Cub," he and "Second Baseman," Gene Baker formed the first African-American double-play combination in the Major Leagues. Banks produced four consecutive years of more than forty home runs between 1957 and 1960.

1968 -   Coretta Scott King became the first woman of any race to preach at Saint Paul's Cathedral in London, England.

1995 -   "Left-Fielder," Lou Brock was inducted to the National Baseball Hall of Fame. During his nineteen year Major League career, Brock was recognized as one of Baseball's most complete and clutch players of the 20th Century. He was known as a stolen base specialist.

2002 -   "Shortstop," Ozzie Smith was inducted to the National Baseball Hall of Fame, nicknamed "The Wizard" for his defensive brilliance, he set Major League records for career assists (8,375) and double plays (1,590) by a "Shortstop." Smith was the only inductee in 2002, approximately 18,000 fans were in attendance along with 47 of the living Hall of Famers.

On this Day in History...

July 29th

1947 - The Brandford Modeling Agency was founded by Edward Brandford, it was the first licensed African-American Modeling Agency in the United States. Their models were known as "Brandford Lovelies."

1971 - Benjamin L. Hunton became the first African-American Army Officer that was commission as Brigadier General in the U.S. Army Reserves. Hunton was also employed for twenty-two years in the public schools of Washington, D.C. He then served at the Departments of Interior and Health, Education and Welfare.

1972 - Kellis E. Parker became the first African-American Law Professor at Columbia University. Parker, along with four other African-American students is credited with integrating the University of North Carolina. In 1968, Parker was a Law Clerk for Judge Spottswood W. Robinson III, who was the first African-American to serve on the U.S. Court of Appeals in Washington, D.C. Parker also taught Law at the University of California in 1969-72.

1996 - Track and Field Athlete, Michael Johnson became the first man ever to win both the 200 and 400-meter sprints in the same Olympics, a feat he accomplished at the Summer Games in Atlanta. He secured a place in Track and Field history when he won the 400-meter event again in the 2000 Olympics in Sydney, making him the first man to win this event in back-to-back Olympics. Johnson is widely considered one of the greatest and most consistent sprinters in the history of Track and Field, he once had a string of fifty-five straight wins in the 400-meter race.

On this Day in History...

July 30th

1958 - Irma Dixon and Verda Freeman Welcome were the first African-American women elected to the Maryland House of Delegates. The two represented the Democratic Party. In 1962, Welcome became the first African-American woman elected to the State Senate.

1966 - Spottswood William Robinson III was appointed by President Lyndon B. Johnson to the United States Court of Appeals for the District of Columbia Circuit, he was the first African-American appointed to that post. He later became the first African-American to serve as Chief Judge of the District of Columbia Circuit. In 1948, he joined the National Association for the Advancement of Colored People (NAACP) Legal Defense and Educational Fund where he worked on several important civil rights cases including Brown vs. Board of Education. During his time with the NAACP, Robinson and Thurgood Marshall worked on several cases together.

1995 - Negro Leagues "Pitcher," Leon Day was inducted to the National Baseball Hall of Fame.

2006 - College and Professional Football "Cornerback" Tye Hill was drafted into the National Football League (NFL) by the St. Louis Rams. He attended Clemson University, where he played for the Clemson Tigers Football Team from 2001 to 2005. Hill was well known for his speed, along with being a star Football Player, he was also an accomplished member of the Track and Field Team at Clemson, winning three ACC Championships and several all-conference accolades. He was named Rams Rookie of the Year and was voted to the 2006 All-Rookie honors by the Pro Football Writers Association (PFWA).

On this Day in History…

July 31st

1971 - Football Player, Activist and Actor, Jim Brown was inducted to the National Football League (NFL). Considered to be among the greatest Football Players of all time, Brown was a Pro Bowl invitee for every season he was in the league and won an NFL Championship with the Cleveland Browns in 1964. He led the league in rushing yards in eight out of his nine seasons, by the time he retired, he had shattered most major rushing records.

1979 - "Rapper's Delight" was a single released by Hip-Hop trio The Sugarhill Gang. While it was not the first single to feature rapping, it is generally considered to be the song that first popularized Hip-Hop in the United States and around the world. Since this single was released, Hip-Hop has evolved into a multi-billion dollar industry worldwide.

1985 - Jazz Singer, Sarah Vaughan was inducted into the Hollywood Walk of Fame and awarded a star on Hollywood Boulevard. Vaughan was a four-time Grammy Award winner, including a "Lifetime Achievement Award." The National Endowment for the Arts bestowed upon her its "Highest Honor in Jazz," the NEA Jazz Masters Award in 1989.

1988 - "Left-Fielder," Willie Stargell became the 200th member of the National Baseball Hall of Fame and just the 17th player elected in his first year of eligibility.

1997 - Negro Leagues "Shortstop," Willie Wells was inducted to the National Baseball Hall of Fame. Known as one of the finest "Shortstops" in history, Wells was also a mentor to younger players such as Jackie Robinson and Monte Irvin.

On this Day in History...

August 1st

1948 - Alice Coachman became the first African-American woman to win a gold medal at the Olympic Games in London, England for the High Jump Competition.

1982 - Frank Robinson was inducted to the National Baseball Hall of Fame. He won the Triple Crown in 1966 and was the first player in major league history to win the MVP Award in both leagues. As a 12-time All-Star, he also took home World Series MVP honors in 1966 and the All-Star Game MVP Award in 1971.

1982 - Hank Aaron was inducted to the National Baseball Hall of Fame. Shortly after Aaron's record breaking 715th home run, Georgia Congressman Andrew Young declared, "Through his long career, Hank Aaron has been a model of humility, dignity, and quiet competence." Boxing Legend, Muhammad Ali once called Aaron "The only man I idolize more than myself." Hall of Famer, Mickey Mantle said "As far as I'm concerned, Aaron is the best Baseball player of my era."

1993 - Reggie Jackson became the 216th member inducted National Baseball Hall of Fame. Nearly 10,000 fans and 38 living Hall of Famers attended the ceremony. Chants of "Reg-gie! Reg-gie!" greeted Jackson as he was the only inductee of that year. Jackson was nicknamed "Mr. October" for his clutch hitting in the postseason with the Oakland Athletics and the New York Yankees. He helped the Athletics win three consecutive World Series Titles from 1971 to 1975. He also helped the Yankees two win back-to-back World Series Titles, from 1977 to 1978. Jackson hit three consecutive home runs at Yankee Stadium in the clinching game 6 of the 1977 World Series.

On this Day in History...

August 2nd

1879 - Mary Eliza Mahoney graduated from the Nursing program at the New England Hospital for Women and Children, she became the first African-American to graduate from a Nursing School. In 1908, Mahoney co-founded the National Association of Colored Graduate Nurses (NACGN) with Adah B. Thoms. This organization attempted to uplift the standards and everyday lives of African-American registered nurses. The NACGN had a significant influence on eliminating racial discrimination in the registered nursing profession. In 1951, the NACGN merged with the American Nurses Association. Mahoney was inducted into the American Nurses Association Hall of Fame in 1976 and to the National Women's Hall of Fame in 1993.

1962 - Jackie Robinson was commemorated on the U.S. postage stamp. Throughout his career, he was the recipient of the Inaugural Major League Baseball (MLB) Rookie of the Year Award in 1947, an All-Star for six consecutive seasons from 1949 through 1954, he also won the National League Most Valuable Player (MVP) Award in 1949. Robinson played in six World Series and contributed to the Dodgers 1955 World Series Championship.

1996 - Teresa Edwards became the only four-time Olympian in Basketball, for 1984, 1988, 1992 and 1996. She has won twelve international medals, including nine golds. USA Basketball named her the "Female Athlete of the Year" in 1996, for the third time.

2012 - Sixteen year-old Gymnastic Phenomenon, Gabrielle "Gabby" Douglas became the first African-American to win a gold medal in the women's all-around final competition. She was also a member of the U.S. Women's Gymnastics team at the Summer Olympics held in London.

On this Day in History...

August 3rd

1936 - Track and Field Athlete, Jesse Owens achieved International Fame by winning four gold medals as well as breaking two Olympic records at the Summer Olympics in Berlin, Germany. He was the most successful Athlete at the Games and as an African-American man, he was credited with "single-handedly crushing the Nazi myth of Aryan supremacy." In all, the United States won eleven gold medals, six of them by African-American Athletes. Owens was easily the most dominant Athlete to compete.

1973 - Negro Leagues "Left-Fielder," Monfors "Monte" Irvin was inducted to the National Baseball Hall of Fame. Irvin made a relatively seamless transition from the Negro Leagues to the Major Leagues. He was a five-time Negro League All-Star and he won the Negro League Batting Title twice. Moving over to the big leagues, Irvin played eight seasons for the New York Giants and Chicago Cubs.

1983 - The first African-American Quintuplets in the world were born. "The Gaither Quintuplets" Ashlee, Joshua, Renee, Rhealyn and Brandon were all born four weeks premature to Sidney and Suzanne Gaither. The Gaither quintuplets attracted worldwide attention when they were born at Indiana University Hospital at a collective weight of 19 pounds, 3 ounces. They were the first surviving set of African-American quintuplets that were conceived naturally without the aid of fertility drugs. Sidney and Suzanne Gaither averaged changing 50 bottles and 50 diapers per day.

1996 - Negro Leagues "Pitcher," Bill Foster was inducted to the National Baseball Hall of Fame.

On this Day in History...

August 4th

1858 - Sarah Jane Woodson Early became the first African-American woman College Instructor in the United States. She taught at Wilberforce College, located in Wilberforce, Ohio.

1984 - Dr. Alexa Canady became the first African-American woman Neurosurgeon in the United States. Canady specialized in Pediatric Neurosurgery and was the Chief of Neurosurgery at the Children's Hospital in Michigan from 1987 until her retirement in 2001. Canady was inducted into the Michigan Women's Hall of Fame, she also received the American Medical Women's Association President's Award.

1999 - Negro Leagues "Pitcher," Joe Williams was inducted to the National Baseball Hall of Fame. Williams was one of them most feared Negro Leagues Pitcher's in the first half of the 20th century. He was known for his fastball, smooth motion and great control.

2015 - Paulette Brown became the first African-American woman to be President of the American Bar Association (ABA). Brown became the first woman of color and third African-American person elected as President.

2017 - Briana Scurry was elected to the National Soccer Hall of Fame, she became the first woman "Goalkeeper" and first African-American woman to be awarded the honor. Scurry was the starting Goalkeeper for the United States women's National Soccer Team at the 1995 World Cup, 1996 Summer Olympics, 1999 World Cup, 2003 World Cup, and the 2004 Summer Olympic Games.

On this Day in History...

August 5th

1979 - Willie Mays was inducted to the Baseball Hall of Fame, nicknamed "The Say Hey Kid," Mays played Major League Baseball for twenty-two seasons. He won Rookie of the Year in 1951, two National League Most Valuable Player (MVP) Awards and ended his career with 660 "home runs." Mays shares the record of most All-Star Games played with 24, along with Hank Aaron and Stan Musial, he is also one of five National League Players to have had eight consecutive 100-RBI seasons. In 2017, Major League Baseball named its World Series Most Valuable Player (MVP) Award after Willie Mays.

2001 - Negro Leagues "Pitcher," Hilton Smith was inducted to the National Baseball Hall of Fame. He pitched alongside Leroy "Satchel" Paige for the Kansas City Monarchs between 1932 and 1948.

2001 - "Center-Fielder," Kirby Puckett was inducted to the National Baseball Hall of Fame. The six-time Gold Glove Award winner was named to ten consecutive All-Star teams from 1986-1995 and was named Most Valuable Player (MVP) of the game in 1993. He finished in the top ten in MVP voting seven times during his twelve year career. He won two World Series with the Twins in 1987 and 1991.

2001 - "Right Fielder," Dave Winfield was inducted to the National Baseball Hall of Fame. Winfield is the only Athlete in history to be drafted by four different Sports Leagues. He chose Major League Baseball over the NFL, the ABA and the NBA. The "Outfielder" didn't spend a single day in the Minor Leagues, he began his career with the San Diego Padres.

On this Day in History...

August 6th

1965 - The Voting Rights Act was signed into law by President Lyndon B. Johnson during the height of the Civil Rights Movement, Congress later amended the Act five times to expand its protections. Designed to enforce the voting rights guaranteed by the Fourteenth and Fifteenth Amendments to the United States Constitution, the Act secured voting rights for minorities throughout the country, especially in the South. According to the U.S. Department of Justice, the Act is considered to be the most effective piece of federal civil rights legislation ever enacted in the United States.

1984 - Track and Field Athlete, Carl Lewis won four gold medals at the 1984 Olympics in Los Angeles, matching the record set by Track and Field legend, Jesse Owens at the 1936 Olympics in Berlin.

1990 - William "Bill" Pinkney became the first African-American to navigate a sailboat single-handedly around the world. At the age of fifty-five, Pinkney began his odyssey, setting sail from Boston Harbor. He sailed on a 47-foot boat called "The Commitment," which had been specially rigged so one man could operate it. Out of all the possible routes, Pinkney chose the most difficult one, which would take him around the five capes. He made stops in Bermuda, Brazil, South Africa and Tasmania, then finally around Cape Horn (the most difficult part of the voyage). His voyage took him 22 months, including a six month delay in Australia due to weather, he covered a total of 27,000 miles.

2009 - Cadet, Jacqueline Fitch became the U.S. Coast Guard Academy's first African-American woman Regimental Commander, the highest-ranking cadet in the academy.

On this Day in History...

August 7th

1948 - John H. Davis became the first African-American Heavyweight Weightlifting Champion. Throughout his career he won 2 Olympic Gold Medals, 2 World Championships, 12 National Titles and set 16 World Records. Known as "The World's Strongest Man," he was the first weightlifter known to lift 400 pounds over his head, he accomplished this in 1951 at the National AAU Senior Championship in Los Angeles, CA.

1954 - Attorney, Charles H. Mahoney was nominated by President Dwight Eisenhower and confirmed by the Senate as the first African-American permanent member of the Delegation to the United Nations.

1972 - Josh Gibson became the second player from the Negro Leagues elected to the National Baseball Hall of Fame. Baseball historians consider Gibson to be among the very best power hitters and catchers in the history of any league.

1972 - Walter "Buck" Leonard became the third player from the Negro Leagues inducted to the National Baseball Hall of Fame. He was one of the best pure hitters to play in the Negro Leagues.

1974 - Beverly Johnson became the first African-American Supermodel to appear on the cover of American Vogue. The Model, Actress, and Singer was also the first African-American woman to appear on the cover of the French Magazine, Elle. When she appeared on the cover of Glamour Magazine during the mid-1970's, its circulation doubled and set a record. By 1992, Johnson had appeared on the covers of over five-hundred magazines.

On this Day in History...

August 8th

1977 - Negro Leagues "Shortstop" and Manager, John Henry "Pop" Lloyd was inducted to the National Baseball Hall of Fame. He is generally considered the greatest shortstop in Negro League History, fellow Hall of Fame inductee, Babe Ruth and Sportswriter, Ted Harlow both reportedly believed Lloyd to be the greatest Baseball Player ever.

1977 - Chicago Cubs "First Baseman" Ernie Banks was was inducted to the National Baseball Hall of Fame. Banks was an excellent defensive player at two positions, "Shortstop" from 1953-61 and First Baseman from 1962-71. As a First Baseman, he led the league in put-outs five times, assists three times, double plays and fielding percentage once each. He was a member of eleven National League All-Star teams.

1981 - Diane Durham became the first African-American woman to win the United States Gymnastics Championship, she won the title for two consecutive years. Durham was also the first internationally ranked African-American woman Gymnast.

2018 - Adrienne Bennett became first African-American woman licensed Master Plumber, Plumbing Contractor, Plumbing Inspector and Certified Medical Gas Inspector and Installer. She remains Michigan's first and only woman licensed Master Plumber and Plumbing Contractor. She served the City of Detroit as a Plumbing Inspector and Code Enforcement Officer. Bennett specialties include: medical gas systems, plumbing code compliance, water conservation, plumbing and piping systems for all facility types. She is an active member of American Society of Plumbing Engineers (ASPE) and the American Society of Sanitary Engineering.

On this Day in History...

August 9th

1971 - Known as perhaps the Greatest Pitcher in Baseball History, Leroy "Satchel" Paige was inducted into the Baseball Hall of Fame. At the age of forty-two, he became the oldest rookie to play in the Major Leagues. Before his move to the Majors, Paige was one of the most famous and successful players from the Negro Leagues.

1976 - Negro Leagues "Center-Fielder," Oscar Charleston was inducted to the National Baseball Hall of Fame. He is considered one of the best players in the history of the league.

1985 - I. S. Leevy Johnson became the first African-American President of the South Carolina Bar Association. He also served in the South Carolina House of Representatives from 1970 to 1980.

1988 - "Shooting Guard" Michael Jordan, who played fifteen seasons in the National Basketball Association (NBA) for the Chicago Bulls and Washington Wizards appeared on the breakfast cereal box "Wheaties." Jordan's individual accolades and accomplishments include six NBA Championships, six NBA Finals Most Valuable Player (MVP) Awards and ten scoring titles.

1992 - Hubert Anderson became the first African-American elected to the Board of the National Association of the Deaf. He was also the first African-American Coach at the 1985 World Games for the Deaf.

1994 - John Paris Jr., became the first African-American Professional Hockey Coach. He coached the Atlanta Knights of the International Hockey League (IHL). His team won the Turner Cup Championship in 1994.

On this Day in History...

August 10th

1863 - As the Civil War developed, Frederick Douglass convinced President Abraham Lincoln to free all slaves so they might enlist in Union Forces, the Emancipation Proclamation was issued and Douglas became one of the main recruiters of free African-Americans in the Northern territories. Douglass was a prominent Abolitionist, Author and Orator. Born into slavery, he escaped at age twenty and went on to become a world renowned Anti-Slavery Activist. After escaping from slavery in Maryland, he became a national leader of the Abolitionist Movement, gaining notoriety for public speaking.

1969 - Constitutional Law Scholar, Derrick A. Bell Jr., became the first African-American Law Professor at Harvard Law School. In 1971, he became the first African-American tenured Law Professor.

1977 - Jesse Hill Jr., became the first African-American President of the Atlanta Chamber of Commerce and the first to head a Major Metropolitan Chamber of Commerce in the Nation. Hill was also the President and Chief Executive Officer of the Atlanta Life Insurance Company.

1994 - Bernette Joshua Johnson became the first African-American woman to sit on the Louisiana Supreme Court. Throughout her career, Johnson was Chief Justice for the Civil District Court as well as a community organizer with the NAACP Legal Defense Fund from 1964 to 1966. From 1977 to 1981, she was also Director of the AFNA National Education Foundation, she then became Deputy City Attorney for the City of New Orleans.

On this Day in History...

August 11th

1962 - James Meredith became the first African-American student admitted to the segregated University of Mississippi after the intervention of the Federal Government, an event that was a flashpoint in the Civil Rights Movement. Inspired by President John F. Kennedy's inaugural address, Meredith decided to exercise his constitutional rights and apply to the University of Mississippi. His goal was to put pressure on the Kennedy Administration to enforce Civil Rights for African-Americans. In 1966, Meredith planned a solo 220-mile "March Against Fear" from Memphis, Tennessee to Jackson, Mississippi. He wanted to highlight continuing racism in the South and encourage voter registration after passage of the Voting Rights Act of 1965.

1966 - Rommie Loudd became the first African-American Assistant Coach in the American Football League, as a former Star Linebacker at UCLA, he coached for the New England Patriots. Loudd is also the first African-American Majority Owner of a Major League Sports Team.

1973 - "Hip Hop," an African-American Musical form was born. As one of the founders of Hip Hop, DJ Kool Herc and his sister Cindy organized a "Back to School Jam" in the recreation room of their apartment block at 1520 Sedgwick Avenue in the Bronx, NY. The main components of Hip-Hop were Rapping, Break Dancing and Graffiti. Since its introduction, Hip-Hop has evolved into a Multi-Billion Dollar Industry worldwide. Sedgwick Avenue was renamed "Hip Hop Boulevard," as it was the birthplace of Hip Hop.

On this Day in History...

August 12th

1974 - Considered by many to be "The fastest man to ever play the game of Baseball," Negro Leagues "Center-Fielder" James "Cool Papa" Bell was inducted to the National Baseball Hall of Fame.

1983 - The African-American Museum and Library at Oakland (AAMLO) was added to the National Register of Historic Places. This museum and non-circulating library was dedicated to preserving the history and experiences of African-Americans in Oakland, CA., it contains an extensive archival collection of artifacts, diaries, correspondence, photos and periodicals.

1990 - Dolores E. Cross became the first African-American woman President of Chicago State University, making her the first woman to head a Four-Year College in the Illinois System of Public Higher Education. In 1999, Cross was also appointed as the first African-American woman President of Morris Brown College in Atlanta, GA.

1993 - Michelle Burton Mitchell became the first African-American woman to serve as Sheriff in the State of Virginia. She has also held several posts in the Virginia Department of Corrections.

2004 - Track and Field Athlete, Jackie Joyner-Kersee, who ranked among the all-time Greatest Athletes in the Heptathlon as well as Long Jump, appeared on the breakfast cereal box "Wheaties." She won three gold, one silver and two bronze Olympic medals, in those two events at four different Olympic Games.

On this Day in History...

August 13th

1937 - The women's Track Team of Tuskegee University became the first African-American team to win the National AAU women's Track and Field Championship.

1946 - Ella Josephine Baker was elected President of the New York Branch of the National Association for the Advancement of Colored People (NAACP), becoming the first woman to hold the post. Baker was also a Community Organizer, Consultant in Education, Civil Rights and Domestic Activist.

1977 - Augustus G. Jenkins Jr., founded "The Black Tennis and Sports Foundation." Throughout his career, Jenkins was also a Flight Instructor.

1984 - Jacqueline Barbara Vaughn became the first African-American woman President of the Chicago Teachers Union. In 1968, she also became Secretary for the Illinois Federation of Teachers.

1990 - Errol B. Davis Jr., became the first African-American to head a major utility company, Wisconsin Power and Light. Throughout his career, he also served as a member of the Corporate Finance staff for Ford Motor Company as well as Xerox Corporation.

1996 - Judith Alane Colbert became the first African-American woman in the State of Oklahoma to be named a Shareholder and Partner in a Major Law Firm. She became a Partner with Hall, Estill, Hardwick, Gable, Golden & Nelson, P.C., located in Tulsa.

On this Day in History...

August 14th

1876 - (HBCU) Prairie View A&M University was founded in Prairie View, TX. Prairie View was the first state supported College in Texas for African-Americans, it was established during the Reconstruction period after the Civil War. The University was established by Article 7 of the Texas Constitution of 1876. State Senator Matthew Gaines along with State Representative William H. Holland, both former slaves, became the leading political figures who crafted legislation for the creation of a State supported "Agricultural and Mechanical" College.

1942 - Lawrence Bailey Sr., became the first African-American named Deputy Clerk of the U.S. District Court in Washington, D.C.

1969 - A Nuclear Powered Submarine was launched and commissioned, it was named in honor of George Washington Carver, becoming the first Submarine to honor an African-American.

1971 - Gerald Edgerton Talbot became the first African-American member of the Maine Legislature. He later introduced legislation to congress for a Dr. Martin Luther King Jr., Holiday. Among his numerous other achievements, he served as Chair of the Maine Board of Education in 1983-84.

1977 - Fredda Witherspoon became the first African-American President of the Metropolitan St. Louis Young Women's Christian Association (YWCA). She was also one of the first African-Americans to integrate St. Louis University.

On this Day in History...

August 15th

1938 - Cornelius Coffey became the first African-American Registered Pilot. He was also the first African-American to create a Non-University affiliated Aeronautical School in the United States. Coffey obtained his commercial license in order to teach at his own school in Chicago, IL. He helped integrate African-American pilots into the American Aviation Industry. Coffey was inducted into the Illinois Aviation Hall of Fame in 1984. The Cornelius R. Coffey Aviation Education Foundation was established at the American Airlines Maintenance Academy in Chicago in his honor to train young pilots.

1973 - The National Black Feminist Organization was established by Eleanor Holmes Norton, the organization addressed the concerns of African-American women in terms of sexism and racism. Within a year, ten new chapters were organized, they all met in a national conference. In 1977, President Jimmy Carter appointed Norton as the first woman to Chair the Equal Employment Opportunity Commission (EEOC).

1991 - Thelma Marie Harper became the first African-American woman elected to the State Senate of Tennessee. She was already a noted entrepreneur and leading member of the Nashville City Council at the time of her election.

2006 - Lizzie Bolden turned one-hundred sixteen years old, making her the "World's Oldest Woman," according to the Guinness Book of World Records. Bolden was the daughter of former slaves. Only 2 of her 7 children survived her. Other survivors included 40 grandchildren, 75 great grandchildren, 150 great-great grandchildren, 220 great-great-great grandchildren and 75 great-great-great-great grandchildren.

On this Day in History...

August 16th

1963 - Internationally known Graphic Designer, George Olden became the first African-American Artist to design a U.S. postage stamp. The stamp featured a broken link in a large black chain against a blue backdrop and was designed to commemorate the 100th anniversary of the Emancipation Proclamation. Olden was named as one of fifteen leading graphic designers in the United States. His work is included in the permanent collection of the Amsterdam Museum in Harlem, NYC.

1969 - Ewart Guinier became the first Chairperson of Harvard University's Department of Afro-American Studies. His daughter, Carol Lani Guinier gained national recognition in 1993, when President Bill Clinton chose her to head the U.S. Department of Justice's Civil Rights Division.

1972 - The Johnson Publishing Company Headquarters was completed. The eleven-story structure was the first building built by African-Americans in downtown Chicago, IL. Architect, John Warren Moutoussamy designed the building.

1975 - Negro Leagues "Third-Baseman" and Manager, William "Judy" Johnson was inducted to the National Baseball Hall of Fame.

1996 - "Outfielder," Ken Griffey Jr., who played twenty-two years in Major League Baseball (MLB) appeared on the breakfast cereal box "Wheaties." He made a second appearance in 2000. Griffey is one of the most prolific "home run" hitters in Baseball history, his 630 "home runs" rank as the seventh in MLB history.

On this Day in History...

August 17th

1876 - Meharry Medical College became the first Medical School founded solely for the education of African-American students. Located in Nashville, TN., Meharry was part of Walden University.

1891 - Franklin A. Denison became the first African-American appointed to Chicago's Law Department, serving for six years under two Mayor Administrations, he was the Assistant City Prosecuting Attorney. In 1915, Denison also served in the military, he was Commander of the 8th Illinois Infantry, which he led an expedition into France during World War I.

1966 - Samuel M. Nabrit became the first African-American member of the United States Atomic Energy Commission (AEC), a government agency established after WWII to foster and control the peacetime development of Atomic Science and Technology. In 1955, Narbrit became President of Texas Southern University.

1974 - Sidney John Barthelemy became the first African-American elected to the State Senate in the 20th century, for Louisiana. In 1986, he was elected Mayor of New Orleans, he served two terms in office.

1988 - Jacqueline Murray became the first African-American woman Commander on the Chicago Police Department. Murray served the City of Chicago on the police force for twenty-one years.

1995 - Ronnie L. White became the first African-American named to the Missouri Supreme Court. He was previously a Judge in the Missouri Court of Appeals, an Assistant Public Defender, a member of the State Legislature and served on the St. Louis City Council.

On this Day in History...

August 18th

1969 - Guitarist, Singer-Songwriter, Jimi Hendrix headlined the Woodstock Musical Festival near Bethel, New York. Woodstock is widely regarded as a pivotal moment in Popular music history, 32 acts performed outdoors before an audience of more than 500,000 people, making the event one of the largest musical concerts in history. During this time, Hendrix was the world's highest-paid Rock Musician.

1980 - Rayford Logan was awarded the NAACP Spingarn Medal. In the 1940's, he was the Chief Advisor to the NAACP on International Affairs. President Franklin D. Roosevelt later appointed Logan to his Cabinet, he drafted Roosevelt's Executive Order prohibiting the exclusion of African-Americans from the military in World War II. Logan was also the 15th General President of Alpha Phi Alpha, the first Intercollegiate African-American Greek-letter fraternity.

1988 - Dolores Spikes became the first woman to head a University System in the United States, she was named President of the Southern University and A & M College System in Louisiana. She is the first African-American woman to earn a PhD in Mathematics from Louisiana State University in 1971. Throughout her career, Spikes was also named President of the University of Maryland Eastern Shore from 1997 to 2001.

2000 - Governor, Paul Patton appointed Ishmon F. Burks as Commissioner of the Kentucky State Police, making him the first African-American to head Kentucky's top Law Enforcement Agency. Burks was a retired Military Officer, he also served as Executive Vice President and Chief Operating Officer of Spaulding University in Louisville.

On this Day in History...

August 19th

1942 - Mollie Moon became founder and first President of the National Urban League Guild, a fund-raising organization to raise money for Urban League programs that promote racial equality. The guild has grown to include 30,000 volunteers in 80 groups across the country.

1946 - Charles Spurgeon Johnson became the first African-American President of Fisk University. He was also a lifelong advocate for racial equality and the advancement of civil rights for African-Americans as well as all ethnic minorities.

1985 - United States Air Force Pilot, Military Engineer and NASA Astronaut, Frederick Drew Gregory led the Shuttle Challenger on a seven day mission, becoming the first African-American to Pilot a Space Shuttle. Gregory was the nephew Dr. Charles Drew, the world famous doctor who developed Blood Plasma Storage and invented the "Blood Bank." From 1985 to 1991, Gregory spent over 455 hours in outer space, he commanded three major space missions.

1987 - Deborah Boutin Prothrow-Stith became the first woman and the youngest Commissioner of Public Health for the Commonwealth of Massachusetts. Between 1984 and 1987, she was the Principal Investigator on numerous adolescent violence projects. She held a number of positions with Boston City Hospital and Harvard University. She was recognized nationally for her work on violence, and the prevention of violence among adolescents.

1994 - Illinois Congresswoman, Cardiss Collins became the first woman to head the Congressional Black Caucus Foundation, Inc.

On this Day in History...

August 20th

1948 - Forty-two year old Leroy "Satchel" Paige pitched the Cleveland Indians to a 1-0 victory over the White Sox in front of 78,382 fans, a Baseball game attendance record that still stands. Paige holds the record for the oldest MLB "rookie" debut at forty-two years old, he is also the oldest player to compete in an MLB game at fifty-nine years old.

1964 - President Lyndon B. Johnson signs the Economic Opportunity Act, initiating the federally-sponsored War on Poverty. The Act includes Head Start, Upward Bound and Volunteers in Service to America (VISTA).

1971 - Samuel "Top" Carson became one of the first African-American Service Station Owners in Brooklyn, N.Y. Growing up in St. George S.C., he moved to New York City in 1960. Serving as a community leader, he established a relationship with local political figures such as Congresswoman Shirley Chisholm and Senator Robert F. Kennedy. He became one of the most respected Businessmen and Entrepreneurs in NYC. Earlier in his career, he was also one of the first African-Americans to work for United Parcel Service (UPS) in Manhattan. Continuing in the Trucking Industry, he later joined Roadway Corp. In 2005, he retired and relocated with his family to Atlanta, GA.

2002 - Heavyweight Champion of World, Muhammad Ali was inducted to the Hollywood Walk of Fame. Out of an estimated 2500 entertainers, Ali became the only person to have his star embedded on a wall instead of on the ground. Ali indicated it was a matter of religious conviction, he bared the name of prophet Muhammad and he did not want people to trample over his name.

On this Day in History...

August 21st

1831 - Nat Turner lead the only effective slave rebellion in U.S. history. He inherited a passionate hatred of slavery from his African born mother, he saw himself as anointed by God to lead his people out of bondage. Turner and a small band of followers murdered his owners, the Travis family, then set off toward the town of Jerusalem where they planned to capture an armory and gather more recruits. The rebels went from plantation to plantation, gathering horses and guns, freeing other slaves along the way as well recruiting others who wanted to join their revolt.

1967 - Private First Class, James Anderson Jr., became the first African-American Marine to receive the Medal of Honor. During the Vietnam War, he threw himself on a grenade to save his comrades. Anderson was acknowledged by the naming of a military supply ship in his honor. Some of his medals and photographs are on display in Paris, France in the Museum Legion of Honor.

1990 - Blues Singer, Electric Guitarist and Songwriter, B.B. King was inducted into the Hollywood Walk of Fame and awarded a star on Hollywood Boulevard. King is considered one of the most influential Blues Musicians of all time. Throughout his career, he was known for performing tirelessly throughout his musical career, appearing at more than 200 concerts per year on average well into his 70's.

1997 - Actress and Fashion Model, Cicely Tyson was inducted into the Hollywood Walk of Fame and awarded a star on Hollywood Boulevard.

1998 - Actor, Producer and Martial Artist, Wesley Snipes was inducted into the Hollywood Walk of Fame and awarded a star on Hollywood Boulevard.

On this Day in History...

August 22nd

1898 - The North Carolina Mutual Life Insurance Company was founded in Durham N.C., it is the first African-American insurance company to attain $100 million in assets. The success of the company was largely due to the abilities of Charles Clinton Spaulding, who was General Manager of the company in 1900 and became President in 1923.

1950 - Charles M. Stokes became the first African-American elected to the Washington State House of Representatives. Ten years later he became the first African-American in the State to run for Lieutenant Governor.

1953 - Lorraine Williams became the first African-American to win a nationally recognized Tennis Title when she won the Junior Girl's Championship.

1993 - David Satcher became the first African-American appointed Director of the Centers for Disease Control and Prevention (CDC) in Atlanta, GA. In 1997, President Bill Clinton nominated Satcher to become the U.S. Surgeon General.

2011 - The Dr. Martin Luther King Jr., Memorial opened in West Potomac Park next to the National Mall in Washington, D.C., it covers four acres and includes the Stone of Hope, a Granite Statue of Civil Rights Movement Leader, Dr. King. The inspiration for the memorial design is a line from King's, "I Have A Dream" speech, "Out of the mountain of despair, a stone of hope." Dr. King is the first African-American honored with a memorial on or near the National Mall and the fourth non-President to be memorialized, his memorial is administered by the National Park Service.

On this Day in History...

August 23rd

1861 - James Stone became the first African-American to fight with the Union forces during the Civil War. He was a very light-complexioned former slave who enlisted in the First Fight Artillery of Ohio, he fought with the unit in Kentucky. His racial identity was revealed only after his death from a service-related injury.

1931 - Walter White was named NAACP Executive Secretary, he went on to become one of the major architects of the modern African-American freedom struggle. His leadership mounted a new strategy for the NAACP to began using lawsuits to end racial discrimination.

1985 - Alyce Griffin Clarke became the first African-American woman member of the State House of Representatives for Mississippi. Throughout her career, she also worked as a Public School Teacher and Nutritionist.

2018 - Author, Advocate for children and families with special needs, Tameka Carn founded the non-profit organization, Unique Minds. As a proud mother of four beautiful children: three daughters, Jamiya, Taliyah, Jayla, and one son, Jayden, she began researching Autism and how to become an advocate after her daughter Taliyah's diagnosis. Carn has emerged as an inspiration for millions of parents with her leadership and courage, her organization has enhanced the lives of parents with children with special needs by motivating, educating and inspiring them. Located in Charleston, S.C., Unique Minds also offers families financial and emotional support as well as community awareness and engagement. Carn's relationship with God, fueled her pursuit to help families of special needs children.

On this Day in History...

August 24th

1854 - Dr. John V. DeGrasse became the first African-American Physician to join a Medical Society, he was admitted to the Massachusetts Medical Society. He received his Medical Degree from Bowdoin College (Brunswick, Maine) in 1849. He studied in Europe, then returned home to Boston where he established a medical practice. De Grasses was a volunteer in the Union Army and was one of the eight African-Americans commissioned Surgeons in the Army during the Civil War.

1943 - Josephine Groves Holloway founded the first African-American Girl Scout Troop in Middle, TN, she was also served as its first executive.

1946 - Harold L. Trigg became the first African-American President of Saint Augustine's College in Raleigh, N.C. The College was founded in 1867 by the Freedman's Commission of the Protestant Episcopal Church, a group that included clergy and laymen of North Carolina's Episcopal diocese.

1988 - Henry Tomes Jr., became the first African-American Commissioner of the Department of Mental Health.

1997 - Robert G. Stanton became the first African-American Director of the National Park Service (NPS). He also served as an Administrator for the National Park Service for four decades.

2004 - Civil Rights Activist and Federal Judge, Robert L. Carter was awarded the NAACP Spingarn Medal, for his extraordinary achievement of winning 21 cases argued before the Supreme Court. In 1956, Carter succeeded Thurgood Marshall as the General Counsel of the NAACP.

On this Day in History...

August 25th

1960 - Regarded as one of the best all-around Athletes ever, Rafer Johnson became the first African-American Flag Bearer for team USA during the Olympic games opening ceremony in Rome, Italy. He went on to shatter the record in the Decathlon with 8,392 points, easily winning the gold medal. Johnson also lit the Olympic cauldron during the Opening Ceremonies at the Los Angeles Olympic Games in 1984.

1964 - During the Democratic National Convention, Civil Rights Activist, Fannie Lou Hamer was part of the Mississippi Freedom Democratic Party, an integrated group of activists who openly challenged the legality of Mississippi's all-white, segregated delegation. Working with the Student Nonviolent Coordinating Committee (SNCC), Hamer helped organize the 1964 Freedom Summer African-American voter registration drive in Mississippi.

1984 - Michelle V. Agins became the first African-American woman Still Photographer admitted to the International Photographers of the Motion Picture and Television Industries Union. She was a personal photographer of then Chicago Mayor Harold Washington.

2008 - David Alexander Paterson become the first African-American Governor of New York, he is also the State's first Legally Blind Governor. In 2006, he ran on a ticket with Eliot Spitzer and became the State's first African-American Lieutenant Governor. Paterson succeeded Spitzer, who resigned amid a scandal. Paterson completed Spitzer's term which ended in 2010.

On this Day in History…

August 26th

1839 - Joseph Cinqué and a group of West-Africans who were abducted for the slave trade, led a revolt and seized the slave ship Amistad. They killed the ship's Captain and most of the crew, they were tried for murder in New Haven, CT. The Supreme Court found they had the right to resist slavery and the 35 surviving Africans were returned to Africa, they were defended in court by former President John Quincy Adams. These events inspired to 1997 film, "Amistad."

1947 - Dan Bankhead became the first African-American "Pitcher" in the Major League Baseball, he and his teammate Jackie Robinson were the first African-American players to compete in the World Series.

1992 - Denise H. Hoover became the first woman to graduate from the U.S. Marine Corps Security Force Training Company in Chesapeake, VA.

2017 - Floyd Mayweather became the first Professional Boxer to reach a record of 50-0. During his career, he held multiple World Titles in five weight classes and the Lineal Championship in four weight classes (twice at Welterweight), he retired with an undefeated record.

2018 - West Virginia State University honored NASA Mathematician, Katherine Johnson during her 100th birthday celebration with a bronze statue and scholarship dedication in her honor. Hundreds of people including seventy-five of Johnson's children, grandchildren and great-grandchildren attended the event honoring the woman who was portrayed by Actress, Taraji P. Henson in the 2016 film, "Hidden Figures." In 2015, Johnson was also awarded the Presidential Medal of Freedom by President Barack Obama.

On this Day in History...

August 27th

1895 - Mary Church Terrell became the first African-American woman to serve on the Washington, D.C., Board of Education, she served until 1911. Terrell was also active in church and community work, she founded the Lincoln Temple Congregational Church in Washington.

1917 - Eugene Bullard became the first African-American Combat Pilot to fly during World War I, he was also the only African-American Pilot to fly during the War. When the United States entered the War, American Pilots who flew for France were eligible for a U.S. Army commission. Bullard, who had been a member of the French Foreign Legion and the French Army, presented himself to the Army, but his application was rejected. He flew more than twenty combat missions for the French Air Service. For his daring flights, he was nicknamed the "Black Swallow of Death," and became a highly decorated combat pilot.

1981 - Johnny Grier became the first African-American Referee in the NFL. Grier also officiated Super Bowl XXII, which was his final game as a Field Judge, it was the same game Doug Williams became the first African-American "Quarterback" to win the Super Bowl.

1988 - Actress, Beah Richards won a Primetime Emmy Award for her guest role in the television series "Frank's Place," she won her second Emmy for her role in "The Practice" in 2000. Richards was nominated for an Academy Award and a Golden Globe for her supporting role in the film, "Guess Who's Coming to Dinner" in 1968. She also received a Tony Award nomination for her performance in the 1965 production of The Amen Corner.

On this Day in History...

August 28th

1963 - The March on Washington for Jobs and Freedom was held in Washington, D.C. The purpose of the march was to advocate for civil and economic rights for African-Americans. Dr. Martin Luther King Jr., stood in front of the Lincoln Memorial and delivered his historic "I Have a Dream" speech, which he called for an end to racism and injustice. This was a peaceful demonstration to focus national attention on equality for African-Americans as well as advance the civil rights bill that was before Congress. A quarter of a million people participated, making it the largest single protest march in the country up to that time. Dr. King's iconic speech went down as one of the greatest speeches in history.

1986 - Singer, Songwriter, Dancer and Actress, Tina Turner was inducted into the Hollywood Walk of Fame and awarded a star on Hollywood Boulevard. Turner's career has spanned for more than five decades. She has won numerous awards and her achievements in the Rock music genre have earned her the title "The Queen of Rock & Roll." The film, "What's Love Got to Do with It" starring Actress, Angela Bassett, opened in 1993, tells her life story.

2008 - Senator Barack Obama gave his acceptance speech at the Democratic National Convention in Denver, CO., he became the first African-American to secure the nomination as a candidate for U.S. President by a major political party.

2018 - Serving as Mayor of Tallahassee, FL., Andrew Gillum became the first African-American to win the Florida Democratic Party's nominee for Governor of Florida.

On this Day in History...

August 29th

1904 - Private School "Mother Academy" was established, it was the first Catholic school for African-Americans in the State of Tennessee. Founder, Katherine Mary Drexel was canonized as a "Saint" by Pope John Paul II in 2000.

1945 - Camilla Ella Williams became the first African-American woman to sing with the New York City Opera, she performed the title role in "Puccini's Madama Butterfly." The next year she became the first African-American to sign a full contract with a major opera company in the United States. In 1954, she was also the first African-American Singer to appear on the stage of the Vienna State Opera.

1960 - As an Amateur Boxer, Cassius Clay, who later changed his name to "Muhammad Ali" won the gold medal at the Olympic Games in Rome, Italy.

1979 - Singer, Aretha Franklin, commonly referred to as "The Queen of Soul" was inducted into the Hollywood Walk of Fame and awarded a star on Hollywood Boulevard. Throughout her career, Franklin recorded a total of 112 charted singles on Billboard, including 77 Hot 100 entries, 17 top ten Pop singles, 100 R&B entries and 21 R&B singles, becoming the most charted female Artist in the chart's history.

1998 - The Student Union opened on the campus of the University of California at Berkeley, it was named in honor of Dr. Martin Luther King Jr.

On this Day in History...

August 30th

1966 - Constance B. Motley became the first African-American woman Federal Judge, she was also the first African-American State Senator for New York. Throughout her career, she was a Civil Rights Activist and Borough President of Manhattan, New York City. She was also Assistant Attorney to Thurgood Marshall while he argued the case Brown vs. Board of Education.

1967 - Thurgood Marshall was confirmed as the first African-American U.S. Supreme Court Justice. Marshall was Chief Attorney of the NAACP for twenty-three years. During his tenure, he distinguished himself for using the legal system to break racially discriminatory practices in voting, housing, transportation as well as other areas. He left the NAACP in 1962 and was confirmed a Judge on the U.S. Court of Appeals, Third Circuit. He was then confirmed as Solicitor General in 1965. He was nominated to the U.S. Supreme Court by President Lyndon B. Johnson.

1979 - John Heartwell Holland became the first African-American Chairman of the Board of Governors of the American National Red Cross.

1983 - Aerospace Engineer, U.S. Air Force Officer, Fighter Pilot and NASA Astronaut, Dr. Guion Stewart Bluford Jr., became the first African-American to travel into space as a member of the Orbiter Challenger crew, on the mission STS-8. He participated in four Space Shuttle flights between 1983 and 1992.

1994 - William B. Gould IV became the first African-American Chairman of the National Labor Relations Board (NLRB).

On this Day in History...

August 31st

1868 - Francis L. Cardozo became the first African-American Secretary of State for South Carolina, he served for four years in the position. He was the first African-American to hold a Statewide office in the United States. Throughout his career, he served as Professor of Latin at Howard University. Cardozo also became the Secretary of the Treasury for South Carolina, he was elected to two terms in 1872 and 1874. In 1864, Cardozo was Pastor of the Temple Street Congregational Church in New Haven, CT.

1907 - Pleasant Grove Missionary Baptist Church was founded by Sister Addie E. Thomas in Marbury, MD. Over the years, Pleasant Grove Baptist Church has been a continuously moving Christian lifeline for its congregation. Reverend Arthur J. Patterson now serves as the Pastor of the Church, he has served as Pastor for more than seventeen years in the West Virginia, Virginia, Washington D.C., and Maryland areas. Along with God's guidance, Reverend Patterson trained and ordained many Deaconesses, Deacons and Ministers to the Gospel Service. He resides in Fairfax VA., with his wife Sandra and their two sons Darin and Darius.

1960 - Wilma Rudolph became the first woman to win three Track and Field Gold Medals in a single Olympics. Rudolph was an American Sprinter who won in the 100 and 200-meter individual events as well as the 4 x 100-meter relay at the Summer Olympics in Rome, Italy.

1990 - Ken Griffey Sr., and Ken Griffey Jr., made Baseball history as the first father and son duo to appear in the same lineup playing for the Seattle Mariners, this was the the first time a father and son had played together while serving the same team.

On this Day in History...

September 1st

1939 - World War II began, more than 3 million African-Americans registered for service. The war's first African-American hero emerged from the attack on Pearl Harbor, when Dorie Miller, a young Navy Steward on the U.S.S. West Virginia carried wounded crew members to safety and manned a machine gun post, shooting down several Japanese planes.

1952 - John Saunders Chase opened the first Architectural Firm owned and operated by African-Americans in the State of Texas, he was also the first African-American licensed to practice Architecture in the State. He later opened branches of his firm in Houston, Dallas and Washington, D.C. In 1971, Chase and twelve other African-American Architects from across the country formed the National Organization of Minority Architects (NOMA). In 1980, President Jimmy Carter appointed Chase to the U.S. Commission on the Fine Arts, the first African-American to hold that appointment. The Commission later picked his firm to design the famous Vietnam Veterans Memorial. His work at Texas Southern University (TSU) included the Thurgood Marshall School of Law, several residence halls, the Martin Luther King School of Education and the student center. He was also Associate Architect for the Federal Reserve Bank of Dallas.

1969 - The John Brown Russwurm African-American Center opened on the campus of Bowdoin College, it was named in honor of 1826 graduate John Brown Russwurm. He founded the Nation's first African-American newspaper.

1981 - Clarence M. Pendleton Jr., became the first African-American to Chair the United States Civil Rights Commission.

On this Day in History...

September 2nd

1945 -   (Known as Victory over Japan -VJ Day) Japan surrendered to the United States, ending World War II. Towards the end of the war, over one million African-American men and women served in the U.S. Military and assisted with the victory.

1948 -   First Lt. Nancy Leftneant-Colon became the first African-American accepted in the regular Army Nursing Corps.

1962 -   Mildred Mitchell-Bateman became the first African-American woman in the United States to head a State Mental Health Department, she was also the first African-American to have Cabinet position in the West Virginia State Government.

1975 -   Joseph Hatchett was sworn in as the first African-American State Supreme Court Justice for the the State of Florida. In 1979, Hatchett was also nominated by President Jimmy Carter to the United States Court of Appeals for the Fifth Circuit.

1984 -   Aulana Louise Peters became the first African-American woman appointed to the Securities and Exchange Commission.

1988 -   Gospel Singer, Mahalia Jackson was inducted into the Hollywood Walk of Fame and awarded a star on Hollywood Boulevard. She was one of the most influential Gospel Singers in the world and was recognized internationally as a singer and civil rights activist. Jackson recorded more than thirty albums during her career, selling millions of records. Jackson once said "I sing God's music because it makes me feel free, it gives me hope."

On this Day in History...

September 3rd

1870 - Jonathan Jasper Wright became the first African-American State Supreme Court Justice in the United States (South Carolina). He studied law in Pennsylvania, where he became the first African-American admitted to the State Bar in 1866.

1987 - Ronald M. Sharpe became the first African-American Commissioner of the Pennsylvania State Police. He was a twenty-five year Veteran of the Police Department at the time of his appointment.

1992 - Spelman College in Atlanta, GA., became the first Historically Black College and University (HBCU) to receive a single gift of $37 million, the largest gift ever made to a Historically Black College. The gift from the DeWitt Wallace/Spelman College fund was established in the New York Community Trust by the Reader's Digest Association. The funds were earmarked for scholarships and to build a curriculum development program within the honors program.

1994 - Ernest A. Finney Jr., became the first African-American Chief Justice of the State Supreme Court of South Carolina since Reconstruction Era. Senator Ernest Hollings praised him on the floor of the United States Senate for his work with the civil rights movement. Finney was also the first African-American Circuit Court Judge in the State and a resident Judge in the Sumter County Courthouse.

1998 - The National League of Women Voters (LWV) elected Carolyn Jefferson-Jenkins as their 15th President. L.W.V is a civic organization that was formed to help women take a larger role in public affairs. She became the first African-American to hold that post.

On this Day in History...

September 4th

1863 - Sarah J. Thompson Garnet became the first African-American woman appointed as a Principal in the New York City Public School System. Prior to her appointment, she was a teacher at the African Free School in Williamsburg, Brooklyn. Garnet was also the founder of Brooklyn's first equal rights organizations, "The Equal Suffrage League" and she was superintendent of the Suffrage Department of the National Association.

1986 - Niara Sudarkasa became the first ever woman President of Lincoln University in Pennsylvania. She was the unanimous choice of the Board of Trustees, chosen from a field of 103 candidates. Sudarkasa holds thirteen Honorary Degrees, she is also the recipient of nearly 100 civic and professional awards.

1988 - Charles and Chester Smith became the first African-American Identical Twins ordained as Priests in the Catholic church.

1994 - "Quarterback" for the Minnesota Vikings, Warren Moon, opened the season, it was the first time in National Football League (NFL) history that an African-American quarterback opened the season for an African-American Head Coach, Dennis Green. In 1995, Moon also became the first quarterback to eclipse 60,000 yards in passing.

2000 - Barbara Christian Hall opened on the campus of the University of California at Berkeley, it was named in honor of Barbara Christian. She was the long-time African-American Studies Professor at Berkeley.

On this Day in History...

September 5th

1870 - The Preparatory High School for Colored Youth became the first Public High School for African-Americans students in the country, it opened in the basement of the Fifteenth Street Presbyterian Church in Washington, D.C. In 1891, the school relocated to a location on M Street, it then became known as M Street High School. Twenty-five years later, the school was renamed to honor Poet and Novelist, Paul Laurence Dunbar. In 1986, the M Street/Dunbar High School was listed on the National Register of Historic Places.

1895 - Nathan Francis Mossell founded first Hospital primarily for African-American Patients, "The Frederick Douglass Memorial Hospital and Training School for Nurses," which is located in Philadelphia, PA.

1994 - San Francisco 49ers "Wide Receiver" Jerry Rice scored touchdown number 127, he broke the all-time career touchdown record set by Jim Brown, becoming the first player to reach that level. Rice is widely considered to be the greatest wide receiver in NFL history and often called the greatest NFL player of all time. He was inducted into the College Football Hall of Fame in 2006 and the Pro Football Hall of Fame in 2010.

2018 - Actress, Cicely Tyson becomes the first African-American woman to receive an Honorary Oscar. Throughout her career, she has won a Tony, two Emmys and a Presidential Medal of Freedom, she was also nominated for an Academy Award as "Best Actress" in the 1972 film Sounder. Tyson began her career as a Model and Stage Actress, she received her big feature-film break in "The Heart Is a Lonely Hunter." (1968)

On this Day in History...

September 6th

1935 - Alvin Demar Loving Sr., became the first African-American High School Teacher in the Detroit Public Schools. He later became a Professor and Associate Dean at the University of Michigan. Loving set up universities in the countries of Nigeria and India, as a result, he became an important figure in international education. The Indian government hired him as a consultant to advise them on the reorganization of their secondary school system.

1986 - Massachusetts Institute of Technology (MIT) named a building after Ronald McNair, a MIT graduate who was one of the Astronauts onboard the Space Shuttle Challenger at the time of its tragic accident. The McNair Building houses the Center for Space Research, a division of the Aeronautics and Astronautics Department at the University.

1988 - Lee Roy Young became the first African-American Texas Ranger in the 165-year history of the law enforcement agency. Young had a considerable amount of experience in law enforcement in Texas, including his service as State Trooper and Criminal Intelligence Investigator.

2016 - Actress, Cree Summer became the the most popular Voice Actress of all time. Known for playing Winifred "Freddie" Brooks on the NBC sitcom "A Different World," Summer has voiced over 150 animated characters during her career. These roles have spanned video games, cartoon television series, animated films and commercials. Among her most famous roles were "Penny" in Inspector Gadget and "Beast Girl" in Teen Titans Go!

On this Day in History...

September 7th

1781 - Peter Hill became one of the first known African-American Clock-Makers in United States during the late 18th and early 19th centuries. He was one of the few African-Americans who opened a small business during this period. Other African-American entrepreneurs of this period were barbers, restaurateurs, caterers, merchants and tailors. Although Hill was not an inventor, his contribution to the art of clock-making during that period was a historic achievement.

1927 - (HBCU) Texas State University was founded in Houston, TX. TSU is one of the largest and most comprehensive Historically Black Universities in the Nation, it is also one of only four independent public Universities in Texas. TSU is the only HBCU in Texas recognized as one of "America's Top Colleges."

1977 - Civil Rights Attorney and Activist, Randall Robinson founded Trans Africa, a private advocacy organization committed to influencing American foreign policy toward Africa and the Caribbean, particularly in matters relating to human rights abuses, immigration reform and foreign aid. Robinson was the most prominent and effective activist in the fight against South African apartheid, persuading Congress to pass an anti-apartheid law in 1986 overriding President Reagan's veto and helping to achieve the release of Nelson Mandela from prison.

1989 - Norman Blann Rice became the first African-American elected as Mayor of Seattle WA., he took office in 1990 and was re-elected in 1993. Rice also spent eleven years on the Seattle, City Council.

On this Day in History...

September 8th

1908 - Vertner W. Tandy, Sr., became the first African-American Architect registered in New York State. Tandy is also known as a founder of Alpha Phi Alpha Fraternity at Cornell University. In 1909, he established a partnership with Architect George Washington Foster. Through the partnership, they received several significant commissions, including St. Philips Episcopal Church and the Harlem townhouse of hair care magnate, Madame C. J. Walker. Their other works include Small's Paradise, the Harlem Elks Lodge and in the Abraham Lincoln Houses in the Bronx.

1981 - Founded in 1836, Bethel African Methodist Episcopal (AME) Church was added to the National Register of Historic Places, it is the oldest African-American Church in the State of Indiana.

1992 - Willie L. Williams became the first African-American Chief of Police in the City of Los Angeles, CA. During his career, he was also the first African-American Police Commissioner of the Philadelphia, PA., Police Department.

1999 - Diane Boardley Suber was appointed as the tenth President of Saint Augustine's University in Raleigh, N.C.

2011 - When promoted from Brigadier General to Major General in the U.S. Army, Marcia Anderson became the Army's first African-American woman Two-Star General. The ceremony took place at Fort Knox, Kentucky. After her promotion, she moved to the office of the Chief of the U.S. Army Reserve in Washington, D.C.

On this Day in History...

September 9th

1937 - Zelda Jackson "Jackie" Ormes became the first Nationally Syndicated African-American woman Cartoonist. She began her cartoon "Torchy Brown in Dixie to Harlem," that ran in the Pittsburgh Courier. She also created the strips "Patty Jo n' Ginger," and "Candy."

1945 - The first and only School of Veterinary Medicine in a Historically Black College or University (HBCU) was established at Tuskegee Institute in Alabama. Veterinarian and then President of Tuskegee, Frederick D. Patterson, founded the school.

1989 - Herbert Carter became the first African-American Chairman of the Board of Directors of United Way Organization. Carter was also Executive Vice Chancellor at California State University at Los Angeles.

1996 - Businesswoman, Corporate Leader and Author, Pamela Thomas Graham was named Partner in the largest management consulting firm in the world, McKinsey & Company. She began her career at Goldman Sachs & Co., where she was a Summer Associate in the Investment Banking Division while she was a student at Harvard Business School.

2001 - San Francisco Giants "Outfielder," Barry Bonds, who is regarded as one of the greatest players in Baseball history, appeared on the breakfast cereal box "Wheaties." Throughout his career, Bonds received seven National League MVP awards and fourteen All-Star selections.

On this Day in History…

September 10th

1917 - Roland Hayes became the first African-American to sing in Symphony Hall in Boston. He was also the first African-American give a recital at Carnegie Hall in 1924.

1967 - Barbara Charline Jordan became the first African-American to sit in the Texas Senate since 1883. In 1972, she became President Pro Tempore of the Senate, the first African-American woman to preside over a legislative body in the United States as well as the first acting Governor of the State. Later that year, she was elected to the U.S. House of Representatives. In 2001, the City Council of Austin approved a seven-foot-tall bronze statue of Jordan to be placed in the Austin-Bergstrom International Airport at the Barbara Jordan Passenger Terminal.

1973 - Henry Ossawa Tanner was commemorated on the U.S. postage stamp. Tanner was the first African-American Painter to gain International acclaim. His most famous painting, "The Banjo Lesson," featured an older gentleman teaching a young boy how to play the banjo was created while visiting his family in Philadelphia in 1893. The following year, he painted another masterpiece "The Thankful Poor."

1994 - The UniverSoul Circus was founded by Cedric Walker, an African-American man who had a vision of creating a circus with a large percentage of people of color performing. He began searching for people from all around the world with incredible talents. The circus has performers from more that twenty countries around the world. Headquartered in Atlanta, GA., the circus tour has grown to more than forty cities.

On this Day in History...

September 11th

1869 - Henry McNeal Turner became the first African-American to serve as a United States Postmaster. He served as Postmaster for Macon, GA.

1933 - Ethel Thompson Overby became the first African-American woman Principal in the Richmond, VA., school system. Overby encouraged her teachers to become active in their State Teachers Association and to know their rights. She insisted that they become registered voters and she urged her teachers to participate in voter drives and local and State teacher organizations. Overby demanded that her teachers be role models and advocates for democracy through their own participation in civic affairs.

1953 - Paul Revere Williams became the first African-American Architect to become a Fellow of the American Institute of Architects. Certified in California in 1915, he designed homes and buildings for Hollywood stars. His clients included Frank Sinatra, Zsa Zsa Gabor, William "Bojangles" Robinson, Lucille Ball and Desi Arnaz. In addition to designing more than three-thousand homes, ranging in value from $10.000 to $600,000, Williams served as Associate Architect for the $50 million Los Angeles International Airport.

1993 - Julius Erving, commonly referred to as "Dr. J," was inducted into the Basketball Hall of Fame. Erving helped to legitimize the American Basketball Association (ABA) and was the best-known player in that league when it merged with the National Basketball Association (NBA). He was well known for slam dunking from the free throw line in slam dunk contests, he is the only player ever voted Most Valuable Player in both the ABA and the NBA.

On this Day in History...

September 12th

1912 - Howard Porter Drew became the first African-American to hold the record for the 100-yard dash. He was called the "World's Fastest Human" and won the National Amateur Athletic Union Championship.

1977 - Serving as the 36th Treasurer of the United States during the Carter Administration, Azie Taylor Morton became the first African-American woman whose signature appeared on U.S. currency.

1992 - Engineer, Physician and NASA Astronaut, Mae C. Jemison became the first African-American woman Astronaut to travel into space. She flew into space with six other Astronauts aboard the Endeavour on mission STS47. Jemison was also the first African-American woman to be admitted into NASA's Astronaut training program. During her eight days in space, she conducted experiments on weightlessness and motion sickness on the crew as well as herself. She spent more than 190 hours in space before returning to earth. Following her historic flight, Jemison noted that society should recognize how much both women and members of other minority groups can contribute if given the opportunity.

1999 - Professional Tennis Players, Serena Williams and her sister Venus Williams became the first African-American women's Team to succeed at the U.S. Open, they won the Doubles Title defeating Chandra Rubin of America and Sandrine Testud of France. They also won gold medals in Doubles at the 2000 Olympic games in Sydney, Australia. They were the first sisters to win Olympic gold in Doubles and extended their Doubles winning streak to twenty-two matches.

On this Day in History...

September 13th

1872 - Abolitionist, Author and Orator, Frederick Douglass became first African-American nominee for Vice President of the United States by the Equal Rights Party.

1881 - Inventor, Lewis Latimer received a U.S. patent for a Carbon Filament for the Incandescent Lightbulb. His creation was an improvement to Thomas Edison's lightbulb, which made electric lighting more practical and affordable for the average household, he was also directly involved with the invention of the Telephone. Latimer patented several other inventions including an improved Railroad Car Bathroom and an early Air Conditioning Unit. Latimer was inducted into the National Inventors Hall of Fame in 2006.

1886 - (HBCU) The University of Maryland Eastern Shore was founded in Princess Anne, MD. Initiated under the support of the Delaware Conference of the Methodist Episcopal Church, the Delaware Conference Academy was established in Princess Anne with nine students and one faculty.

1994 - Jazz Musician and Singer, Billie Holiday was commemorated on the U.S. Postage Stamp. Holiday's singing career spanned over thirty years. Nicknamed "Lady Day" she is considered one of the greatest Jazz Vocalist of all time.

1999 - Heavyweight Champion of the World, Muhammad Ali, who is regarded as one of the most significant and celebrated sports figures of the 20th century, appeared on the breakfast cereal box "Wheaties." Ali made a second appearance in 2012, he is the only Heavyweight Champion to win the title three times.

On this Day in History...

September 14th

1983 - Representing the State of New York, Vanessa Williams became the first African-American Miss America, she was also the first to resign with the title in 1984. Suzette Charles, who was the the first African-American runner up representing New Jersey, took Williams's place.

1992 - William K. Finney became the first African-American Chief of Police of St. Paul, MN., he was a twenty-one year Veteran of the Police Department at the time of his appointment.

1994 - Vocal Group "The Temptations," who released a series of successful singles and albums with Motown Records during the 1960's and 1970's, were inducted into the Hollywood Walk of Fame and awarded a star on Hollywood Boulevard. Group members David Ruffin, Melvin Franklin, Paul Williams, Otis Williams and Eddie Kendricks were known for their choreography and distinct harmonies. Having sold tens of millions of albums, the Temptations are one of the most successful groups in music history.

1995 - R&B and Disco Band, "Earth Wind and Fire" was inducted into the Hollywood Walk of Fame and awarded a star on Hollywood Boulevard. The Band has won six Grammy Awards and four American Music Awards. They have also been inducted into both the Rock & Roll Hall of Fame and the Vocal Group Hall of Fame.

1998 - Leonard Washington Jr., became the first African-American State Trooper in Pennsylvania that was appointed to Major. He commanded the force in the Western part of Pennsylvania. Throughout his career in law enforcement, Washington served as a State Trooper, Corporal, Sergeant, Lieutenant, Captain and Major.

On this Day in History...

September 15th

1956 - Rock & Roll Singer and Songwriter, Frankie Lymon became the first African-American teen heartthrob. He inspired a number of younger musicians, including Michael Jackson. Lymon became a lead singer of Doo-Wop, performing with his friends for donations on the streets of New York. They later created the quartet that would be known as the "Teenagers."

1978 - Muhammad Ali became the first and only Boxer to ever win the Heavyweight Championship of the world a total of three times when he defeated Leon Spinks at the Superdome in New Orleans, LA.

1988 - Charles Lakes became the first African-American man to be a member of the United States Olympic Team for Gymnastics, he participated in the Summer Games in Soul, Korea.

1991 - Inventor, Jan Ernst Matzeliger was commemorated on the U.S. Postage Stamp. Matzeliger invented the automatic shoe making machine in 1883. His machine was able to create hundreds of pairs of shoes in a single day, vastly increasing production in the Shoe Making Industry. He was also inducted into the National Inventors Hall of Fame in 2006.

1997 - Veroman D. Witcher Jr., became the first African-American to win the State Trooper of the Year Award. The Ohio State Officer joined the patrol in 1985 and graduated in the 115th Academy class. He previously worked as a Background Investigator and Field Training Officer, he also addressed safety issues through education and enforcement.

On this Day in History...

September 16th

1984 - Bishop Robinson became the first African-American Commissioner of the Baltimore Police Department, he was a thirty-two year Veteran of the Police Department at the time of his appointment. Robinson is also a founder, and a past President of the National Organization of Black Law Enforcement Executives.

1989 - Virginia Fields became the first African-American woman elected to the City Council from Manhattan, NYC, she served for two terms. In 1997, she was elected Manhattan Borough President. New York Supreme Court Justice, Leland DeGrase swore her in office at a ceremony at the Metropolitan Museum of Art. Fields vowed to help rebuild lower Manhattan, she also supported plans for a memorial to those who lost their lives in the terrorist attacks on September 11, 2001.

1990 - Dana Tyler and Reggie Harris formed the first African-American News Anchor Team in a Major Metropolitan City for WCBS-TV, in New York City. Tyler is the great-granddaughter of Ralph Waldo Tyler, the first African-American War Correspondent during World War I.

1993 - Joann Horton became the first woman President of Texas Southern University, one of the Nation's largest Historically Black Colleges and Universities (HBCU's). Throughout her career, Horton has also headed fifteen institutions and twenty-eight campuses of the Iowa Community College System. In 1998, she became President of Kennedy-King College in Chicago, IL.

On this Day in History...

September 17th

1849 - Abolitionist, Humanitarian and Spy for the United States Army during the American Civil War, Harriet Tubman made use of the network known as the "Underground Railroad." She began her journey to freedom and traveled nearly 90 miles from Maryland to Philadelphia, PA. Tubman then bravely returned back to Maryland to rescue her family. Slowly, one group at a time, she brought relatives with her out of the State and eventually became the most famous "Conductor" of the Underground Railroad, over time she guided several hundred other slaves to freedom.

1966 - Frank Robinson became the first African-American Baseball Player named the Most Valuable Player (MVP) in both National and American Leagues, playing for the National League Cincinnati Reds in 1961 and the American League Baltimore Orioles in 1966. He was also was the first African-American to win the Triple Crown which is the most home runs, highest batting average and most runs batted in.

1970 - Comedian, Flip Wilson became the first African-American man to have a weekly primetime comedy television show in his own name. "The Flip Wilson Show" earned him a Golden Globe and two Emmy Awards, it was the second highest rated show on network television. Wilson also won a Grammy Award in 1970 for his comedy album.

2000 - Maurice Greene became the "fastest man on earth," he won two gold medals (an individual gold in the 100-meter dash and a second as a member of the U.S. 4x100 Relay team) and set a World Record in the 100-meter dash at the Olympics held in Sydney, Australia.

On this Day in History...

September 18th

1924 - Sidney Bechet became the first African-American to achieve recognition on the soprano saxophone. As an outstanding representative of the New Orleans tradition, he was also one of the first African-Americans recognized in Classical music circles. A statue of Bechet was erected in Antibes in honor of his work in France.

1935 - (HBCU) Norfolk State University was founded in Norfolk, VA. The University was brought to life in the midst of the Great Depression, provided a setting in which the youth of the region could give expression to their hopes and aspirations.

1989 - Robert T. Johnson became the first African-American District Attorney for New York City. Throughout his career, he was also appointed as a Judge for New York Criminal Court, he was then promoted to Acting Justice of the New York State Supreme Court.

1994 - Langston Hall opened on the campus of Oberlin College, it is named after John Mercer Langston, an 1849 graduate of the college. Unable to gain admittance to Law School because of his race, Langston studied on his own for the Bar. In 1868, he moved to Washington where he founded the Howard University School of Law, serving as its first Dean. In 1890, he was elected to Congress from Virginia and served as a Diplomat in Haiti and the Dominican Republic. He also served as President of Virginia State University. Langston is also the great-uncle of the famous Poet, Langston Hughes.

On this Day in History...

September 19th

1919 - Lucie Campbell Williams published "Something Within," she became the first African-American woman composer to have a Gospel song published.

1982 - Bernice Bouie Donald became the first woman Judge in the State of Tennessee, she was appointed as General Sessions Court Judge in Shelby County. In 1988, Donald also became the first African-American woman to serve on a U.S. Bankruptcy Court.

1992 - Herman Williams Jr., became the first African-American Fire Chief of Baltimore, MD. In 1954, he became one of the first African-Americans to join the City's Fire Department. Williams is the father of famed talk show host Montel Williams.

1993 - The Reginald F. Lewis International Law Center opened on the campus of Harvard University, it was named after the late CEO of TLC Beatrice Holdings, Inc. Lewis gave $3 million to Harvard Law School in 1992, he was a 1968 graduate of the Law School.

1996 - Multi-Grammy Award winning musician, George Benson was inducted into the Hollywood Walk of Fame and awarded a star on Hollywood Boulevard. Benson's recording career began at the age of twenty-one as a Jazz Guitarist, he is also known as a Pop, R&B and Scat Singer.

2000 - Track and Field Athletes, Alvin and Calvin Harrison became the first twins in Olympic history to run in the same relay and to win a gold medals. They were teammates for the U.S. Olympic 4x400 Relay Team in Sydney, Australia.

On this Day in History...

September 20th

1894 - Julia A. J. Foote became the first woman in the United States to be ordained as a Deacon, she was a member of the African Methodist Episcopal church (AME). In 1898, she also became the second Methodist woman to be ordained an Elder.

1934 - Willa Brown-Chappell became the first African-American woman in the United States to hold a commercial pilot's license, she was also the first African-American woman to run for United States Congress. She later became the first African-American Officer in the U.S. Civil Air Patrol.

1942 - Perry B. Jackson became the first African-American Judge in the State of Ohio, he was appointed to the Municipal Court of Cleveland.

1980 - The Betty Shabazz Cultural Center opened on the campus of Mount Holyoke College, in South Hadley, MA. The center was named in honor of Betty Shabazz, a Political Activist and widow of Malcolm X.

1992 - Paul A. Stephens became the first African-American President of the Academy of General Dentistry, which is the second largest Dental Association in the country.

2004 - Singer, Songwriter and Composer, Barry White was posthumously inducted into the Dance Music Hall of Fame. During the course of his career, White was a three-time Grammy Award winner, had 106 gold albums worldwide, 41 of which also attained platinum status. He also achieved worldwide record sales in excess of 100 million. White is one of the world's best-selling Artists of all time.

On this Day in History...

September 21st

1964 - Harold Gordon Tillman Sr., became the first African-American Judge in the State of Texas, he was appointed as a Municipal Judge.

1979 - Matthew J. Perry Jr., became the first African-American Federal Judge in the State of South Carolina.

1985 - Lu Valle Commons opened on the campus of University of California at Los Angeles (UCLA). The building was named in honor of James Ellis Lu Valle, a graduate of UCLA who won a bronze medal at the 1936 Olympics in Berlin. Lu Valle later conducted research for Eastman Kodak and became Director of Research at the Stanford University chemistry laboratories.

2001 - George Garwood Jr., became the first African-American Mayor in the State of Utah, for the City of South Ogden. For six years, Garwood served on the City Council, he also served as President of the Utah League of Cities and Towns.

2006 - Julius Erving, commonly referred to as "Dr. J," appeared on the breakfast cereal box "Wheaties." Erving won three Championships, four Most Valuable Player (MVP) Awards and three Scoring Titles with the New York Nets (now the Brooklyn Nets) and the Philadelphia 76ers.

2009 - President Barack Obama appointed Mignon Clyburn as the first African-American woman to head the Federal Communications Commission (FCC).

On this Day in History...

September 22nd

1919 - Dr. Dorothy Lavinia Brown became the first African-American woman Surgeon in the U.S. Later in her career she entered politics, she became the first African-American to serve in the Tennessee General Assembly having been elected to the Tennessee House of Representatives.

1944 - Elizabeth B. Murphy Moss became the first African-American woman certified as a war correspondent during World War II. Moss later became Vice President and Treasurer of the Afro-American Company, she was also the publisher of the largest African-American chain of weekly newspapers in the United States.

1950 - Ralph Bunche became the first African-American to be awarded the Nobel Peace Prize, for his peace efforts in the Middle East. Bunche served as a Professor at Howard University, Undersecretary General of the United Nations and a Diplomat. In 1963, he was awarded the Presidential Medal of Freedom by President John F. Kennedy. Bunche's home was placed on the National Register of Historic Places.

2017 - NASA dedicated a facility to honor "Hidden Figure" Katherine Johnson. Known as the human computer, she was behind some of NASA's biggest advancements. Johnson, along with Dorothy Vaughan and Mary Jackson, shattered the segregational norms within the agency in the 1960s to push forward some of the country's greatest aerospace advancements. The Katherine G. Johnson Computational Research Facility is a state-of-the-art facility run by NASA's Langley Research Center. The building consolidates four of the organization's data centers as a part of Langley's twenty-year revitalization plan.

On this Day in History...

September 23rd

1915 - Frederick D. Patterson became the first African-American to own and operate a Car Manufacturing Business. Greenfield-Patterson cars were built in Greenfield, Ohio. Over the next five years, the company produced approximately 150 vehicles. Considered to be a better quality vehicle than Henry Ford's Model T, the company's two models were the Roadster and a four-door Touring, both cars were sold for the price of $850.

1951 - The Ben Moore Hotel was founded in Montgomery, AL., it was the first-American owned hotel in the City. The Owner, Matthew F. Moore named the business in honor of his father, Ben Moore, who was a former slave born in Alabama.

1981 - Billie Anne Willis became the first woman of any race to be a Police Precinct Commander in Detroit, MI. She served on the force for twenty-three years.

1988 - Zina Lynna Garrison become the first African-American Olympic winner in Tennis. She won a gold medal in Doubles and a bronze in the Singles at the 1988 Olympics games in Seoul, Korea. Garrison was also the first African-American Tennis Player to rank in the top ten on the Women's Professional Tour.

2000 - Fifty-Meter Freestyler, Anthony Ervin became the first African-American Swimmer to compete in the Olympic Games and to win a gold medal at the Sydney Olympics. Throughout his career, Ervin has won four Olympic medals and two World Championship gold medals.

On this Day in History...

September 24th

1909 - Wade Hammond, Alfred Jack Thomas, William Polk and Egbert Thompson were promoted to the rank of Chief Musicians, they became the first African-American Bandmasters in the U.S. Army.

1941 - Charlie Christian became the first African-American Electric Guitarist to use single-string solos. He was also a pioneer in the development of the Jazz revolution later named Bop. Christian was one of a group of musicians meeting after hours at Minton's Playhouse, a Harlem nightclub. The group included Thelonious Monk, Kenny Clarke and Dizzy Gillespie.

1978 - Carolyn R. Payton became the first woman and African-American to head the Peace Corps. Payton was also a pioneer in African-American women's leadership within the American Psychological Association and the field of Psychology.

1994 - Harold Hairston became the first African-American Fire Commissioner for the the City of Philadelphia, PA. He was a twenty-nine year Veteran of the Fire Department at the time of his appointment.

2016 - The National Museum of African-American History and Culture (NMAAHC) which is a Smithsonian Institution Museum opened with a ceremony led by U.S. President Barack Obama. Located on the National Mall in Washington, D.C., the Museum has close to 37,000 objects in its collection related to subjects such as community, family, the visual and performing arts, religion, civil rights, slavery and segregation.

On this Day in History...

September 25th

1917 - Fort Des Moines, Iowa became the first U.S. Army Camp for training African-American Officers in World War I. About half (639) of the Officers commissioned during the war were trained there.

1941 - Dean Charles Dixon became the first African-American to conduct the New York Philharmonic, he was also the first African-American recognized as a symphonic conductor of international stature.

1960 - Edmund Stanley Dorsey became the first African-American White House Broadcast Correspondent with radio station WWDC. Three years later, while he was News Director with radio-television station WOOK, he became the first African-American television news reporter in Washington, D.C. In 1964, he joined station WIND and was sent to Saigon (South Vietnam), where he became the first African-American Bureau Chief for the Washington Broadcasting Network. In 1949, while serving with the United States Army in Tokyo, Japan, he became the first African-American Managing Editor of the military publication, "Stars and Stripes."

1974 - Katie Geneva Cannon became the first African-American woman in the United States ordained in the Presbyterian Church.

1996 - Lieutenant Colonel, Paulette Francine Ruffin became the first woman Director of the Georgetown University Army Reserve Officer Training Corps (ROTC). Ruffin began her career in the Army in 1978 by attending the U.S. Army Ordinance School.

On this Day in History...

September 26th

1843 - Norbert Rillieux revolutionized the Sugar Industry, he invented a refining process that was responsible for transforming sugar into a household item. Rillieux was inducted into the National Inventors Hall of Fame in 2004.

1974 - U.S. Air Force General, Lloyd "Fig" Newton became the first African-American Pilot to join the "Thunderbirds," an aerial demonstration squadron for the Air Force. In 1995, he was promoted to the rank of Three-Star General and named Air Force Assistant Vice Chief of Staff. Two years later he was promoted to the rank of Four-Star General. Newton was the third African-American in the Air Force to achieve that rank, he was one of only twelve Four-Star Generals of any race at the time.

1990 - George A. Stallings Jr., established the first African-American Catholic Church. He was its first Bishop, having been consecrated by Richard Bridges, who broke away from the Independent Old Catholic Church. Stallings left the Roman Catholic Church over what he saw as its neglect of the spiritual needs of African-Americans. He founded the Imani Temple African-American Catholic Congregation, an African-American-led form of Catholicism.

2001 - "Right Fielder," Dave Winfield, who played for six teams in Major League Baseball (MLB) over a twenty-two year career, appeared on the breakfast cereal box "Wheaties." Winfield is a twelve-time MLB All-Star, seven-time Gold Glove Award winner and a six-time Silver Slugger Award winner.

On this Day in History...

September 27th

1887 - Railroad Worker, Engineer and Inventor, Granville T. Woods patented a Multiplex Telegraph. This device allowed train operators to communicate with each other, it also helped them avoid collisions and other dangers on the tracks. Woods made railways much safer, he has nearly 60 patents to his name and he revolutionized the Railroad Industry. Woods was also inducted into the National Inventors Hall of Fame in 2006.

1969 - Mal Johnson became the first African-American woman television reporter to cover the White House. In 1970, she became the first woman National Correspondent for Cox Broadcasting Corporation, on WKBS-TV, she hosted "Coffee Break and Let's Talk About It." Johnson later became President of Media Linx International in Washington, D.C. In 1975, she founded the National Association of Black Journalists. She was also a member of various Professional Journalism organizations and has been honored widely for her achievements in the field.

1990 - Singer, Marvin Gaye was inducted into the Hollywood Walk of Fame and awarded a star on Hollywood Boulevard. Throughout his career, Gaye was crowned as "The Prince of Motown" as well as "The Prince of Soul." His later recordings influenced several contemporary R&B sub-genres such as "Quiet Storm" and "Neo-Soul."

1991 - Pamela Lynn Carter became the first African-American woman to serve as an Attorney General for the State of Indiana.

1996 - Emmett Turner became the first African-American Chief of Police for the City of Nashville, TN.

On this Day in History...

September 28th

1892 - (HBCU) Winston Salem State University was founded as Slater Industrial Academy in Winston Salem, N.C., by Simon Green Atkins. Atkins had a vision to create an institution where each student would meet the everyday challenges equipped with an education designed to intellectually prepare the "Head, Hand and Heart."

1944 - Harold Robert Perry became the first African-American Bishop of the Roman Catholic Church in the United States.

1975 - Daniel H. "Chappie" James Jr., became the first African-American Four-Star General in the U.S. Air Force, he was later named Commander-in-Chief of North American Air Defense Command (NORAD). James was not only the first African-American Air Force Four-Star General, but also the first to be promoted to that rank in any of the U.S. Armed Forces.

1981 - Ed Bradley became the first African-American Co-Editor of "60 Minutes," a CBS television network weekly news program, he replaced Dan Rather. His previous assignments included serving as Principal Correspondent for CBS, including CBS News White House Correspondent, Anchor of the CBS Sunday Night News and reports shown on CBS Evening News with Walter Cronkite.

2007 - Melodie Mayberry-Stewart became the first African-American woman Chief Information Officer in New York State. As the Governors top Information Technology Adviser, she developed and oversaw 190,000 employees and Information Technology investments for the $134 billion State enterprise.

On this Day in History...

September 29th

1910 - The National Urban League was founded in New York City. The League is Nonpartisan Civil Rights Organization that advocates on behalf of African-Americans and against racial discrimination in the United States.

1923 - Downhearted Blues/Gulf Coast Blues became the first record by an African-American to sell more than one million copies. Singer, Bessie Smith became one of the most important women in the history of American music, both as a stage performer and recording star. She was the most popular woman Blues Singer of the 1920s and 1930s. Regarded as one of the greatest Singers of her era, Smith was a major influence on other Jazz singers.

1970 - Nathan G. Conyers opened an Automobile Dealership in Detroit, MI. As of 2002, it became the oldest dealership in the United States owned and operated by African-Americans, and the only one in Detroit. Conyers began his career as an Attorney for the Small Business Administration, in private law practice, and as special assistant to the Attorney General for the State of Michigan. Before he become Partner in the Law Firm Keith, Conyers, Anderson, Brown & Wahls, P.C., Conyers served as the company's President.

1972 - Marian Wright Edelman became the first African-American woman admitted to the Mississippi State Bar. In 1973, she founded the Children's Defense Fund (CDF), an organization that served as an advocacy and research center for children's issues, documenting the problems and possible solutions to children in need. In 1980, she also became the first African-American and the second woman to head the Spelman College Board of Trustees.

On this Day in History...

September 30th

1873 - (HBCU) Bennett College was founded in Greensboro, N.C. The school began in the basement of the Warnersville Methodist Episcopal Church. In 1878, a group of emancipated slaves purchased the site of the school, College level courses and permanent facilities were later added. In 1926, The Women's Home Missionary Society joined with the board of education and the church to established Bennett College.

1952 - Major League "Pitcher" Joe Black became the first African-American Pitcher to win a World Series game. As a member of the Brooklyn Dodgers, he was the 1952 Rookie of the Year. The Dodgers defeated the New York Yankees by a score of 4-2. Black later became a Vice President of Greyhound Corporation. In 1995, he was inducted into the Brooklyn Dodgers Hall of Fame at the Brooklyn Museum.

1968 - Carl Fields became the first African-American Assistant Dean at an Ivy League School. In 2002, Princeton University dedicated a building in his honor "The Carl Fields Center for Equality and Cultural Understanding."

1971 - "Soul Train," a Music/Dance Television Program aired in syndication. The show primarily featured performances by R&B, Soul, Pop and Hip Hop Artists, although Funk, Jazz, Disco and Gospel Artists also appeared. The series was created by Don Cornelius, who also served as its first host and Executive Producer. Originally a Journalist who was inspired by the Civil Rights Movement, Cornelius recognized that in the late 1960's, there was no television venue in the United States for Soul music. He introduced many African-American musicians to a larger audience as a result of their appearances on Soul Train. The show had a thirty-five year history on television.

On this Day in History...

October 1st

1975 - The "Thrilla in Manila" was the final installment in the bitter trilogy between Boxing Champions, Muhammad Ali and Joe Frazier which took place in Manila, Philippines. The action inside the ring was brutal, it was a seesaw battle, Frazier dominating the middle rounds. As the fight continued, Ali began to take control, Frazier's left eye was swollen shut, his corner stopped the fight heading into the 15th round. Frazier protested and was on his feet, ready to fight when the bell rang. When the fight was over, Ali said, "It was like death, closest thing to dying that I know of." Frazier added, "Man, I hit him with punches that would bring down the walls of a City."

1992 - Robert O. Evans became the first African-American Head Coach of the University of Mississippi (Ole Miss) Basketball Team. He also served as Head Coach for Arizona State University from 1998 to 2006.

1995 - The home of Investigative Journalist, Educator and Leader in the Civil Rights Movement, Ida B. Wells was listed as a Chicago Landmark and National Historic Landmark. Wells was one of the founders of the National Association for the Advancement of Colored People (NAACP) and one of the the most famous African-American woman in the United States during the early 20th century. She also owned a newspaper called "Memphis Free Speech and Headlight." Wells was active in women's rights and the women's suffrage movement, establishing several notable women's organizations.

1997 - Gilda Jackson became the first African-American woman Colonel in the U.S. Marine Corps, she received the honor in a ceremony at Marine Corps Air Station in Cherry Point, N.C.

On this Day in History...

October 2nd

1870 - The first African-American Camp Meeting occurred at Shady Grove in Saint George, South Carolina. Shady Grove began shortly after the Civil War by former slave, Ceasar Wolfe. While returning home from church service, Wolfe persuaded others to help a local rice farmer in need to gather his crops before they were destroyed by an approaching storm. The farmer, Sam M. Knight, expressed his appreciation and granted the group the deed to the land to be used exclusively for religious purposes. Many local African-American residents living nearby wanted a place to worship with their families and praise God in unity. The land was later named Shady Grove, after the large trees on site that provided shade to the bush arbors, makeshift huts or tents that were built. The Shady Grove Camp Meeting became an annual tradition on the first Sunday in October, families come together from across the country to pay homage to their ancestors, attend church services, prepare meals and have fellowships with everyone together in several hundred tents.

1942 - The first Liberty Ship named in honor of an African-American was the "S.S. Booker T. Washington." World renowned Singer, Marian Anderson christened the ship when it was launched from a New Jersey shipyard. The ship carried war cargo to Europe during World War II.

1975 - WGPR-TV went on the air as the first Television Station fully owned and operated by African-Americans in the United States. WGPR-TV stood for "Where God's Presence Radiates," and the station, situated in Detroit, MI, was founded by William Venoid Banks. The station first aired on channel 62 in Detroit, it was marketed towards the urban audience.

On this Day in History...

October 3rd

1887 - (HBCU) Florida Agricultural and Mechanical University (FAMU) was founded in Tallahassee FL. The introduction of legislation leading to the foundation of the College was due to the initiative of the Superintendent of Public Instruction and Abolitionist, Jonathan C. Gibbs.

1904 - (HBCU) Bethune-Cookman University was founded in Daytona, FL. Dr. Mary McLeod Bethune originally opened the Daytona Literary and Industrial Training School for Negro Girls with $1.50, faith in God and five little girls. In 1923, the school merged with Cookman Institute of Jacksonville and became co-ed, it also gained the prestigious United Methodist Church affiliation. The school's name was officially changed to Bethune-Cookman College to reflect the leadership of Dr. Bethune.

1966 - Political Activist, Huey P. Newton along with Bobby Seale, co-founded the "Black Panther Party for Self Defense." The organization instituted a variety of community social programs, most extensively the free breakfast for children and community health clinics. The party enrolled the largest number of members and made the greatest impact in the Oakland-San Francisco Bay Area, New York, Chicago, Los Angeles, Seattle and Philadelphia.

1994 - Marian C. Bennett became the first African-American Inspector General for the United States Information Agency. Throughout her career, she has served as Investigator and Staff Attorney for the National Labor Relations Board and various positions with the Department of Energy.

On this Day in History...

October 4th

1871 - (HBCU) Alcorn University was founded as a result of the people of Mississippi's efforts to educate the descendants of formerly enslaved Africans, it was named in honor of the sitting Governor of Mississippi, James L. Alcorn. The campus is located in Lorman, Mississippi.

1965 - Carl Maxie Brashear became the U.S. Navy's first African-American Diver and Master Diver. While suffering an injury to his leg in the line of duty, he later became the first amputee to earn a master diver certificate, to everyone's astonishment except his own. Brashear went on to become a Master Chief, the highest rank in the Navy for an enlisted man. The film, "Men of Honor" starring Actor, Cuba Gooding Jr., opened in 2000, tells Brashear's life story.

2001 - San Francisco Giants "Outfielder," Barry Bonds made "home run" history when he hit number 71, he broke the single-season home run record. Bonds ended the season hitting 73 "home runs," he also became the first player to hit 400 "home runs" and steal 400 bases.

2008 - Actor, Playwright, Screenwriter, Director, Television and Film Producer, Tyler Perry opened Tyler Perry Studios. He became the first African-American Owner of a major Television and Film Studio. Located on over 30-acres in Atlanta, G.A., his studio is housed in a 200,000-square-foot production complex featuring five sound stages, a post-production facility, a 400-seat theater, private screening rooms as well as areas for entertaining and other events.

On this Day in History...

October 5th

1881 - Former slave and Veteran of the Union Army, William Washington Browne, founded the Grand Fountain of the United Order of True Reformers. This was an African-American fraternal organization that became the largest and most successful African-American business enterprise in the United States between 1881 and 1910.

1930 - Nella Marian Larsen became the first African-American woman recipient of a Guggenheim Fellowship in creative writing. Her novels, Quicksand (1928) and Passing (1929), were highly acclaimed.

1970 - Larry Ellis became the first African-American Coach in any Ivy League sport. Hired at Princeton from 1970 to 1992, he coached indoor and outdoor Track and Field for twenty years, and cross-country for twenty-two years.

1977 - Alberta Hunter became the first African-American to record a best-selling album at the age eighty-three. Her career began in 1921, she cut her first record for the Black Swan label, but, feeling neglected in favor of Ethel Waters, she switched to Paramount, where she recorded her own "Down Hearted Blues." Hunter worked in Paris and on the French Riviera in 1927, a year later she opened in the London production of Show Boat. She later undertook a USO tour of Europe and Korea, she became the first African-American woman performer to visit the war zone in Korea.

1989 - Clarence Page became the first African-American Columnist to be Awarded a Pulitzer Prize. He was senior member of the Chicago Tribune Editorial Board.

On this Day in History...

October 6th

1871 - Fisk University's Jubilee Singers begin their first national tour. The Jubilee Singers became world-famous Singers of African-American spirituals, they performed before the Queen of England and also the Emperor of Japan. The money they earned financed the construction of Jubilee Hall on the Fisk University campus.

1943 - Sculptor, Educator and School Founder, Selma Hortense Burke became the first African-American Sculptor to design a United States coin. She won a competition to design the portrait of President Franklin D. Roosevelt that appeared on the dime. She later founded the Selma Burke School of Sculpture in New York. In 1983, the Selma Burke Gallery opened at Winston-Salem State University, where many items from her private collection are gathered. That marked the first time a gallery was named after an African-American woman Artist.

1994 - Virgil A. Starkes and Sheldon D. Starkes were both promoted to U.S. Air Force Colonel. They were the first African-American brothers that were simultaneously elevated to that rank. The brothers have a history of following similar paths, they were commissioned simultaneously as Second Lieutenants and then promoted at each grade through the rank of Colonel. When promoted to Colonel, Virgil Starkes was Chief of the Personnel Program in the Directorate of Personnel at Wright-Patterson Air Force Base, Ohio. Sheldon Starkes was the associate dean for operations at the Armed Forces Staff College in Virginia.

1998 - Gregory Johnson became the first African-American Chief Resident of Johns Hopkins Hospital Radiology Department in Baltimore, MD.

On this Day in History…

October 7th

1957 - Aubrey Lewis became the first African-American Captain of an Athletic Team at the University of Notre Dame. He starred on the Track squad from 1957 to 1958. Having been one of New Jersey's greatest High School Athletes and an all-American "Halfback" at Montclair High School in the early 1950s, he received some 200 scholarship offers from various schools. At Notre Dame he was also a member of the Football Team, playing the halfback position from 1955 to 1957.

1993 - The Benjamin Mays Center opened on the campus of Bates College, it was named in honor of 1920 graduate, Benjamin Mays. He went on to become president of Morehouse College, Mays is often referred to as the mentor of Dr. Martin Luther King Jr.

1996 - Robert Mack Bell became the first African-American Chief of the Court of Appeals in the State of Maryland. He was a Judge of Maryland District Court in Baltimore, MD., from 1975 to 1980. When Bell took office, he was the youngest Judge in the State.

1997 - Bradley International Hall opened on the campus of University of California at Los Angeles (UCLA). The building honors the first African-American Mayor of Los Angeles, Thomas Bradley, he graduated from UCLA in 1941.

2008 - Former frontman with the Rock Band, Hootie & the Blowfish, Darius Rucker, made his debut in Country Music. Releasing his debut album, "Learn to Live," the album went No. 1 on the Country charts. Along with Ruker's success, he became the first African-American Singer to win the "Best New Artist Award" at the Country Music Awards.

On this Day in History...

October 8th

1950 - Charlotte Andrews Stephens became the first African-American to have a school named in her honor, in Little Rock, AR. Stephens worked with her parents to establish a school to educate African-Americans in Little Rock as early as 1864. The first school was established in her father's small Methodist church. Stevens later became a teacher, she taught at every level in Little Rock's schools for over seventy years until she retired in 1939. She was Little Rock's first African-American Teacher. Her dedication to teaching led officials to name a school in her honor.

1963 - Walter Harris became the first African-American "Chess Master" in the United States.

1980 - Odell Horton became the first African-American Federal Judge in the State of Tennessee. Prior to his appointment he was President of Le Moyne-Owen College.

1987 - The "King of Rock & Roll," Chuck Berry was inducted into the Hollywood Walk of Fame and awarded a star on Hollywood Boulevard. Berry was a pioneer who influenced generations of musicians, perhaps the best measure of his influence is the extent to which other popular Artists sampled his work. The Beach Boys, the Rolling Stones and the Beatles have all covered various Chuck Berry songs.

2001 - Lloyd D. Ward became the first African-American elected as Chief Executive Officer of the United States Olympic Committee (USOC).

On this Day in History...

October 9th

1798 - Joshua Johnston of Baltimore, MD., became the first African-American Portrait Painter to gain widespread recognition in the United States. Johnston was the first African-American Professional Artist in America. An advertisement in the Baltimore Intelligencer Newspaper described Johnston as a "Self-Taught Genius." He painted many prominent citizens in the 18th century and his works are in many museum collections.

1934 - Sculptor and Educator, Augusta Christine Savage became the first African-American member of the National Association of Women Painters and Sculptors. One of her major commissions was the creation of a sculpture for the New York World's Fair. Lift Every Voice and Sing, a sculptural group symbolizing African-Americans contribution to music became Savage's best known and most widely recognized work. In 1937 she became the first Director of the Harlem Community Art Center and organized programs in education, art, and recreation.

1968 - Louise Smith became the first African-American State Trooper in the United States, she joined the Connecticut State Police.

2016 - Ballet Dancer for American Ballet Theatre (ABT), Misty Copeland was recognized by Barbie as a "Shero" honoree, she was honored with her very own Barbie doll. The Barbie Collection defines a "Shero" as a hero who inspire young girls by breaking boundaries and expanding possibilities for women everywhere. Copeland became the first African-American woman to be promoted to Principal Dancer in American Ballet Theatre's seventy-five year history.

On this Day in History...

October 10th

1925 - (HBCU) - Xavier University of Louisiana was founded in New Orleans, LA. Xavier is the only Historically Black Roman Catholic institution of higher education in the United States.

1955 - Maude Eudora McClennan Boxley became the first African-American woman to host a Southern television cooking show. "The Eudora Boxley Cooking Show" aired on WLAC, Channel 5, in Nashville, TN. It aired during an era when African-Americans were rarely seen on television, especially with their own show. Boxley and her daughters also had a successful catering business in Nashville, it was regarded as the number one business of its kind in Nashville. The business catered to wealthy families and had a staff of approximately fifty employees.

1967 - Businessman, Albert William Johnson Sr., became the first African-American to be awarded an Oldsmobile Car Dealership. His dealership franchise opened in a suburb of Chicago, IL. In less than four years, his success led to a Cadillac Car Dealership.

1975 - "The Wiz," became the longest running African-American musical on Broadway, with 1,672 shows. The musical starred Stephanie Mills, Ted Ross, Hinton Battle, Andre DeShields and Mabel King.

2016 - Channing Dungey became the first African-American President of a Major Broadcast TV Network (ABC). Dungey worked as ABC's Head of Drama and oversaw the development of ABC Studios shows such as "Scandal, Criminal Minds, How to Get Away with Murder, Army Wives, Nashville, Quantico and Once Upon A Time."

On this Day in History...

October 11th

1887 - Inventor, Alexander Miles created a method for opening and closing elevator doors automatically. His new automated process dramatically improved passenger safety and saved countless lives. Miles was inducted into the National Inventors Hall of Fame in 2007.

1925 - Florence Mills became the first African-American woman to headline at a Broadway venue. Mills was a child prodigy who later demonstrated her talent as a singer and dancer.

1986 - Nathan A. Chapman Jr., became the Founder and Chief Executive Officer of the Chapman Company, the first Investment Banking Firm in America owned and operated by African-Americans.

1991 - Actress, Dancer, Choreographer and Television Director, Debbie Allen was inducted into the Hollywood Walk of Fame and awarded a star on Hollywood Boulevard. Allen is known as a member of the President's Committee on the Arts and Humanities and her work on the 1982 musical-drama television series Fame.

2009 - Command Sergeant Major, Teresa King became the first woman to serve as Commandant of the School for U.S. Army Drill Sergeants. She was stationed at the U.S. Army Drill Sergeant School in Fort Jackson, S.C., the Army's largest training installation. Her Battalion Commander said that she was selected because she knew "the business of taking civilians and making them into soldiers." She became the first female Sergeant to serve in the 18th Airborne Corps from 1997-2001 and also command other battalions.

On this Day in History...

October 12th

1973 - Lois Mailou Jones became the first African-American Artist to have a solo exhibit at the Boston Museum of Fine Arts. Jones was responsible for organizing the Art Department at Palmer Memorial Institute in Sedalia, North Carolina. She later became a Professor at Howard University, where she remained for nearly fifty years. She was highly successful as a Professor and Artist, throughout her career she influenced the lives of many African-American Artists.

1990 - Emma Carolyn Chappell became the first Chair and Chief Executive Officer of the newly founded United Bank of Philadelphia. She helped raise funds by soliciting in churches and searching for small investors. The Board of Directors contributed funds themselves and asked large banks to provide start-up money. The bank began growing in the community. In 1995, it was named Black Enterprise Magazine's Financial Company of the Year. Through her efforts, Chappell contributed significantly to economic development of Philadelphia's African-American community.

1995 - Orlando "Tubby" Smith became the first African-American Head Basketball Coach at the University of Georgia.

1996 - Carlette "C.J." Jones, a Lieutenant Colonel, became the first woman named as Commanding Officer of the Air Force ROTC program at North Carolina Agricultural and Technical State University in Greensboro. Her duties included service as a Personnel Officer at the institution. During her career, she was also the Regional Director of Admissions for the Southeastern United States and Central America at the U.S. Air Force Academy.

On this Day in History...

October 13th

1994 - R&B and Soul, Singer-Songwriter, Anita Baker was inducted into the Hollywood Walk of Fame and awarded a star on Hollywood Boulevard. Throughout her career, Baker has won eight Grammy Awards and has four platinum albums and two gold albums to her credit.

1995 - The Pennsylvania State Police promoted Virginia L. Smith to the rank of Major, she became the first woman in the department's eighty-nine year history to hold that rank. During her twenty-year tenure with the department, she also became the first African-American woman to reach the rank of Corporal, Sergeant, Lieutenant and Captain.

2010 - Lisa Lunsford became the CEO and co-founder of Global Strategic Supply Solutions (GS3 Global). She was also Vice President of Sales and Marketing for the Livonia, Michigan-based Deshler Group, which includes GS3 Global. Under her leadership, the manufacturing and engineering company grew to more than 100 employees and generated more than $36 million in revenue in 2015. GS3 Global was named to Black Enterprise Magazine's 2017 Top 100s list, recognizing the Nation's largest African-American businesses.

2018 - Singer, Composer and Producer, John Legend became the youngest person ever to achieve "EGOT Status. This honor is for individuals who have won all four major annual American entertainment awards, the Emmy, Grammy, Oscar, and Tony (EGOT) Awards. Respectively, these awards honor outstanding achievements in television, recording, film, and theater. Winning all four awards has been referred to as winning the "Grand Slam" of American show business.

On this Day in History...

October 14th

1834 - Inventor, Henry Blair became the second African-American man to receive a U.S. patent, he patented the Corn Seed Planter. This apparatus allowed farmers to plant their corn more than 30 times faster than manually planting by hand, which saved a tremendous amount of time and eased the burden of labor. Blair also invented the Cotton Planter in 1836.

1964 - Dr. Martin Luther King Jr., became the youngest African-American awarded the Nobel Peace Prize. In 1963, he led his massive March on Washington, in which he delivered his famous "I Have a Dream" address. In 1964, the civil rights movement achieved two of its greatest successes, the ratification of the Twenty-forth Amendment, which abolished the poll tax and the Civil Rights Act of 1964, which prohibited racial discrimination in employment and education and outlawed racial segregation in public facilities. Dr. King donated the prize money, valued at $54,600 to the Civil Rights Movement.

1989 - Eric Gregg became the first African-American Umpire to officiate in a World Series game. He appeared in the contest between the Oakland Athletics and the San Francisco Giants in a series known as the "Battle of the Bay" as the two participant cities lie on opposite sides of San Francisco Bay, connected by the San Francisco/Oakland Bay Bridge.

1994 - Upon the nomination of President Bill Clinton, John W. Marshall became the first African-American U.S. Marshal for the Eastern District of Virginia. He is the youngest son of U.S. Supreme Court Justice Thurgood Marshall. He also became Director of the U.S. Marshal's Service.

On this Day in History...

October 15th

1859 - Abraham Molineaux Hewlitt became the first African-American Director of Physical Culture at Harvard University. The course was offered to students who desired to study the proper care of their bodies and those who needed an introduction to medicine.

1881 - (HBCU) Morris Brown College was founded in Atlanta, GA., by African-Americans affiliated with the African Methodist Episcopal (AME) Church and named to honor the denomination's second Bishop, Morris Brown. The school opened its doors with 107 students and 9 teachers. Morris Brown was the first educational institution in the State of Georgia to be owned and operated independently by African-Americans. For more than a century, the College enrolled many students from poor backgrounds, large numbers of whom returned to their hometowns as teachers. Education was a mission of high priority at the college.

1958 - Willie O'Ree became the first African-American to play Professional Hockey in the National Hockey League (NHL) for the Boston Bruins.

1973 - Maynard H. Jackson Jr., was elected as the first African-American Mayor of Atlanta, GA. As Mayor, he completed the terminal at Atlanta Hartsfield International Airport ahead of schedule and under budget. In 2003, the airport was renamed Hartsfield-Jackson International Airport in his honor. He served three terms in office.

1993 - Brigadier General, Larry Jordan became the first African-American General Post Commander at Fort Knox, KY.

On this Day in History...

October 16th

1901 - President Theodore Roosevelt invited Tuskegee Institute's President Booker T. Washington to have dinner at the White House, marking the first time an African-American had been entertained there as a guest. After dinner, Washington and Roosevelt discussed the President's plans for the South.

1968 - During their medal ceremony at the Summer Olympics in the in Mexico City. Athletes, Tommie Smith and John Carlos won the gold and bronze medals respectively in the 200-meter Track and Field event. Smith and Carlos turned on the podium to face their flags and heard the American National Anthem, each Athlete raised a black-gloved fist in the air and kept them raised until the anthem was over. Smith later stated that the gesture was not a "Black Power" salute, but a "Human Rights"salute. The event is regarded as one of the most overtly political statements in the history of the modern Olympic Games.

1995 - The first Million Man March, masterminded by Louis Farrakhan was held twenty-one blocks from the Capitol Building in Washington, D.C. This was to be a national day of atonement, with thousands gathering for spiritual, economic, or political reasons. The men were to unite and pledge to take responsibility for themselves. Joining in the protest were African-American leaders from all walks of life, included Rep. Charles Rangel, Rev. Jesse Jackson, Isaac Hayes and Stevie Wonder.

2013 - Cory Booker became the first African-American to represent the State of New Jersey in the United States Senate. As Senator, Booker brought an innovative and bipartisan approach to tackling some of the most difficult problems facing New Jersey and the country.

On this Day in History...

October 17th

1964 - As an Amateur Boxer, "Smokin" Joe Frazier won the gold medal at the Olympic Games in Tokyo, Japan. In 1970, he became the Heavyweight Champion of the World.

1968 - Ruth Lucas became the first African-American woman Colonel in the U.S. Air Force. At the time of her promotion, Colonel Lucas was a General Education and Counseling Services Assistant in the Office of the Deputy Assistant Secretary of Defense for Education at the Pentagon.

1971 - Barbara Gardner Proctor became the first African-American in Chicago, IL., to opened her own Advertising Agency.

1984 - Stephen L. Hightower became founder, President and CEO of Hightowers Petroleum Co. (HPC), one of the premier marketers of gasoline and diesel fuels in America. Hightower built a $300 million business enterprise consisting of five National and International businesses, all providing energy solutions. He was was recognized as National Minority Supplier Development Council (NMSDC) Supplier of the Year in 2010.

1995 - Kwame Clark became the first woman in the United States ever to play on a mens Varsity Football Team, she played at Bishop Rosecrans High School in Zanesville, Ohio. The "Tailback" and "Linebacker" scored two touchdowns her first season. Football was her way of staying in shape for the women's Basketball Team, her usual pre-Basketball preparation activity was Cross-Country Running, but when that program was not offered, she turned to Football.

On this Day in History...

October 18th

1900 - (HBCU) Coppin State University was founded in Baltimore, MD. The institution was named after Fanny Jackson Coppin, an African-American woman who was a pioneer in education. Born a slave in Washington, D.C., she gained her freedom, graduated from Oberlin College in Ohio and founded the Philadelphia Institute that was the forerunner of Cheyney State University.

1949 - Don Newcombe became the first player in history to win all three of Major League Baseball Awards, he was named "Rookie of the Year," "Most Valuable Player" and a recipient of the "Cy Young Award."

1968 - As an Amateur Boxer, George Foreman won the gold medal at the Olympic Games in Mexico City, Mexico.

1973 - Henry Minton Frances became the first African-American Deputy Assistant Secretary of Defense. He later served with the Department of Housing and Urban Development as Executive Assistant to the First Secretary.

1977 - Robert L. Harris became the first African-American elected to the Utah House of Representatives. He was elected in a predominantly Caucasian District. Harris was also a Minister at the Church of God in Christ.

1996 - Irvin B. Lee became the first woman and the first African-American Chief of Police in the City of Dunbar, West Virginia. Earlier in her career, she was also the first African-American woman Officer and Sergeant in the City of Charleston, West Virginia.

On this Day in History...

October 19th

1950 - Chuck Cooper, Nathaniel Clifton and Earl Lloyd became the first African-Americans to play Professional Basketball in the National Basketball Association (NBA). Cooper played for the Boston Celtics, Clifton played for the New York Knicks and Lloyd played for the Washington Capitols.

1968 - Track and Field Athlete, Madeline Manning became the first African-American woman to win a gold medal for the 800-meter race, during the Summer Olympics in Mexico City. Manning set an Olympic record time of 2 minutes 0.9 seconds. She also won the 800-meter race six times while attending Tennessee State University. While in college, she won ten National Titles and set a number of American records.

1972 - Alma Woodsey Thomas became the first African-American woman to have a solo exhibit at the New York's Whitney Museum of American Art. Her works show a variety of themes, including science, religion and economics. Woodsey was deeply inspired by the space program, she did a number of "Space Paintings." Her most popular painting, "The Eclipse," features a dark circle surrounded by mosaic squares in many colors. She was eighty-one years old at the time of the Whitney exhibit.

1993 - Historian and Educator, David Levering Lewis won a Pulitzer Prize for "W.E.B. Du Bois: Biography of a Race." In 2001, he published the second volume of the Du Bois biography, "W.E.B. Du Bois: The Fight for Equality and the American Century," and again won a Pulitzer Prize, becoming the first biographer to win twice for back-to-back books on the same subject.

On this Day in History...

October 20th

1914 - Inventor, Garrett Morgan patented the Gas Mask, his creation was later used in World War I to protect soldiers from poison gas. In 1916, he personally used his newly invented gas mask to rescue men trapped after an explosion in a tunnel 250 feet beneath Lake Erie. Morgan also supported the African-American community throughout his lifetime, he was a member of the newly formed NAACP.

1994 - Vanessa D. Gilmore became the only African-American Federal District Judge in the State of Texas. Appointed by President Bill Clinton, she became the youngest sitting Federal Judge in the United States.

1998 - Comedian and Actor, Richard Pryor was awarded the first ever Mark Twain Prize for American Humor. During his successful career as a comedian, Pryor also won an Emmy Award along with five Grammy Awards. In 1974, he won two American Academy of Humor Awards and the Writers Guild of America Award. The albums that he made in the 1970's and 1980's filled with adult language and humor, sold millions of copies.

2018 - Staff Sergeant, Dana Petty became the first member of her family to join the U.S. Air Force. As a new mother, she represents the many soldiers who balance family and career. Petty discovered new techniques and tools on how to manage her career and life. As a newlywed, she enlisted in the Air Force Reserves at Seymour Johnson Air Force Base in Goldsboro, NC., then gave birth to her son in 2014. As an inspiration to many, she resides in Greensboro, N.C., with her husband Alex and their son Alex Jr.

On this Day in History...

October 21st

1958 - Choreographer and Activist, Alvin Ailey formed his own group, "Alvin Ailey American Dance Theater." Ailey's choreographic masterpiece "Revelations" is believed to be the best known and most often seen modern dance performance. In 2014, President Barack Obama selected Ailey as a posthumous recipient of the Presidential Medal of Freedom.

1968 - Wyomia Tyus became the first Athlete to win an Olympic Sprint Title twice. She won a gold medal for the 100-meter dash at the 1964 Olympics in Tokyo and a silver medal for the 4 X 100-meter relay at the same event. In 1968, she won the gold medal for the 100-meter dash and the 4 X 100-meter relay in Mexico City. She set the Olympic and World Record in the 100-meter dash in both Olympic games. Tyus was also inducted into the Georgia Sports Hall of Fame as well as the U.S. Olympic Hall of Fame.

2005 - Jazz Trumpeter, Bandleader, Composer and Singer, Dizzy Gillespie was inducted into the Hollywood Walk of Fame and awarded a star on Hollywood Boulevard. Gillespie is one of the greatest Jazz trumpeters of all time, he taught and influenced many other musicians, including Trumpeters Miles Davis, Fats Navarro, Clifford Brown, Arturo Sandoval, Lee Morgan, Chuck Mangione and Johnny Hartman.

2011 - Gospel Music brother and sister duo, BeBe "Benjamin" and CeCe "Priscilla" Winans were inducted into the Hollywood Walk of Fame and awarded a star on Hollywood Boulevard. Together they have performed for over three decades and received several awards, including three Grammys.

On this Day in History...

October 22nd

1865 - Michael Augustine Healy became the first African-American appointed to the U.S. Coast Guard, he was assigned to command the famous "Cutter Bear" and became the Chief Federal Law Enforcement Officer in the Northern waters around Alaska. He was nicknamed "Hell-Roaring" Mike Healy.

1915 - Fritz Pollard became the first African-American Head Coach in the National Football League (NFL). Pollard was also the first African-American to play in the Rose Bowl. He was inducted into the Pro-Football Hall of Fame in 2005.

1924 - Ida Bell Robinson founded the first African-American Pentecostal Denomination headed by a woman. Mount Sinai Holy Church of America (MSHCA) was chartered in Philadelphia, PA. Today the church has approximately 130 congregations in 14 States and located in 4 Countries, its membership of over 50,000.

1988 - Blenda Jacqueline Wilson became the first African-American woman to head a Public University in Michigan when she was appointed Chancellor of the University of Michigan, Dearborn.

2002 - Tahirah Lamont Brown became the first African-American woman Pilot for Federal Express (Fedex). After receiving her Pilot's license, she taught as a flight instructor for two years and then worked for Great Lakes Airlines (United Express) as a Pilot. While at Fedex, Brown became a Line Check Airman, as an Instructor and Evaluator. She was designated by the FAA to train, evaluate and certify the competency of FedEx Pilots.

On this Day in History…

October 23rd

1877 - (HBCU) Jackson State University was founded. The school was established during the reconstruction era in Natchez, MS., as "Natchez Seminary" by the American Baptist Home Mission Society of New York City. The Society moved the school to the State Capital, Jackson in 1882, renaming it Jackson State College.

1930 - Earl Wiley Renfro became the first African-American Orthodontist in the United States. For many years, he was acknowledged as one of the best hands-on Clinical Orthodontics instructors in the world.

1980 - Attorney, George Albert Dalley became the first African-American member of the Civil Aeronautics Board (CAB), an agency of the Federal Government of the United States.

2014 - Record Producer, Quincy Jones was awarded the NAACP Spingarn Medal. Jones is one of the founders of the Institute for Black American Music (IBAM), whose events aim to raise enough funds for the creation of a National Library of African-American Art and Music. He also founded the Black Arts Festival in his hometown of Chicago.

2017 - Entrepreneur and Businesswoman, Janice Bryant Howroyd became the first African-American woman to operate a company that generates more than $1 billion in annual revenue. She is founder and Chief Executive Officer of Act 1 Group, an employment agency that also provides consulting and business services, including background checks and screening. Act 1 includes other brands such as Agile 1, A-Check Global and AppleOne, the company has contracts with 17,000 clients in 19 countries and 2,600 employees worldwide.

On this Day in History...

October 24th

1935 - "Mulatto" by Langston Hughes opened at the Vanderbilt Theatre, it was the first play by an African-American Author to be a long-running Broadway hit. Mulatto played continuously until December 9, 1937.

1985 - Professional Basketball Player, Lynette Woodard became first woman member of the Harlem Globetrotters. She was also Captain of the woman's Basketball Team that won the gold medal at the 1984 Los Angeles Olympic Games. She was the first player to have her jersey retired after she played four years of College Basketball at the University of Kansas.

1989 - Gwendolyn S. King became the first African-American woman to serve as Commissioner of the U.S. Social Security Administration. King was also employed by the U.S. Department of Health and Human Services in 1971.

1996 - Founder of Motown Records, Berry Gordy was inducted into the Hollywood Walk of Fame and awarded a star on Hollywood Boulevard. In 2016, he also received the National Medal of Arts from President Barack Obama for helping to create a trailblazing new sound in American Music. As a record producer and songwriter, he created Motown, launching the music careers of countless legendary Artists. His unique sound helped shape our Nation's story for decades.

1997 - Marcus E. Spigner became the first African-American Postmaster in the State of Idaho. Along with a twenty-year career in the U.S Postal Service, Spigner also served in the U.S. Air Force along with the Idaho National Guard.

On this Day in History...

October 25th

1922 - Joseph H. Ward became the first African-American appointed to Head a Veterans Administration Hospital. He was named Medical Officer/Chief of the Veterans Hospital in Tuskegee, AL.

1992 - Cito (Clarence Edward) Gaston became the first African-American Manager to lead a Major League Baseball Team to win a World Series Title, he managed the Toronto Blue Jays. Gaston was also the manager for two American League All-Star teams. During his career as a player, Gaston was a "Center Fielder" for the Atlanta Braves and the San Diego Padres.

1998 - Former Professional Football Player, Leland Melvin became the only person drafted into the National Football League to have flown in space. Before becoming an Astronaut, Melvin was drafted by the Detroit Lions in the 1986 College Draft to play Professional Football, but a hamstring injury thwarted his NFL career with Detroit and then later with the Dallas Cowboys. Melvin has a Bachelor of Science Degree in Chemistry and a Master's Degree in Materials Science Engineering. He worked at NASA Langley Research Center in the area of non-destructive testing, creating optical fiber sensors for measuring damage in aerospace vehicles, his work was published in numerous scientific journals. Melvin has traveled on two Space Shuttle missions to help build the International Space Station. After he retired as the head of NASA Education, he served as the Co-Chair on the White House's Federal Coordination in STEM Education Task Force and was the United States Representative and Chair of the International Space Education Board (ISEB).

On this Day in History...

October 26th

1951 - Simeon Saunders Booker Jr., became the first African-American Reporter for the Washington Post. His work as a journalist appeared in leading news publications for more than 50 years. He was known for his journalistic works during the civil rights movement, he also worked for Jet and Ebony magazines. In 2013, Booker was inducted into the National Association of Black Journalists Hall of Fame. In In 2017, seventeen members of the U.S. House of Representatives introduced a bipartisan bill nominating Booker for a Congressional Gold Medal.

1997 - The first Million Woman March was held, involving more than 500,000 women in Philadelphia, PA. Speakers included Congressman Maxine Waters, Winnie Mandela, Attallah and Ilyasah Shabazz, who were the daughters of Malcolm X. Organizers of this march aimed to strengthen the cohesiveness of African-American women from all walks of life. The women addressed such issues as women in prison, the beginning of independent African-American schools, employment as well as women in politics and business.

2017 - Breanna Holbert became the first African-American woman elected President of The National Future Farmers Organization (FFA). As an Agricultural Education Major at California State University, Holbert along with five other National Officers commit to a year of service to the National FFA Organization. Each officer travels more than 100,000 National and International miles to interact with business and industry leaders, thousands of FFA members, teachers, corporate sponsors, government and education officials.

On this Day in History...

October 27th

1891 - Inventor, Philip Downing patented the Street Letter Box, which is known today as the Mailbox. Downing was also elected as a member of the Wisconsin State Senate in 1940.

1909 - (HBCU) North Carolina Central University was founded in Durham, N.C., as the National Religious Training School and Chautauqua by Dr. James Edward Shepard. The school became the first public liberal arts institution for African-Americans in the Nation.

1971 - Founded in 1819, Congdon Street Baptist Church was added to the National Register of Historic Places, it is the oldest African-American church in the State of Rhode Island.

2002 - Dallas Cowboys "Running Back" Emmitt Smith passed the 1,000-yard season mark and became the first "Running Back" in the National Football League (NFL) to gain 1,000 yards in eleven consecutive seasons. He set the record on a 13-yard run in the third quarter when the Cowboys played the Detroit Lions at the Silverdome in Pontiac, MI. The Hall of Famer also surpassed Walter Payton to become the NFL's all-time career rushing leader.

2004 - The African-American Civil War Memorial was established in Washington, D.C., it commemorates the service of 209,145 African-American Soldiers, 2,145 Latino Soldiers and approximately 20,000 Navy Sailors who fought for the Union in the American Civil War. The memorial includes a 9-foot bronze sculpture "The Spirit of Freedom," and a walking area with curved panel short walls inscribed with the names of the men who served in the war.

On this Day in History...

October 28th

1923 - Dewey Gatson better known as Rajo Jack became the first African-American Racer in America. He won races up and down the West Coast of the United States in stock cars, big cars and motorcycles. He was inducted in the West Coast Stock Car Hall of Fame in 2003 and the National Sprint Car Hall of Fame in 2007.

1987 - Entrepreneur, Patricia Williams was encouraged to take the leap of faith and leave her career as a Rehabilitation Therapist and become her own boss, she cashed out her 401k and took out a small business loan and purchased a McDonald's location in Compton, CA. A few years later, she began working along with her daughters, Nicole Enearu and Kerri Harper-Howie. Together, the three women have built an empire and now own 13 McDonald's franchises. Between the three of them, they provide employment for more than 700 people in their community and generate $50 million in annual revenue. Williams and her daughters also give back to the community through scholarships for local students and funding for local and national charities.

1990 - Actor, Director and Author, Lavar Burton was inducted into the Hollywood Walk of Fame and awarded a star on Hollywood Boulevard. Burton first came to prominence portraying Kunta Kinte in the 1977 award-winning ABC television miniseries "Roots" based on the novel by Alex Haley.

2017 - Danielle Outlaw became the first African-American woman Chief of Police for Portland, OR. Outlaw was a nineteen year Veteran of the Oakland Police Department where she previously served as Deputy Chief.

On this Day in History...

October 29th

1979 - Barbara J. Wilson became the first African-American woman to franchise an Automobile Dealership. In 1979, she became President of Porterfield-Wilson Pontiac, GMC Truck, Mazda, Honda. In 1987, Wilson received the Candace Award for Business Woman of the Year.

1981 - Arnette Rhinehart Hubbard became the first woman President of "The National Bar Association," a national association for African-American Lawyers. As a Chicago Attorney, Hubbard was also the first woman President of the Cook County (Illinois) Bar Association.

1983 - Barbara J. Mahone became the first African-American woman to Chair the United States Federal Labor Relations Authority.

1998 - Great Britain's Prince Charles named Colleen Harris Deputy Press Secretary, making her the first African-American member of the English Royal household.

2015 - Film Director, Producer and Screenwriter, Ava Duvernay was recognized by Barbie as a "Shero" honoree, she was honored with her very own Barbie doll. The Barbie Collection defines a "Shero" as a hero who inspire young girls by breaking boundaries and expanding possibilities for women everywhere. Duvernay was nominated for two Academy Awards and four Golden Globes for her film, "Selma" which chronicled the historic 1965 voting rights campaign led by Dr. Martin Luther King Jr., She won the "Best Director" Prize at the Sundance Film Festival in 2012 for her acclaimed feature "Middle of Nowhere." In 2010, she founded Array, an independent film distribution and resource organization for filmmakers of color and women filmmakers.

On this Day in History...

October 30th

1972 - Richard J. Arlington was elected as the first African-American Mayor of Birmingham, AL. In 1977, he was also the first African-American elected to the Birmingham City Council.

1974 - Arguably one the greatest sporting events of the 20th century, "The Rumble in the Jungle" was a historic Boxing match in Kinshasa, Zaire (now Democratic Republic of the Congo) between undefeated World Heavyweight Champion George Foreman against challenger Muhammad Ali. Ali told his trainer, Angelo Dundee along with his fans that he had a secret plan for Foreman, a strategy he later dubbed the "Rope-A-Dope." Ali won by the fight by knocking Foreman out just before the end of the eighth round with 60,000 fans in attendance. The fight was watched by a record estimated television audience of one billion viewers worldwide, becoming the world's most-watched live television broadcast at the time. This included a record estimated 50 million viewers watching the fight pay-per-view on closed-circuit theatre TV. The fight grossed an estimated $100 million in worldwide revenue.

2017 - Tonya Boyd became the first African-American woman to attain the rank of Deputy Chief with the Fire Department New York (FDNY). As a FDNY's Emergency Medical Services (EMS) Veteran with twenty-one years on the job, she was the highest-ranking African-American woman in the entire department. Her promotion marked the first time in more than one-hundred fifty years that the FDNY had an African-American woman as a Deputy Chief.

On this Day in History…

October 31st

1798 - James Forten Sr., established the first major Sail Making Shop in Philadelphia, PA., that was owned and operated by African-Americans. Forten was also a leader in the radical abolitionist movement, he was an organizer of the American Anti-Slavery Society, he supported women's suffrage and temperance.

1951 - Football Player, Bernard Custis became the first African-American to play professional as a "Quarterback." Custis was a Star Quarterback at Syracuse University, he was then drafted by the the Cleveland Browns. After playing with the Browns, he left the National Football League (NFL) and joined the Canadian Football League (CFL) to play for the Hamilton Tiger-Cats.

1975 - Entrepreneur, Catherine "Cathy" Hughes became the first woman Radio General Station Manager in Washington, D.C. She began her career in radio at Howard University's station, WHUR-FM, increasing station revenue from $250,000 to $3 million in her first year. In 1980, Hughes then founded Radio One. As the CEO, her company went on to own 70 radio stations in 9 major markets in the U.S. In 1999, Radio One became publicly traded under the NASDAQ stock exchange.

1990 - Ezra C. Davidson Jr., became the first African-American President of the American College of Obstetricians and Gynecologists. He later became Chair of the Obstetrics and Gynecology Department of Charles Drew University of Medicine.

1994 - Loretta C. Argrett became the first African-American woman member of the Joint Committee on Taxation of the U.S. Congress.

On this Day in History...

November 1st

1804 - Absalom Jones became the first African-American in the United States to be ordained as an Episcopal Priest in Philadelphia, PA. Jones wanted to establish an African-American congregation, after a successful petition, the African Episcopal Church of St. Thomas became the first African-American church in Philadelphia.

1901 - (HBCU) Grambling State University was founded in Grambling, LA. The school was founded by the North Louisiana Colored Agriculture Relief Association, a group of African-American farmers who wanted to operate a school for African-Americans in their region of the State. In the Association's request for assistance, Tuskegee Institute's Booker T. Washington sent Charles P. Adams to help the group organize an industrial school. Adams became its founding President.

1945 - Founded by John H. Johnson, Ebony Magazine released its first issue. Ebony provided a much needed National forum for African-Americans, its content centered on entertainment, business, health, personalities, occupations and sports. The magazine highlighted accomplishments of African-Americans and earned a strong National reputation for its celebration of history and culture.

1951 - Founded by John H. Johnson, JET Magazine released its first issue. Initially billed as "The Weekly Negro News Magazine," JET is notable for its role in chronicling the Civil Rights Movement from its earliest years. The magazine contained fashion and beauty tips, entertainment news, dating advice, political coverage, health tips and diet guides. The cover photo usually corresponded to the focus of the main story.

On this Day in History...

November 2nd

1863 - The Nation's first Hospital for African-American soldiers opened in Beaufort, South Carolina. The first patients were from the 1st South Carolina Volunteers, the Nation's first officially sanctioned African-American Regiment. They mustered with Colonel, Thomas Wentworth in command. While the wounded were hospitalized, they were visited by Civil War Nurse, Susie King, the first African-American Army Nurse in the United States.

1886 - Inventor, Henry Brown patented the improvement to the Strongbox, known today as the Safe. His revolutionary invention has evolved into the world's most trusted device to protect valuables.

1976 - Utica Blackwell was elected as the first African-American woman Mayor in the State of Mississippi (Meyersville). Blackwell was a leading figure in the civil rights movement, she was also the first woman President of the National Conference of Black Mayors.

1987 - Bert Norman Mitchell became the first African-American President of the New York State Society of Certified Public Accountants. In addition to his work as an accountant and an administrator for various organizations, Mitchell has published more than fifty professional articles.

1996 - Joseph Paul Reason became the first African-American Four-Star Admiral in the U.S. Navy. He was Commander-in-Chief of the U.S. Atlantic Fleet in Norfolk, Virginia. At the time of his promotion, he was assigned to the Pentagon, serving as Deputy Chief of Naval Operations for Plans and Policy. Reason was also Naval Aide to President Jimmy Carter, from December 1976 to June 1979.

On this Day in History...

November 3rd

1975 - James Benton Parsons became the first African-American to serve as Chief Judge of a U.S. District Court. He served the Court for the Northern District of Illinois.

1978 - Jack Tanner became the first African-American Federal Judge in the State of Washington.

1983 - John Charles Thomas became the first African-American member of the State Supreme Court of Virginia.

1992 - Carol Moseley Braun of Illinois became the first African-American woman elected to the United States Senate. She served on the Senate Finance, Banking and Judiciary Committee, the Small Business Committee as well as the Housing and Urban Affairs Committee. After her tenure as Senator, President Bill Clinton nominated Braun to the post of U.S. Ambassador to New Zealand and Samoa, a post she held until 2001.

2017 - Dr. Shayla Creer and Robert McCray became the founders of Live Alkaline Water, the first water brand owned and operated by African-Americans to be sold in Walmart. With its headquarters based in Jacksonville, FL., the company uses water that comes from a natural alkaline water spring that McCray's family has owned in North Carolina for more than 100 years. McCray's Aunt once took him out to the spring and said, "you're the blood of your ancestors crying out, you're responsible for this." The water is sourced from a natural underground spring, an aquifer, and a mineral rock bed that lies 800 feet below the ground making it extremely pure and fresh to the taste.

On this Day in History...

November 4th

1846 - Businessman, William Leidesdorff became the first African-American to open a hotel in San Francisco, CA. He was also President of the San Francisco School Board and elected as City Treasurer. He later served as U.S. Vice Consul to Mexico at the Port of San Francisco.

1879 - Inventor, Dr. Thomas Elkins received a U.S Patent for his invention of the "Improved Refrigerator," known today as the modern day refrigerator. This device utilized metal cooling coils that became very cold, it produced cool air that filled an enclosed area within a sealed refrigerated box. This unit included a vacuumed sealed door that was designed to keep cool air inside, which allowed perishable items inside to remain fresh for longer periods of time.

1881 - Allen Hall, located on the Huston-Tillotson College campus in Austin, Texas, is the first building in Texas (as well as the first west of the Mississippi) built to educate African-Americans. The College was founded in 1876, when Sam Huston College and Tillotson College merged.

2002 - "Running Back," Emmitt Smith, who became the National Football League's (NFL) all-time leading rusher during his fifteen seasons in the league, appeared on the breakfast cereal box "Wheaties."

2008 - Senator Barack Obama of Illinois was elected as the 44th President of the United States, he became the first African-American President. He was also re-elected as President in 2012 on this date.

On this Day in History...

November 5th

1952 - Cora M. Brown became the first African-American woman in the United States elected to a State Senate. After supporting Dwight Eisenhower in the 1956 Presidential election, she was appointed Special Associate General Counsel of the U.S. Post Office Department in 1957, becoming the first African-American woman member of the department's legal staff.

1966 - Henry W. McGee was appointed by President Lyndon B. Johnson as Postmaster of Chicago, IL., the largest Postal District in the United States, he became the first African-American in the City to hold that post. McGee was also active in the Chicago Branch of the National Association for the Advancement of Colored People (NAACP). In 1946, at the age of thirty-six, he was elected as President, making him the youngest person ever chosen to lead the Branch. In 2000, the new post office building in Chicago was named in his honor.

1974 - Mervyn Dymally was elected as Lieutenant Governor for the the State of California, George Brown was also elected as Lieutenant Governor for the State of Colorado. They are the first two African-Americans to hold these posts in the 20th century.

1994 - At the age of forty-five, George Foreman became the oldest Boxer to win the Heavyweight Championship when he defeated twenty-seven year-old Michael Moore. In 1997, Foreman retired from Boxing with a record of 76-5. After retirement, he began promoting his grilling machine commonly known as the "George Foreman Grill." Since its introduction, over 100 million of his signature grills have been sold worldwide.

On this Day in History...

November 6th

1881 - James Sidney Hinton became the first African-American elected to the Indiana House of Representatives.

1895 - (HBCU) Fort Valley State University was founded in Fort Valley, GA. A group of 15 African-American men, half of whom were former slaves petitioned the Superior Court of Houston County, GA., to legalize the creation of a school to "Promote the cause of Mental and Manual Education in the State of Georgia," and the Fort Valley High and Industrial School was born. FVSU is one of few colleges founded by former slaves.

1972 - Andrew Young was elected to the U.S. Congress for the State of Georgia. He came into prominence as a Civil Rights Activist and close associate of Dr. Martin Luther King, Jr., his civil rights work was largely done with the Southern Christian Leadership Conference (SCLC) where he served as an Executive Director and Vice President. President Jimmy Carter appointed Young to serve as the U.S. Ambassador to the United Nations, he is the first African-American to hold that post. Young was also Mayor of Atlanta, GA., from 1981 - 1990.

1973 - Coleman A. Young was elected as the first African-American Mayor of Detroit, MI. During World War II, Young also served in the 477th Medium-Bomber Group (Tuskegee Airmen) of the United States Army Air Forces as a Second Lieutenant, Bombardier and Navigator. In 1968, Young was also the first African-American to serve on the Democratic National Committee. Young served an unprecedented five terms as Mayor.

On this Day in History...

November 7th

1983 - Harvey B. Gantt was elected as the first African-American Mayor of Charlotte, N.C. During his career he served on the Charlotte City Council from 1974 until 1983. Gantt was also the first African-American student admitted to Clemson University. In 2009, the Afro-American Cultural Center and the City of Charlotte honored Gantt by building the Harvey B. Gantt Center for African-American Arts + Culture, recognizing his contributions to the Civil Rights Movement and as the City's first African-American Mayor.

1990 - Actor and Comedian, Arsenio Hall was inducted into the Hollywood Walk of Fame and awarded a star on Hollywood Boulevard. He is best known for hosting "The Arsenio Hall Show," a late-night talk show that ran from 1989 until 1994, then again from 2013 to 2014.

1990 - Sharon Pratt Kelly was elected the first African-American woman Mayor of Washington, D.C., she became the first African-American woman to lead a large American City.

1997 - William E. Kennard became the first African-American Chairman of the Federal Communications Commission (FCC). He was also nominated as Ambassador to the European Union by President Barack Obama and confirmed by the U.S. Senate.

2006 - Deval Patrick became the first African-American elected as Governor of Massachusetts. Serving as the 71st Governor, he was re-elected in 2010. Patrick also served as the United States Assistant Attorney General for the Civil Rights Division under President Bill Clinton.

On this Day in History...

November 8th

1966 - Edward Brooke was elected as the third African-American to serve in the United States Senate, he represented the State of Massachusetts. During his Senate career he championed the causes of low-income housing, increasing minimum wage and promoted commuter rail and mass transit systems. He also worked tirelessly to promote racial equality in the South.

1966 - Publisher of Ebony and Jet Magazines, John H. Johnson, was awarded the NAACP Spingarn Medal, for his productive imagination in the perilous field of publishing and for his contributions to the enhancement of the African-American self image through his publications. His magazines were among the most influential African-American businesses in media in the second half of the 20th century.

1990 - Eddie Robinson of Grambling State University became the first College Coach of any race to win 408 games in their career. He is recognized by many College Football experts as one of the greatest coaches in history. During his fifty-six year career, Robinson coached every game from the field and was inducted into the College Football Hall of Fame in 1997. More than 200 of his players went on to compete in the National Football League, including NFL Hall of Fame members Willie Davis, Willie Brown and Buck Buchanan.

2016 - Kamala D. Harris was elected as the first African-American woman to serve in the United States Senate, representing the State of California. Harris was also the first African-American and first woman elected as District Attorney for the City of San Francisco as well as Attorney General for the State of California.

On this Day in History...

November 9th

1875 - Jeremiah Haralson was elected to the (44th) Congress, as a member of the U.S. House of Representatives from Alabama's 1st District.

1875 - John A. Hyman was elected to the (44th) Congress, as a member of the U.S. House of Representatives from North Carolina's 2nd District.

1875 - Charles E. Nash was elected to the (44th) Congress, as a member of the U.S. House of Representatives from Louisiana's 6th District.

1875 - Robert E. Smalls was elected to the (44th - 45th and 47th - 49th) Congresses, as a member of the U.S. House of Representatives from South Carolina's 5th District.

1883 - James E. O'Hara was elected to the (48th - 49th) congresses, as a member of the U.S. House of Representatives from North Carolina's 2nd District.

1890 - John M. Langston was elected to the (51st) Congress, as a member of the U.S. House of Representatives from Virginia's 4th District.

1890 - Thomas E. Miller was elected to the (51st) Congress, as a member of the U.S. House of Representatives from South Carolina's 5th District.

1890 - Henry P. Cheatham was elected to the (51st - 52nd) Congresses, as a member of the U.S. House of Representatives from North Carolina's 2nd District.

On this Day in History...

November 10th

1931 - Inventor, Benjamin F. Thornton patented the world's first Telephone Answering Machine. His device was able to record multiple telephone messages from several callers using a turntable along with a recordable record. The device also featured an electric motor as well as an electric switch that was connected directly to the telephone line.

1945 - Frederick C. Branch became the first African-American commissioned Officer in the Marine Corps. In 1995, on the occasion of the 50th anniversary of his commissioning, a United States Senate resolution was passed honoring Branch, a base building was named in his honor at Camp Lejeune, North Carolina.

1948 - "Running Back," Levi Jackson became the first African-American Football Captain at Yale University. Only one other African-American player had been Captain of an Ivy League team, that was in 1893 when William Lewis was named Captain at Harvard. Jackson did not go the professional route. In 1950, he took a position with the Ford Motor Company and went on to hold major executive positions in Labor Relations and Urban Affairs. He was a Vice President at Ford when he retired in 1983.

1957 - Charlie Sifford became the first African-American to win a major Professional Golf Tournament, "The Long Beach Open." He was also the first African-American to play on the PGA Tour. He won the Greater Hartford Open in 1967 and the Los Angeles Open in 1969. For his contributions to Golf, Sifford was inducted into the World Golf Hall of Fame in 2004. He was awarded the Old Tom Morris Award in 2007 and a Presidential Medal of Freedom in 2014.

On this Day in History...

November 11th

1942 - Surgeon and Medical Researcher, Dr. Charles Drew patented an Apparatus for Preserving Blood. He conducted research in the field of blood transfusions while developing improved techniques for blood storage. He also pioneered the first large-scale Blood Collection Program in the United States during World War II. Dr. Drew was inducted into the National Inventors Hall of Fame in 2015.

1956 - Jazz Pianist and Vocalist, Nat King Cole became the first Major African-American Performer to host his own television show, "The Nat King Cole Show," which aired on ABC.

1960 - Rock Singer, Chubby Checker released his recording of "The Twist." The song remains the first and only record to have reached number one on the Pop charts two times, in 1960 and 1962. He introduced a dance by the same title and set off one of the greatest dance crazes in the 20th century.

1994 - Joyce Stephens became the first African-American woman promoted to Captain of the New York Police Department, she was a thirteen year Veteran of the Police Department at the time of her appointment.

2000 - Ruth J. Simmons became the first African-American woman President of an Ivy League School, she served as the 18th President of Brown University in Providence, Rhode Island. Later in her career, she was also named as the 8th President of Prairie View A&M University, becoming the first woman elected to serve as President, where her older brother once was once a star Basketball Student-Athlete.

On this Day in History...

November 12th

1899 - Dr. George Franklin Grant invented the world's first "Golf Tee," he also invented a medical device called the "Oblate Palate." Dr. Grant was the first African-American student to enter the Harvard School of Dental Medicine. One of his patients was Charles William Eliot, President of Harvard.

1977 - Ernest Nathan "Dutch" Morial was elected as the first African-American Mayor of New Orleans, he served two terms. Morial was also the first African-American Judge on the Juvenile Court of the City. In 1972, he was elected to the Louisiana Fourth Circuit Court of Appeals. Morial was the first African-American to graduate from Louisiana State University Law School of Law. He became nationally known for creating the first Office of Economic Development, a City Agency that coordinate efforts to attract and retain businesses. Morial also employed the first Minority Business Enterprise Counselor to work with small and minority-owned businesses. His son, Marc Morial also served as Mayor of New Orleans from 1994 to 2002.

1993 - Sharon Sayles Belton became the first African-American and the first woman Mayor of Minneapolis, MN. Many of her advisors and colleagues were women, who focused on neglected issues such as sexual assault and domestic violence. Earlier in her career, she was Associate Director of the Minnesota Program for Victims of Sexual Assault, she helped to build twenty-six centers to help rape victims throughout the State. She also helped to establish one of the Nation's first shelters for abused women, the Harriet Tubman Shelter. Her work led to her election to the City Council from 1984 to 1993, representing the Eighth Ward of Minneapolis.

On this Day in History...

November 13th

1913 - Dr. Daniel Hale Williams became the first African-American elected to the American College of Surgeons. Dr. Williams later became the first Surgeon in the United States to successfully perform an open heart surgery. His patient, James Cornish fully recovered and would go on to live for another 50 years. Dr. Williams work as a pioneering Surgeon has paved the way for modern day doctors who frequently perform the open heart surgery procedure each day to save countless lives worldwide.

1994 - Frank "Big Hurt" Thomas Jr., became the first Major League Baseball (MLB) player in to win back-to-back Most Valuable Player (MVP) Citations, in 1993 and 1994. Playing with the Chicago White Sox, Thomas was a leader in several offensive and defensive categories in those years and a member of the All-Star Team.

1992 - The Birmingham Civil Rights Institute and Research Center opened in Birmingham, AL., it depicts the struggles of the Civil Rights Movement in the 1950's and 1960's. The Institute is located in the Civil Rights District, which includes the historic 16th Street Baptist Church, Kelly Ingram Park and the Alabama Jazz Hall of Fame. The Institute had more than 25,000 visitors during its first week, it showcases a walking journey through the "living institution," which displays the lessons of the past as a positive way to chart new directions for the future. The permanent exhibitions are a self-directed journey through Birmingham's contributions to the civil rights movement and human rights struggles.

On this Day in History...

November 14th

1853 - William W. Brown became the first African-American Novelist. His novel, "Clotel; Or, The President's Daughter: A Narrative of Slave Life in the United States," was published in England. In 1847, he published his memoir, "The Narrative of William W. Brown," which became a bestseller across the United States, second only to Frederick Douglass Slave Narrative memoir.

1886 - Cathay Williams became the first African-American women to enlist and serve in the United States Army. Williams had to pretend to be a man in order to enlist, she went by the name of William Cathay. Over 400 women posed as male soldiers during the Civil War, most enlisted with their husbands, brothers or other family members.

1950 - Arthur Dorrington, was a Dentist who signed with the Atlantic City Seagulls of the Eastern Amateur League. He became the first African-American to play in organized Hockey in the United States. He also played three seasons with the Johnstown (Pennsylvania) Jets.

1971 - Dorothy Mae Taylor became the first African-American woman elected to the Louisiana Legislature. In 1986, Taylor was elected the first Councilwoman-at-large of New Orleans, she was also the first woman to serve as Acting Mayor of the City.

1991 - Guitarist, Singer and Songwriter, Jimi Hendrix was inducted into the Hollywood Walk of Fame and awarded a star on Hollywood Boulevard. Although his mainstream career spanned only four years, he is regarded as the most influential electric guitarists in the history of Popular music, and one of the most celebrated musicians of the 20th century.

On this Day in History...

November 15th

1866 - Pilgrim Baptist Church was founded in Saint Paul, MN. The church served as the birthplace of St. Paul's National Association for the Advancement of Colored People (NAACP), Urban League, and the Hallie Q. Brown Community Center (now the Martin Luther King Center). This is the oldest African-American church in the State of Minnesota, it is listed on the National Register of Historic Places.

1867 - (HBCU) Morgan State University was founded in Baltimore, MD. Founded as the Centenary Biblical Institute by the Baltimore Conference of the Methodist Episcopal Church, the institution's original mission was to train young men in ministry, it subsequently broadened its mission to educate both men and women as teachers.

1890 - (HBCU) Savannah State University was founded in Savannah, GA. The school was established as a result of the Second Morrill Land Grant Act, which mandated that southern and border States develop land grant Colleges for African-American citizens.

1979 - President Jimmy Carter appointed Anna Diggs-Taylor to the Federal Court for the Eastern District, in the State of Michigan.

2017 - Shonda Rhimes became the third African-American woman inducted into the Television Academy Hall of Fame. She joined the ranks of fellow honorees, Oprah Winfrey who was the first to be inducted in 1993, followed by Actress and Singer Diahann Carroll, who was inducted in 2011. The Hall of Fame is for individuals who have made outstanding contributions in the arts, sciences or management of television.

On this Day in History...

November 16th

2016 - Kareem Abdul-Jabbar received the Presidential Medal of Freedom. He is the National Basketball Association's all-time leading scorer who helped lead the Los Angeles Lakers to five Championships and the Milwaukee Bucks to another. During his career, Abdul-Jabbar was a six-time NBA Most Valuable Player and a 19-time NBA All-Star. In 2012, he was selected by Secretary of State Hillary Clinton to be a U.S. Global Cultural Ambassador. In addition to his Legendary Basketball Career, Abdul-Jabbar has been an outspoken advocate for social justice.

2016 - Michael Jordan received the Presidential Medal of Freedom. He is considered one of the Greatest Athletes of all time. Jordan played 15 seasons in the NBA for the Chicago Bulls and Washington Wizards. Jordan led the Chicago Bulls to six NBA titles, capturing five MVPs, he was third on the all time points scored list in the NBA and appeared in 14 All-Star games. After his retirement from Basketball, he became the Principal Owner and Chairman of the Charlotte Hornets.

2016 - Diana Ross received the Presidential Medal of Freedom. Ross has had an iconic career spanning more than 50 years within the Entertainment Industry in Music, Film, Television, Theater and Fashion. Ross was inducted into the Rock & Roll Hall of Fame and a recipient of the Grammy Awards highest honor, the Lifetime Achievement Award.

2016 - Cicely Tyson received the Presidential Medal of Freedom. Tyson has won two Emmy Awards and a Tony Award, she is known for her performances in "Sounder," "The Autobiography of Miss Jane Pittman" and "The Help." In 2013, she returned to the stage with "The Trip to the Bountiful" and was awarded the Tony Award for "Best Leading Actress."

On this Day in History...

November 17th

1911 - Omega Psi Phi was founded at Howard University, it is the first predominantly African-American Fraternity to be founded at a (HBCU) Historically Black College and University.

1984 - Chicago Bulls "Shooting Guard," Michael Jordan received his own Signature Line of Athletic Footwear, when Nike introduced "Air Jordans." The shoe featured a silhouette of Jordan slam dunking a Basketball, known as the "Jumpman" Logo. The Nike Air Jordans are primarily responsible for the birth of the Sneaker Collection Industry. Since its release, the shoe became a cultural phenomenon, the Air Jordan brand has generated an estimated $3 billion in sales worldwide.

1996 - Julia M. Carson became the first woman of any race elected to Congress from Indianapolis, IN. After serving as Secretary to the United Auto Workers local office and Director of the Area Office for Congressman Andrew Jacobs, she made a successful run for office and was elected a State Representative in 1992. Carson was also elected to the Indiana State Senate in 1976 and held that office until 1990.

2017 - For the first time in North Carolina's history, there were six African-American woman Police Chiefs in six major cities simultaneously. Raleigh's, Cassandra Deck-Brown, Durham's, C.J. Davis, Fayetteville's, Gina Hawkins, Morrisville's, Patrice Andrews, Winston-Salem's, Catrina A. Thompson and Morehead City's, Bernette Morris. Having six African-American woman Police Chiefs set a record for North Carolina as well as all other States in the country; all of the women are close friends with each other.

On this Day in History...

November 18th

1924 - Clifton R. Wharton Sr., became first African-American to pass the Foreign Service Examination. Over the next 30 years he held posts in the Malagasy Republic, Portugal, and Rumania. President Dwight D. Eisenhower appointed Wharton as the first African-American Minister to the Country of Romania. In 1961, he was also sworn in as the first African-American Ambassador to the Country of Norway.

1962 - Thelton Eugene Henderson became the first African-American to join the U.S. Justice Department's Civil Rights Division. After his tenure with the Department of Justice, he held several posts in California, including that as Assistant Dean of the Stanford University Law School. Henderson later became Chief Judge of the Ninth Circuit Court in San Francisco.

1987 - Marilyn Virginia Yarbrough became the first African-American Law School Dean in the country, she was hired at the University of Tennessee at Knoxville. Throughout her career, Yarbrough was a law professor and associate vice chancellor at the University of Kansas. In 1991, she became professor of law at the University of North Carolina, Chapel Hill.

1996 - Harold Ford Jr., son of retired U.S. Representative Harold Ford Sr., was elected to the House of Representatives, becoming the youngest member elected to the 105th Congress and the second youngest member to date. Ford represented the Ninth Congressional District in Tennessee. The election marked the first time in Congressional Black Caucus history that a son had succeeded a father.

On this Day in History...

November 19th

1868 - John Willis Menard became the first African-American ever elected to congress, who represented the State of Florida.

1883 - Hartshorn Memorial College became the first African-American women's College in the country. The institution began in Richmond, VA., in the basement of Ebenezer Baptist Church, with fifty-eight students. It was chartered by the Virginia legislature as "an institution of learning of collegiate grades for the education of young women." The College awarded its first Degrees in 1892, when three young women graduated, Mary Moore Booze, Harriet Amanda Miller and Dixie Erma Williams.

1890 - The Alabama Penny Savings Bank became the first African-American owned Bank in the State of Alabama, it opened in Birmingham and was in business until 1915.

1971 - William "Bill" Rhodman was inducted into the U.S. Bowling Hall of Fame. He was a member of the first African-American Team to participate in the ABC Bowling Tournament. Rhodman was also the first African-American Bowler to win top rank in ABC Competition.

1993 - Eric H. Holder Jr., became the first African-American U.S. Attorney for the District of Columbia. President Bill Clinton nominated him for the position.

1997 - Doctors Paula R. Mahone and Karen L. Drake made medical history when they delivered the first septuplets born alive in the United States, at the Iowa Methodist Medical Center in Des Moines.

On this Day in History...

November 20th

1923 - Inventor, Garrett Morgan patented the Traffic Signal, he was inspired to invent his creation after he witnessed a serious car accident at a busy intersection. Morgan's traffic signal was the first to feature three commands instead of two, which controlled traffic more effectively. Morgan was inducted into the National Inventors Hall of Fame in 2005.

1983 - Husband and Wife, Robert C. Maynard and Nancy Hicks Maynard became first African-American Owners of a major Metropolitan Newspaper "The Oakland Tribune."

1984 - Singer, Song Writer and Dancer, Michael Jackson was inducted into the Hollywood Walk of Fame and awarded a star on Hollywood Boulevard. Referred to as the King of Pop, Jackson was recognized as "The Most Successful Entertainer of All Time" by Guinness World Records. His contribution to music, dance and fashion made him a global figure in popular culture for over four decades. The eighth child of the Jackson family, he debuted on the professional music scene along with his brothers as a member of "The Jackson Five" in the mid-1960's, he began his solo career in 1971.

1990 - Charles E. Freeman became the first African-American elected to the Illinois Supreme Court.

1997 - Dallas Mavericks "Forward," A. C. Green Jr., broke the National Basketball Association (NBA) record for the most consecutive games played, he became the league's new "Iron Man" playing his his 907th game in a row.

On this Day in History...

November 21st

1938 - Crystal Dedra Bird Fauset became the first African-American woman elected to a State Legislature (Pennsylvania) in the United States. Before going into politics, Fauset was known for her superior ability as a public speaker and charming large audiences. She used her public lectures to encourage all citizens, particularly African-American women, to become politically active.

1964 - Activist, Roy Wilkins became the Executive Director of the National Association for the Advancement of Colored People (NAACP). He developed an excellent reputation as an articulate spokesperson for the civil rights movement. He participated in the March on Washington (1963), the Selma to Montgomery marches (1965), and the March Against Fear (1966). When W.E.B. Du Bois left the organization in 1934, Wilkins replaced him as Editor of "Crisis," the official magazine of the NAACP.

1995 - Minyon Moore became the first African-American woman to serve as Political Director for the National Democratic Committee. In 1997, she also became the first African-American Deputy Political Director in the White House.

2001 - State Representative, Helen Giddings of Dallas, TX., was sworn in as the first African-American President of the National Order of Women Legislators (NOWL). The organization represents over 1,000 women in Government at the Local, State, and National level. During the time of her election to NOWL, Giddings won her fifth consecutive term in the Texas House of Representatives.

On this Day in History...

November 22nd

1986 - Mike Tyson became the youngest Boxer to win the World Heavyweight Championship, at age of twenty when defeating Trevor Berbick. He won his first nineteen professional fights by knockout, twelve of them in the first round. He won the WBC Title in after stopping Trevor Berbick in two rounds, later added the WBA and IBF titles after defeating James Smith and Tony Tucker in 1987. This made Tyson the first Heavyweight Champion to simultaneously hold the WBA, WBC and IBF titles, the only Heavyweight to successively unify them.

1986 - George Branham III became the first African-American to win a Professional Bowlers Association, (PBA) Championship. He joined the PBA at the age of twenty-four. Throughout his seventeen years as a Professional Bowler, Branham won five major titles, including the sport's highest honor, the Tournament of Champions, he also rolled 23 games with a perfect score of 300. When he retired from the game in 2004, he remained one of the world's top contenders.

1989 - Author and Journalist, Alex Haley became the first person of any race to receive an Honorary Degree from the Coast Guard Academy.

1994 - Catholic Priest, George H. Clements became known worldwide when he founded his "One Church, One Child" adoption program in the 1980s, he then established the "One Church, One Addict" program. Clements saw the program as an example of a private, community based leadership that was needed to defeat drug use. He called for community institutions, religious congregations, health care and treatment facilities and law enforcement agencies to come together and stay involved in the program.

On this Day in History...

November 23rd

1945 - Irving C. Mollison became the first African-American Judge of a U.S. Customs Court. This was the first time that an African-American served as a Federal Judge in the United States.

1957 - Civil Rights Activist, Anna Arnold Hedgeman became the first African-American woman to serve on the Cabinet of a New York City Mayor. She served on the staff of Mayor Robert Wagner from 1957-1958. Her career spanned more than six decades as an advocate for civil rights. In 1963, she helped Asa Philip Randolph and Bayard Rustin plan the March on Washington and was the only woman among the key event organizers, Hedgeman recruited over 40,000 protesters who participated in the march. She was also Executive Director of Harry S. Truman's 1948 Presidential Campaign, Hedgeman was rewarded with a federal appointment in the Health, Education, and Welfare Department in the new President's Administration. In 1966 she also co-founded of the National Organization for Women.

1996 - First Lady, Hillary Rodham Clinton wanted to acquire a Work of Art by a famous African-American Artist for the White House's permanent Art Collection, she selected Henry Ossawa Tanner's "Sand Dunes at Sunset, Atlantic City." The painting became the first by an African-American Artist to be included in the White House collection. Measuring fifty-eight by thirty inches, the White House Endowment Fund underwrote the $100,000 price tag.

2002 - Harry S. Johnson became the first African-American President of the Maryland Bar Association.

On this Day in History...

November 24th

1866 - (HBCU) Rust College became the first institution of higher learning for African-Americans in the State of Mississippi. Founded by the Methodist Episcopal Church as Shaw University, the name was changed in 1890, presumably to avoid confusion with the school in Raleigh, North Carolina. The school was then named for Richard Rust, a Caucasian anti-slavery advocate who supported the Freedmen's Aid Society of the church, it is the second-oldest Private College in the State.

1956 - Mathematician, Gladys West became the second African-American woman to work at the Naval Surface Warfare Center Dahlgren Division in Dahlgren, VA., where she joined a team of Engineers. West began to collect data from satellites, eventually leading to the development of Global Positioning System (GPS). Her groundbreaking work played a pivotal role in creating the technology. Today, GPS works in any weather conditions anywhere in the world. The U.S. Department of Defense (USDOD) originally put the satellites into orbit for military use, but they were made available for civilian use in the 1980s.

1984 - Leontine T. Kelly became the first African-American woman, and the second woman overall to be ordained by a major Christian denomination. Kelly was a Bishop of the United Methodist Church.

2005 - Civil Rights Attorney, Oliver W. Hill was awarded the NAACP Spingarn Medal, for his key role in the United States Supreme Court Case, Brown v. Board. Hill was known for his determination, quiet and persistent pursuit of justice.

On this Day in History...

November 25th

1939 - George W. Crockett Jr., became the first African-American Attorney with the U.S. Department of Labor. He also served as a National Vice President of the National Lawyers Guild and co-founded of the first racially integrated law firm in the United States. In 1972, he was then elected to the U.S. House of Representatives for the State of Michigan.

1968 - Gordon A. Parks Sr., became the first African-American to Produce, and Direct a Film, "The Learning Tree" for a major studio, Warner Brothers. Parks helped to break down racial barriers in Hollywood. The film, "Seven Arts," was based on his Autobiographical Novel published in 1963, this film became one of the first registered in the Library of of Congress National Film Registry. Other highly commercial films directed by Parks include Shaft (1971), "Shaft's Big Score" (1972) and "The Super Cops," (1974) all for MGM studios.

1977 - Pauli Murray became ordained as the first African-American woman Priest of the Protestant Episcopal Church, she was also a Civil Rights Activist, Women's Rights Activist and Attorney.

1980 - The second Boxing match between "Sugar" Ray Leonard and Roberto Durán, known as the "No Más Fight," it was one of the most famous fights in Boxing history. The match gained its famous name from the moment at the end of the eighth round when Durán turned away from Leonard towards the referee and quit by apparently saying, "No Más," spanish for "no more."

On this Day in History...

November 26th

1911 - Football Player, Coach and Attorney, William Henry Lewis became the first African-American appointed to a sub-cabinet post. President William Howard Taft appointed him an Assistant Attorney General of the United States.

1930 - Bessie Stringfield became the first African-American woman to ride a motorcycle across the United States solo, she was also one of the few civilian motorcycle despatch riders for the US Army during World War II. Known as "The Motorcycle Queen of Miami" she rode through 48 States, Europe, Brazil and Haiti. During this time she earned money by performing motorcycle stunts in carnival shows. Stringfield was inducted into the Motorcycle Hall of Fame in 2002. The American Motorcyclist Association (AMA) named the award "Superior Achievement by a Female Motorcyclist" in her honor.

1956 - Charles Gittens became the first African-American U.S. Secret Service Agent. In 1971, he was later promoted to head the field office in Washington D.C.

1978 - Vel R. Phillips became the first woman, and the first African-American elected as Secretary of State for Wisconsin, her Law Degree from the University of Wisconsin in 1951 was also a first. In 1972, Phillips was first African-American woman Judge in the State.

1990 - Leander J. Shaw Jr., became the first African-American State Supreme Court Chief Justice in the State of Florida. He was also the first African-American to head any branch of government in Florida.

On this Day in History...

November 27th

1885 - Mahlon Van Horne was elected to the Rhode Island General Assembly, making him the first African-American Legislator in the State, an office he held for three terms. He also assumed the Pastorate of Union Congregational Church, one of the few racially integrated churches in the U.S. at that time. In 1896, President William McKinley appointed Van Horne to be U.S. consul to St. Thomas in the Danish West Indies, he became one of the Nation's first African-American Diplomats.

1948 - Entertainer, Comedian and Composer, Timmie Rodgers launched the first all-African-American variety show, "Sugar Hill Times" on CBS. Known for his trademark phrase "Oh, Yeah!," Rodgers inspired other entertainers such as Redd Foxx, Dick Gregory, Nipsey Russell and Slappy White. He also wrote hit songs for Nat King Cole and Sarah Vaughan.

1955 - Ballet Dancer and Choreographer, Arthur Mitchell became the first African-American dancer with the New York City Ballet, he was later promoted to Principal Dancer. In 1986, he founded the first African-American Classical Ballet Company, "Dance Theatre of Harlem." Mitchell received numerous awards in recognition of his groundbreaking work and achievements, including the United States National Medal of Arts and a Fletcher Foundation fellowship.

1957 - Archibald J. Carey Jr., became the the first African-American to head the President's Committee on Government Employment Policy, he was appointed by President Dwight D. Eisenhower. Carey was also an Attorney and two-term Chicago Alderman. From 1953 to 1956, he served as an Alternate Delegate to the United Nations.

On this Day in History...

November 28th

1902 - Robert Herenton Terrell became the first African-American Justice of the Peace in Washington D.C. He taught in the District of Columbia's public schools from 1884 to 1989 and left to become Chief Clerk in the Office of the Auditor for the U.S. Treasury. While serving as Judge, he also taught in the Law School at Howard University.

1945 - Richmond Barthe became the first African-American Sculptor elected to the National Academy of Arts and Letters. In 1946, he was commissioned to sculpt the bust of Booker T. Washington, to be placed in the American Hall of Fame of New York University. He is noted for his small bronzes and monumental statues.

1961 - Wendell Oliver Scott won the Grand National Series Race at Speedway Park in Jacksonville, Florida, becoming the first African-American Driver to win a race at NASCAR's premier level. He was posthumously inducted into the NASCAR Hall of Fame in 2015. The 1977 film, "Greased Lightning" starring Richard Pryor, was based on his life.

1979 - Marcus Alexis became the first African-American to Chair the United States Interstate Commerce Commission. Throughout his career, he was also Deputy Chairman of the Federal Reserve Bank of Chicago.

2016 - Wyatt Worthington II became first African-American to win the Professional Golf Association (PGA) Tournament Series event. He was also the second African-American Club Professional to qualify for the PGA Championship.

On this Day in History...

November 29th

1867 - (HBCU) Fayetteville State University was founded in in Fayetteville N.C., after African-American citizens of Fayetteville decided to establish their own school for the education of their children.

1977 - Clifford Alexander Jr., was confirmed as the first African-American Secretary of the U.S. Army. Throughout his military career, he also served in the U.S. National Guard from 1958 to 1959.

1979 - Joyce London Alexander became the first African-American woman Chief Judge in the State of Massachusetts, she was also one of the first African-American Chief Federal Magistrate in the Nation.

1982 - Reuben M. Greenberg became the first African-American Chief of Police in Charleston, S.C. Throughout his career, he was also Undersheriff in San Francisco, CA., from 1971 to 1973.

2008 - Naomi Mitchell became the youngest African-American Golfer to win the U.S. Kids World Championship, she was eight years old. This is the largest competition for young golfers, ages four through twelve.

2016 - Jade Colin became the youngest African-American woman to own a McDonald's restaurant franchise. Four years after graduating from the University of Louisiana at Lafayette with a Bachelor's Degree in Business Management, the New Orleans native opened her first McDonald's location at the age of twenty-six. Colin later received the Outstanding Restaurant Manager of the Year Award for her region and the Ray Kroc Award, which recognizes the top one percent of Restaurant Managers in the country.

On this Day in History...

November 30th

1807 - The African Meeting House was built, known as the Joy Street Baptist Church, in Boston, MA., it is the oldest surviving building constructed to serve as an African-American Church. It housed the first African-American Baptist congregation in Boston, organized in 1805 by Thomas Paul Sr., who also founded the Abyssinian Baptist Church in New York City in 1809.

1956 - Milt Gray Campbell became the first African-American to win the Decathlon at the 1956 Summer Olympics in Melbourne, Australia. He captured the gold medal with 7937 points.

1982 - "Thriller," the sixth album by Singer and Entertainer Michael Jackson was released. In just over a year, Thriller became, and currently remains, the world's best-selling album, with estimated sales of 70 million copies. It is the best-selling album in the United States and the first album to be certified 33 times multi-platinum, having shipped 33 million units. The album won a record-breaking eight Grammy Awards in 1984, including Album of the Year.

1990 - Thelton Eugene Henderson became the first African-American Chief Judge of the Northern California U.S. District Court.

1993 - Sharon Farmer became the first African-American woman to serve as the White House Photographer, covering President Bill Clinton and the First Family.

1997 - President Bill Clinton appointed Calvin D. "Buck" Buchanan as U.S. Attorney in the Northern District of Mississippi.

On this Day in History...

December 1st

1865 - (HBCU) Shaw University was founded in Raleigh, N.C. The University was founded by Henry Martin Tupper, a native of Monson, Massachusetts. He was also a Soldier in the Union Army during the Civil War, and a graduate of Amherst College and Newton Theological Seminary.

1955 - Civil Rights Activist, Rosa Parks, whom the United States Congress called "the First Lady of Civil Rights" and "the Mother of the Freedom Movement" refused to comply with a Montgomery, AL., City Bus Driver's order to give up her seat in the "colored section" to a Caucasian passenger, after the "whites-only" section was filled. Parks was not the first person to resist bus segregation. Others had taken similar steps. NAACP organizers believed that Parks was the best candidate for seeing through a court challenge after her arrest for civil disobedience in violating Alabama segregation laws. Her act of defiance and the Montgomery Bus Boycott became important symbols of the modern Cvil Rights Movement. She became an International icon of resistance to racial segregation.

1964 - After more than six years in the U.S. Air Force, Captain, Dave Harris decided to seek a position as a Commercial Pilot, he became the first African-American pilot to fly a commercial airline in the United States. Harris went on to have a perfect career before his retirement in 1994, he flew the wide-body MD-11, the country's largest airplane at the time. Harris was honored by the Organization of Black Airline Pilots in August 2008, he was recognized for his thirty-year career as a Pilot for American Airlines.

On this Day in History...

December 2nd

1965 - Michael Lockett Garrett, a University of Southern California (USC) "Halfback" won the Heisman Trophy. Garrett played Professional Football for eight seasons with the Kansas City Chiefs and San Diego Chargers.

1969 - Inventor, Marie Van Brittan Brown patented the World's first Home Security System, she also patented the first ever Closed Circuit Television. Her invention was comprised of a camera, peepholes, monitors and a two way microphone. There was also an alarm button that she could press to contact the Police in the event of an emergency.

1997 - Lee Patrick Brown became the first African-American Mayor of Houston, TX. Prior to politics, Brown had an extensive career in law enforcement, he was the first African-American Chief of Police for the City of Houston. New York City Mayor, David Dinkins invited Brown to run the police force in his City. Brown also became the first African-American Police Commissioner for the City of New York, the largest Police Department in the Nation. President Bill Clinton later appointed Brown as Director of the White House Office of Drug Control Policy.

2008 - Retired NBA Player, Kevin Johnson defeated a two-term incumbent and became the first African-American elected as Mayor of Sacramento, CA. While campaigning, Johnson called on Magic Johnson and several other NBA greats, for support. Since founding St. HOPE Academy in 1989, which is an after school program for children. Johnson continues to be active in education reform.

On this Day in History...

December 3rd

1881 - Moses Fleetwood Walker became the first African-American College Varsity Baseball Player, he was a member of the first Oberlin College Varsity Baseball Team. In 1883 the "Barehanded Catcher" signed for the Northwestern League Toledo Team. He became the first African-American in Major League Baseball when the team entered the American Association in 1884.

1951 - Janet Collins became the first African-American Prima Ballerina at the Metropolitan Opera Company. She had the lead in "Carmen, La Gioconda" as well as "Sampson and Delilah."

1969 - Anna Bailey Coles became the founding Dean of Howard University's College of Nursing. The school was formed when a 1967 Act of Congress called for the transfer of Freedmen's Hospital School of Nursing to Howard.

1990 - Elaine C. Weddington became the first African-American woman Assistant General Manager of the Boston Red Sox. She was also the first African-American woman Executive of Professional Baseball Organization. From 1988 to 1990 she was Associate Counsel for the team.

2000 - Vashti Murphy McKenzie became the first woman elected Bishop in the African Methodist Episcopal (AME) Church. The election came during the church's quadrennial convention held in Cincinnati, OH. She was also the National Chaplain of Delta Sigma Theta Sorority, Incorporated and the granddaughter of one of Delta's founders, Vashti Turley Murphy.

On this Day in History...

December 4th

1906 - Alpha Phi Alpha became the first African-American Intercollegiate Greek Letter Fraternity, it was founded on the campus of Cornell University in Ithaca, N.Y.

1949 - Jesse Leroy Brown became the first African-American Pilot in the Naval Reserve. In 1950, he was also the first African-American Aviator to die in combat, losing his life in Korea. He received the Distinguished Flying Cross, Air Medal and Purple Heart posthumously. In 1973, he was the first African-American Officer to have a Knox-class ocean escort ship, the USS Jesse L. Brown, named after him, the ship was commissioned at the Boston Naval Yard. He was honored again in 1997, when the Jesse L. Brown Memorial Combined Bachelor Quarters were dedicated at the Naval Air Station in Meridian, Mississippi. Another honor came to him in 2000, when a $ 2.6 million County Tax Building in Hattiesburg, Mississippi, was named after him.

1976 - Theodore Roosevelt Newman Jr., was named the Chief Judge of the Washington Court of Appeals, he was the first African-American in the United States to head a court at this level. At the time of his appointment, there were fewer than a dozen African-American Judges on Appeals Courts in the various States.

1988 - Barry Sanders, an Oklahoma State "Running Back" won the Heisman Trophy. He played professionally for the Detroit Lions of the National Football League (NFL). A Pro Bowl invitee in each of his ten NFL seasons and two-time NFL "Offensive Player of the Year," Sanders led the league in rushing yards four times and established himself as one of the most elusive runners in pro Football with his quickness and agility.

On this Day in History...

December 5th

1961 - Ernie Davis, a Syracuse University "Running Back" became the first African-American to win the Heisman Trophy. Davis played College Football for Syracuse University and was the first pick in the 1962 National Football League (NFL) Draft, selected by the Washington Redskins.

1979 - Cowboy and Rodeo Rider, Jesse Stahl was posthumously inducted into Oklahoma City's Rodeo Hall of Fame, he became the second African-American Cowboy (after Bill Pickett) to receive that honor. Stahl set the standard of performance in "Saddle Bronc Riding" that continues to this day. He became famous for his performance at the Salinas Rodeo in California in 1912, performing before 4,000 fans. Stahl invented the rodeo technique of "Hoolihanding," literally leaping from a horse onto the back of a 2,000-pound bull, grabbing its horns, overpowering the animal, and rooting it into the ground tethered by its horns. He wowed sellout audiences with his bravery and exceptional performances until hoolihanding was outlawed. With his reputation growing as one of the great performance riders of the West, Stahl was a contract headliner at rodeo expositions all over the country.

1984 - John W. Heritage III became the first African-American Captain in the New York State Police, he entered the State Police Academy in 1967. In 1986, he became the first African-American Major in the force.

1987 - Robert Davis Glass became the first African-American member of the State Supreme Court of Connecticut.

On this Day in History...

December 6th

1933 - Inventor, Richard Spikes patented the Automatic Transmission Gear Shift for automobiles. This device is now standard on all automobiles with a manual transmission, he sold the patent rights for this invention to a major automobile manufacturer for $100,000.00 in 1934.

1959 - Louis Lomax became the first African-American Television Journalist when he joined WNTA-TV in New York City.

1963 - Marian Anderson and Ralph Bunche became the first two African-Americans to be recipients of the Presidential Medal of Freedom by President John F. Kennedy.

1971 - Larry William McCormick became the first African-American News Anchorman in Los Angeles, CA. After joining Tribune Broadcasting's KTLA, he became a mainstay in local broadcast journalism. In 1994, the Academy of Television Arts and Sciences awarded him its highest annual honor, "The Governor's Award."

1975 - Attorney, Willie E. Gary founded the first Law Firm in the State of Florida that was solely owned and operated by African-Americans.

1977 - Earl Campbell, a University of Texas "Running Back" won the Heisman Trophy. Campbell was drafted first overall by the Houston Oilers and had an immediate impact in the league, earning NFL Rookie of the Year honors. Campbell was also named the NFL's Offensive Player of the Year in each of his first three seasons.

On this Day in History...

December 7th

1958 - Jim Brown became the first African-American Athlete to win the Jim Thorpe Trophy, he won it again in 1965. Once a Football legend at his Alma Mater, Syracuse University, he then played nine years with the Cleveland Browns. In the 1960's, Brown also became the first player to score 126 career touchdowns. He later became an Actor, Producer, Sports Commentator and Marketing Executive. Brown is heralded as one of Football's greatest "Running Backs" ever. He is also noted for his continuing efforts to help the African-American community, reflecting his belief in the power of economic development.

1966 - James O. Patterson Jr., became the first African-American elected to the State Senate of Tennessee. Patterson was also an Attorney and a Bishop of the Church of God in Christ in the City of Memphis.

1972 - W. Sterling Cary became the first African-American President of the National Council of Churches in America. Throughout his career Cary was also a prominent political activist.

1978 - Billy Sims, a University of Oklahoma "Running Back" won the Heisman Trophy. He was the first overall pick in the 1980 NFL Draft and played professionally for the NFL's Detroit Lions.

1986 - Edward Joseph Perkins became the first African-American U.S. Ambassador to the Country of South Africa. He was later appointed as the Director of the U.S. State Department's Diplomatic Corps. Throughout his career Perkins was also the first African-American named Ambassador to the countries of Australia and Liberia.

On this Day in History...

December 8th

1850 - Lucy Ann Stanton became the first African-American woman in the United States to graduate from college. She completed the two-year "ladies" course and received her Bachelor's Degree from Oberlin College. She then taught school in the South during Reconstruction. Two other women also have been called the first African-American woman College Graduate. Grace A. Mapps was the first African-American woman to obtain a Degree from a four-year college, she attended Central College, McGrawville in New York in 1852. Mary Jane Patterson was the first African-American woman to earn a Bachelor's Degree from the four-year "gentleman's" course at Oberlin College in 1862.

1950 - Charline White became the first African-American woman elected to the Michigan Legislature.

1983 - Mike Rozier, a University of Nebraska "Running Back" won the Heisman Trophy. Rozier was also inducted to the College Football Hall of Fame. He played in the National Football League (NFL) for seven seasons.

1987 - Kurt Lidell Schmoke became the first African-American elected Mayor of Baltimore, MD. The first African-American Mayor was Clarence Du Burns, who was not actually elected. In January 1987, Du Burns succeeded then Mayor William Donald Schaeffer, who was elected Governor of the State. Schmoke was a Rhodes Scholar at Oxford, after his graduation from Yale, he earned a Law Degree at Harvard in 1976. He worked as an Assistant United States Attorney and as State's Attorney for Baltimore City, before his election.

On this Day in History...

December 9th

1872 - Pinckney Benton Stewart Pinchback became the first African-American Governor of a U.S. State, he served as the 24th Governor of Louisiana. Pinchback was the first person to be elected to both the House and the U.S. Senate. He was also a founding member of Southern University and A&M College.

1917 - The 369th Infantry Regiment became the first group of African-American Combat Soldiers to arrive in Europe. Cited for bravery eleven times, the regiment was awarded the Croix de Guerre by the French Government.

1975 - Julia P. Cooper became the first African-American woman Judge appointed of the District of Columbia Appellate Court. She was the highest ranking woman in the Federal Courts.

1976 - Tony Dorsett, a University of Pittsburgh "Running Back" won the Heisman Trophy. Dorsett was the first-round draft choice of the Dallas Cowboys, he was the National Football League (NFL) "Offensive Rookie of the Year" and played for eleven seasons. He is a member of the Pro Football Hall of Fame (1994) and the College Football Hall of Fame (1994).

1982 - Herschel Walker, a University of Georgia "Running Back" won the Heisman Trophy. In the NFL, he played for the Minnesota Vikings, Philadelphia Eagles, and New York Giants. Walker was inducted into the College Football Hall of Fame in 1999.

On this Day in History...

December 10th

1921 - Frederick "Duke" Slater became the first African-American to receive the Most Valuable College Player (MVP) Award, he was a "Tackle" with the University of Iowa's undefeated team in 1921. He later became a Municipal Court Judge in Chicago in 1948. Slater was the first African-American elected to the College Football Hall of Fame in 1951.

1979 - Sir. Arthur Lewis of Princeton University was awarded the Nobel Prize in Economics, making him the first African-American to win the award in a category other than Peace. Lewis was honored for his work in Economics, he authored 12 books and had more than 80 technical works in Developmental Economics.

1981 - Marcus Allen, a USC Trojan "Running Back" won the Heisman Trophy. Allen was the first NFL player to gain more than 10,000 rushing yards and 5,000 receiving yards during his career. He is considered one of the greatest goal line and short-yard runners in National Football League (NFL) history. Allen has the distinction of being the only player to have won the Heisman Trophy, an NCAA National Championship, the Super Bowl, named NFL MVP and Super Bowl MVP. He has been inducted into both the College Football Hall of Fame and the Pro Football Hall of Fame.

2009 - The Nobel Peace Prize was awarded to the President Barack Obama, for his "extraordinary efforts to strengthen international diplomacy and cooperation between peoples." The Norwegian Nobel Committee cited Obama's promotion of Nuclear Nonproliferation and a "new climate" in International Relations.

On this Day in History...

December 11th

1934 - Pilot and Civil Rights Activist, Chauncey Spencer joined a group of African-American Aviators, together they organized the National Airmen Association of America (NAAA). In May 1939, he flew a rented Lincoln-Paige biplane on a Ten-City tour that started in Chicago and ended in Washington, DC. Realizing that war in Europe was imminent, he demonstrated the aviation abilities of African-Americans and lobbied Congress to include people of color in the Civilian Pilot Training Program for the U.S. Army Air Corps. His flight drew National attention and proved that African-Americans could fly an airplane, contrary to the beliefs and opinions of most Army Air Corps and government leaders. Born in Lynchburg, VA, he was the son of Edward Spencer and noted Harlem Renaissance Poet, Anne Spencer. The Spencers were one of the most respected families in Lynchburg, visitors to the Spencer home included George Washington Carver, Paul Robeson, James Weldon Johnson, Walter White, Clarence Muse, Dean Pickens, Adam Clayton Powell, Langston Hughes, Thurgood Marshall, and W.E.B. Du Bois.

1964 - Austin T. Walden became the first African-American Judge in the State of Georgia. He was a Municipal Judge in Atlanta.

1974 - Archie Griffin, an Ohio State "Running Back" won the Heisman Trophy. He is College Football's only two-time Heisman Trophy winner (1974-1975). Griffin also won four Big Ten Conference Titles with the Ohio State Buckeyes and was the first player ever to start in four Rose Bowls. Griffin played seven seasons in the NFL with the Cincinnati Bengals.

On this Day in History...

December 12th

1870 - Joseph H. Rainey became the first African-American to serve in the U.S. House of Representatives, serving a total of four terms for the State of South Carolina. Rainey made three speeches on the floor of Congress in support of what was finally passed as the Civil Rights Act of 1875. He also supported legislation that became known as the Enforcement Acts, which were three bills that passed by the United States Congress between 1870 and 1871. They were Criminal Codes which protected African-Americans right to vote, hold office, serve on juries and receive equal protection under the law. Passed under the Presidency of Ulysses S. Grant, the laws also allowed the Federal Government to intervene when States did not act to protect these rights.

1985 - Singer, Actress and Television Show Host, Dionne Warwick was inducted into the Hollywood Walk of Fame and awarded a star on Hollywood Boulevard. Warwick ranks among the 40 biggest hit makers of the entire Rock era. Along with a successful music career, she was also a United Nations Global Ambassador for the Food and Agriculture Organization as well as a United States Ambassador of Health.

1985 - Alburn University "Running Back" Bo Jackson won the Heisman Trophy, he is the only Athlete in history to be named an All-Star in both Major League Baseball (MLB) and the National Football League (NFL), he played both sports professionally. Jackson is widely considered one of the greatest Athletes of all time. In 1996, he was inducted into the College Football Hall of Fame.

On this Day in History...

December 13th

1976 - Clara Stanton Jones became the first African-American elected President of the American Library Association. She was also the Director of the Detroit Public Library, becoming the first African-American Director of a major City Public Library in the United States.

1985 - Anna F. Jones became the first African-American woman to head a Major Community Foundation, "The Boston Foundation." Jones is the daughter of the first African-American President of Howard University, Mordecai W. Johnson..

1994 - Brigadier General, John H. Bailey became the first African-American to Command the Texas Militia. "The Militia," formally known as State Defense Forces, was one hundred fifty-nine years old when he took office. Bailey brought to the office his experience on Active Duty in Vietnam and being a Teacher of Military Science. He was also given the Lone Star Distinguished Service Medal, the highest military honor in the State of Texas.

2004 - Simmie Knox became the first African-American Artist to paint the official portrait of a U.S. President, Bill Clinton. Knox won the commission just before Clinton left office in January 2001. He also painted a portrait of former First Lady, U.S. Senator and U.S. Secretary of State Hillary Rodham Clinton. The oil on linen portraits of both Clintons took two years each to complete, they were unveiled during a ceremony in the East Wing of the White House. President Clinton's portrait hangs alongside those of other former Presidents. In 1989, Knox was also commissioned to paint an official portrait of Supreme Court Justice, Thurgood Marshall.

On this Day in History...

December 14th

1814 - Six hundred African-Americans were among the U.S. Army troops which defeated British forces at the Battle of New Orleans. The troops were led by Major, Joseph Savary, the highest ranking African-American Officer the U.S. Army during that time.

1972 - Adele Nutter became the first African-American woman U.S. Dart Champion, she was also a Founder and Charter Member of the American Dart Foundation.

1977 - Karen Farmer became the first African-American member of the Daughters of the American Revolution. She traced her ancestry to William Hood, a soldier in the Revolutionary Army.

1993 - Florida State University "Quarterback," Charlie Ward won the Heisman Trophy. Despite his NCAA Football success, Ward was one of the very few players who won a Heisman Trophy but was not drafted in the NFL Draft. He won the College Football National Championship Game with the Florida State University Seminoles. Ward is the only Heisman Trophy winner that was drafted into the National Basketball Association (NBA). He played several years with the New York Knicks. He was inducted in the College Football Hall of Fame in 2006.

1996 - Carol Jennifer became the first African-American woman to Direct Operations of an Immigration and Naturalization Service Office (INS), an Agency of the U.S. Department of Labor.

On this Day in History...

December 15th

1920 - Ann Cole Lowe became first African-American noted Fashion Designer. Her one-of-a-kind designs were a favorite among high society matrons from the 1920s to the 1960s. In 1953, she was hired to design a wedding dress for future First Lady Jacqueline Bouvier and the dresses for her bridal attendants for her September wedding to then-Senator John F. Kennedy.

1958 - "Sugar" Ray Robinson Jr., became the first African-American Boxer to hold the Middleweight Title on five separate occasions. In his 202 professional fights, Robinson lost only 19, and was never knocked out. He is widely considered the greatest pound-for-pound Boxer ever.

1966 - Football Player, Coach, Government Official and Broadcaster, Lowell Wesley Perry became the first African-American Assistant Coach in the National Football League (NFL), he was also the first African-American to broadcast an NFL game to a National audience. Later in his career, Perry was appointed as the Commissioner of the Federal Equal Employment Opportunity Commission (EEOC) by President Gerald Ford.

1982 - Singer and Actor, Lou Rawls was inducted into the Hollywood Walk of Fame and awarded a star on Hollywood Boulevard. Throughout his career, Rawls has released more than 60 albums and sold more than 40 million records.

1997 - Conrad L. Mallett Jr., became the first African-American elected Chief Justice of the Michigan Supreme Court, Governor James Blanchard appointed him to the Court.

On this Day in History...

December 16th

1946 - The first U.S. Coin honoring an African-American was issued. The half-dollar, featured the bust of Booker T. Washington, the founder of Tuskegee Institute in Alabama. Artist, Isaac S. Hathaway also became the first African-American to design a U.S Coin. Hathaway later designed the George Washington Carver half-dollar.

1968 - The Robert C. Weaver Federal Building in Washington, D.C., became the first building in the Nations Capital to be named after an African-American. The structure was dedicated to Robert C. Weaver, the first African-American Secretary of Housing and Urban Development (HUD), it houses the Headquarters of HUD.

1981 - Singer, Songwriter, Musician and Composer, Ray Charles was inducted into the Hollywood Walk of Fame and awarded a star on Hollywood Boulevard. Charles was a pioneer in the genre of Soul music during the 1950's by fusing Rhythm & Blues, Gospel and Blues styles into his early recordings. He also helped racially integrate Country and Pop music during the 1960's with his crossover success. Charles became one of the first African-American musicians to be given artistic control by a mainstream record company.

1996 - Detroit Lions Star "Running Back" Barry Sanders rushed for 1,000 yards in his eighth consecutive season and became the first African-American to reach that milestone. During the game in which he set the record, he gained 107 yards, this brought Sanders total rushing yards to 11,271 and pushed him just ahead on the NFL's rushing list.

On this Day in History...

December 17th

1884 - Henry V. Plummer became the first African-American Chaplain in the Army. He also held the rank of Captain and was assigned to the 9th Cavalry, which was one of the Regiments called the "Buffalo Soldiers."

1899 - Mary Annette Anderson became the first African-American woman elected into Phi Beta Kappa, the oldest Collegiate Academic Honor Society in the country.

1994 - Actress and Singer, Pearl Bailey was inducted into the Hollywood Walk of Fame and awarded a star on Hollywood Boulevard. Throughout her career, she has also won a Tony Award, Daytime Emmy Award and a Screen Actors Guild Life Achievement Award.

2007 - Fashion Designer, Dancer and Choreographer, Lisa Danielle founded DaniLi Apparel. While working as a Businesswoman and Dancer early in her career, her passion grew for fashion, she then established her Clothing Company. Her "Anything but Ordinary" custom made designs are a favorite among her clients.

2015 - Jermall and Jermell Charlo became the first Identical Twin Brothers to ascend the ranks in the sport of Boxing, with each sibling having an undefeated record. Jermall "The Hitman" Charlo was 26-0 with 20 knockouts, while Jermell "The Iron Man" was 30-0 with 15 KOs of his own. In 2018, they ranked amongst the world's best active Middleweight Boxers by the Transnational Boxing Rankings Board and BoxRec. The brothers train together at the Charlo Brothers Boxing Academy in Sugarland, Texas, turning every workout session into its own mini competition.

On this Day in History…

December 18th

1865 -   The Thirteenth Amendment to the U.S. Constitution was adopted in the aftermath of the Civil War, it abolished slavery in the United States. The Thirteenth Amendment states: "Neither slavery nor involuntary servitude, except as a punishment for crime whereof the party shall have been duly convicted, shall exist within the United States, or any place subject to their jurisdiction."

1978 -   Aletha Morgan became the first African-American woman Trooper in the South Carolina State Highway Patrol.

1989 -   Bill White became the first African-American elected as President to Head Major League Baseball's National League.

2002 -   Black Entertainment Television (BET) founder Bob Johnson started a National Basketball Association (NBA) expansion franchise in Charlotte, N.C. named "The Charlotte Bobcats," making him the first African-American to hold a majority ownership in a major Professional Sports Franchise.

2010 -   Little Richard's (Richard Penniman) song "Tutti Frutti" (1955) was included in the National Recording Registry of the Library of Congress, which stated that his "unique vocalizing over the irresistible beat announced a new era in music." In 2015, the National Museum of African-American Music honored Little Richard with a Rhapsody & Rhythm Award for his pivotal role in the formation of Popular music genres and in helping to shatter the color line on the music charts, changing American culture significantly.

On this Day in History...

December 19th

1943 - The Army Ground Forces Headquarters called for the activation of the 555th Parachute Infantry Battalion, a volunteer unit with officers and enlisted men who were all African-American. The unit was popularly known as the "Triple Nickels," formally becoming the World's first African-American Paratroopers. The battalion was sent to the West Coast of the United States to remain alert for possible Japanese attacks. Their mission there was also to fight forest fires, they made over 1000 jumps as they fought fires in Oregon and California, which earned them a second nickname, "Smoke Jumpers." After the war the group organized as the 555th Parachute Infantry Association, using the motto "Before them there weren't many, after them there weren't any." Three Buffalo Nickels stacked in pyramid form became their logo.

1971 - Jazz Pianist, Thelonious Monk became the second-most-recorded Jazz composer after Duke Ellington, he wrote about seventy pieces. Monk's musical work was crucial in the formulation of Bebop, which would be continued by other Artists, including Dizzy Gillespie, Charlie Christian, Kenny Clarke, Charlie Parker and later, Miles Davis. In 1993, he was awarded the Grammy Lifetime Achievement Award. In 2006, he was also awarded a special Pulitzer Prize for "A Body of Distinguished and Innovative Musical Composition that has had a significant and enduring impact on the evolution of Jazz." Monk was inducted into the North Carolina Music Hall of Fame in 2009.

1982 - JoAnn Jacobs became the first African-American woman Firefighter in New York City. Jacobs was thirty-one years old and a Physical Education Instructor at the time of her appointment.

On this Day in History...

December 20th

1962 - Mary Carson became one of the first African-American women appointed to the District Attorney's Office in Brooklyn, N.Y. Throughout her career, she continued to serve the citizens of New York City, working at Queens Legal Services and the State Supreme Court New York. After forty years of service, she retired in 2005 and relocated with her family to Atlanta, GA.

2000 - The Guinness Book of World Records declared that Entertainer, Michael Jackson broke the World Record for the "Most Charities Supported by a Pop Star." Jackson supported 39 charitable organizations throughout his lifetime, it's estimated he donated over $500 million to various charities.

2001 - Kenneth Chenault became the Chairman and CEO of American Express. After his appointment, he became the third African-American CEO of a Fortune 500 company.

2004 - Blues, Jazz, R&B and Soul Singer, Nancy Wilson was the recipient of the National Endowment for the Arts (NEA), Jazz Masters Fellowships Award. She was one of the best selling recording Artist in the 1960's, in which she issued five albums in two years. Wilson's career in music spanned over six decades. In 1967, she hosted her own variety series for NBC, "The Nancy Wilson Show," which won an Emmy Award, and she was a frequent guest performer on other programs. Throughout her career, she recorded more than seventy albums and won three Grammy Awards. Wilson was also a major figure in the Civil Rights Movement in the 1960s, in 2005 she was inducted into the International Civil Rights Walk of Fame.

On this Day in History...

December 21st

1939 - Edward Davis became the first African-American to own a new car dealership. The dealership was called "Davis Motor Sales," and it became one of the first African-American franchised car dealers in Detroit, MI. He sold new Studebaker automobiles along with truck models to the City of Detroit and to local businesses. In 1999, Davis also became the first African-American inducted into the Automobile Hall of Fame Museum.

1949 - Wallace Triplett became the first African-American drafted by a National Football League Team (Detroit Lions). In 1948, he was also the first African-American to play in the Cotton Bowl Classic, catching the tying touchdown in Penn State's 13-13 tie with Southern Methodist University. Triplett also co-founded the Gamma Nu Chapter of Alpha Phi Alpha while at Penn State.

1960 - Andrew T. Hatcher became the first African-American Presidential Press Secretary for John F. Kennedy's Administration. Hatcher was the highest-ranking African-American Appointee in the Executive Branch of the Federal Government. In 1963, he also founded the organization "100 Black Men of America."

1966 - Thomas David Parham Jr. became the first African-American Chaplain in the U.S. Navy to attain the rank of Captain. He was the Chaplain assigned to the Naval Air Station at Quonset Point, Rhode Island.

1987 - Marcus Doyle Williams became the first African-American State Judge in Fairfax County, VA., he was also the youngest at the age thirty-four.

On this Day in History...

December 22nd

1960 - William Roscoe Mercer became the first African-American Disc Jockey News Announcer on station WINS in New York. Known by his fans simply as "Rosko," he broke several barriers for African-Americans on the radio.

1977 - Ernesta G. Procope founded the E. G. Bowman Company, the first Commercial Insurance Brokerage Firm on Wall Street owned and operated by African-Americans. She became the Broker of Record for the New York City Housing Authority and the Insurance Broker for the construction of the United States portion of the Alaska Pipeline.

1979 - Wallace E. Orr became the first African-American Secretary of Labor in the State of Florida. He also served as President of the Florida Education Association.

1996 - Margaret Dixon became the first African-American elected President of the American Association of Retired Persons (AARP).

1998 - James A. Johnson became the first African-American Active-Duty Admiral in the Navy Medical Corps. He served in the U.S. Navy for thirty-two years prior to being promoted to Admiral. When he entered the service in 1966, he held the rank of Ensign, and served as Senior Medical Officer aboard the USS New Orleans on his first assignment. Earlier in his career, he held the position of Principal Director for Clinical Services in the Office of the Assistant Secretary of Defense for Health Affairs, in Washington, D.C.

On this Day in History...

December 23rd

1897 - Charles Burleigh Purvis became the first African-American Physician to serve on the Board of Medical Examiners in Washington, D.C.

1977 - Lucille Mason Rose became the first African-American woman named as Deputy Mayor of New York City. Her first efforts were devoted to providing jobs for teenagers, she was also named New York City Commissioner of Employment in 1972.

1987 - Educator and Anthropologist, Dr. Johnnetta B. Cole became the first African-American woman President of Spelman College in Atlanta, GA.

1993 - Judith Nelson Dilday became the first African-American appointed to the Probate and Family Court of Massachusetts, she received a lifetime position. Dilday was one of four African-American women Judges in the State Judiciary.

1997 - Civil Rights Pioneer, Rosa Parks received the first Lifetime Achievement Award from the Federal Transit Administration. During the awards ceremony held in Washington, D.C., she was honored for refusing to give up her seat to a Caucasian passenger on a segregated bus in Montgomery, AL. In 1955, this landmark act spurred the modern Civil Rights Movement. In 1998, Parks also received the first International Freedom Conductor Award. The award honors people who were courageous in public or private actions and who have made significant contributions to freedom and human rights worldwide.

On this Day in History...

December 24th

1943 - Harriet M. Waddy became the first African-American woman Major in the Women's Army Auxiliary Corps (WAAC), which later became the Women's Army Corps (WAC). She was also Chief of Planning in the Bureau of Control Division at WAAC Headquarters in Washington, D.C.

1977 - Geophysicist and Seismologist, Waverly Person became the first African-American Director of the U.S. Geological Survey's National Earthquake Information Center (NEIC) in Colorado. He was assigned to locate earthquakes, compute their size, and disseminate his findings quickly and efficiently to specific sites throughout the world.

1993 - Pearline Motley became the first African-American honored as American Business Woman of the Year. She received the award from the American Business Women's Association. Motley was the Manager of the Federal Women's Program of the Agricultural Stabilization and Conservation Service in Kansas City, Missouri.

1999 - The U.S. Coast Guard commissioned a Cutter in honor of Pulitzer Prize winner Alex Haley, marking the first time a military vessel was named for a Journalist. The vessel is a 282-foot Cutter formerly known as the USS Edenton, once a rescue and salvage vessel for the U.S. Navy, it became part of the Coast Guard's fleet. The Vessel is based in Kodiak, Alaska, and used for law enforcement and search and rescue missions in the Bering Sea, Gulf of Alaska and the northern Pacific Ocean. Haley spent twenty years in the Coast Guard and became the first Head of its Office of Public Affairs.

On this Day in History...

December 25th

1914 - The Spingarn Medal was instituted by Joel Elias Spingarn, then Chairman of the Board of Directors of the National Association for the Advancement of Colored People (NAACP). The Spingarn Medal is awarded annually by the NAACP for outstanding achievement by an African-American. During its annual convention, the NAACP presents the award after deciding from open nominations. The gold medal is valued at $100, Spingarn left $20,000 in his will for the NAACP to continue presenting the award indefinitely.

1947 - Kenneth Bancroft Clark and Mamie Phipps Clark established the Northside Center for Child Development. This was the first comprehensive agency that addressed the psychological and social needs of African-American children.

1994 - Johnny Rivers became the first African-American recipient of the American Culinary Federation Chef Professional Award. He was the Executive Chef at the Disney Village Marketplace in Lake Buena Vista, Florida.

1999 - Actor and Playwright, John Amos became the first Honorary Ambassador from the United States for the Legion of Goodwill, a Brazilian nonprofit group that offers social services to underprivileged children in North and South America.

2008 - Peggy A. Quince became the first African-American woman Chief Justice of the Florida Supreme Court.

On this Day in History...

December 26th

1908 - Boxer and Inventor, Jack Johnson became the first African-American Heavyweight Champion of the World when he knocked out Canadian, Tommy Burns in the 14th round in a Championship bout in Sydney, Australia.

1955 - Inventor and Chemist, Dr. Lloyd Augustus Hall became the first African-American to serve on the Board of Directors of the American Institute of Chemists. Dr. Hall was a Consultant for the George Washington Carver Foundation and for the United Nations Food and Agricultural Organization. He was also a pioneer in the field of Food Chemistry.

1966 - Maulana Karenga founded Kwanzaa, in order to restore and reaffirm African heritage and culture. (Kwanzaa is Swahili for "First Fruits") Although the celebration coincides with Christmas season, it was not intended as a religious celebration or one that promotes ideologies, instead it focuses on family values. Each night for seven nights, one particular family value is celebrated.

1966 - The first observance of the first day of Kwanzaa, "Umoja," which means "Unity," was observed. The celebration honors African Heritage in African-American Culture.

1972 - Allen E. Broussard became the first African-American President of the California Judges Association. He was Judge in the Oakland-Piedmont District Municipal Court and later Judge in the Alameda Superior Court in Oakland. He later became a Partner in the firm Coblentz, Cahen, McCabe and Breyer.

On this Day in History...

December 27th

1893 - Paul Laurence Dunbar became the first African-American Poet to gain National fame. He was accepted wholeheartedly as a Writer and widely recognized in the late 19th century. His literary promise was recognized first when he graduated from High School in 1891.

1921 - "Shuffle Along" became the first African-American Musical to run more than 500 performances on Broadway. The show was written by Eubie Blake, a Pianist and Composer. Soon after it opened, "Shuffle Along" became so popular that crowds gathered on the sidewalk waiting to buy tickets, cars and taxicabs also jammed the streets.

1942 - Hugh Mulzac became the first African-American Captain of an American Merchant Marine Ship. He was Captain of the the liberty ship named after Booker T. Washington. His ship saw antiaircraft action on a number of occasions. In 1920, he also became the first African-American to earn a Ship Master's License.

1961 - Maurice Sorrell became the first African-American member of the White House News Photographers Association. After a thirty-two year record with the Association, he was voted a life member in 1995. He became known for capturing on film, the history of the Civil Rights Movement. Working for the Washington Afro-American newspaper, Sorrell covered President Eisenhower and continued to cover the new Kennedy Administration in 1961.

1966 - The first observance of the second day of Kwanzaa, "Kujichagulia" which means "Self-Determination" was observed. The celebration honors African Heritage in African-American Culture.

On this Day in History...

December 28th

1943 - Guitarist and Singer, Muddy Waters (McKinley Morganfield) became the first Artist to combine Blues and Amplified Guitar to create Urban Blues. In 1948, he signed a recording contract and became known as the "King of the Delta (or Country) Blues." Often cited as the "Father of Modern Chicago Blues," he was an important figure to emerge on the Blues scene.

1966 - The first observance of the third day of Kwanzaa, "Ujima" which means "Collective Work and Responsibility" was observed. The celebration honors African Heritage in African-American Culture.

1968 - Elizabeth Duncan Koontz became the first African-American President of the National Education Association (NEA). Koontz was a classroom Teacher in North Carolina and an active member of NEA until she became President of the Department of Classroom Teachers in the NEA in 1965. After installation as President at the annual meeting, she called for statesmanship as the hallmark of teaching. She saw school as a way for Americans to transform their dreams into reality. From 1969 to 1972, she was also Director of the Women's Bureau of the United States Department of Labor.

1982 - Filmmaker, Director and Civil Rights Activist, Kathleen Collins became the first African-American woman to direct a feature-length film, "Losing Ground," she also wrote the screenplay. Her film won First Prize at the Figueroa International Film Festival in Portugal, garnering much International acclaim. Collins was also an active in the Civil Rights Movement.

On this Day in History...

December 29th

1842 - Robert Scott Duncanson became the first African-American Painter to win worldwide acclaim as a serious Landscape Artist and Muralist. He is considered the first African-American Artist to be internationally known. He operated in the elite cultural circles of Cincinnati, Detroit, Montreal and London.

1901 - Bert Williams and his partner George Walker became the first African-American Recording Artists, they were also among the first best-selling Artists. Williams was also the the first African-American Performer to star on Broadway, he starred in a Musical Comedy.

1963 - Katherine Dunham became the first African-American Choreographer to work at the Metropolitan Opera House. In the early 1940s her professional troupe, "The Dunham Dancers," set the stage for the Alvin Ailey American Dance Theater in Harlem. In 1989, she was awarded the National Medal of Arts. Her other recognition was the Kennedy Center Honor for Lifetime Achievement Award.

1966 - The first observance of the forth day of Kwanzaa, "Ujamaa" which means "Cooperative Economics" was observed. The celebration honors African Heritage in African-American Culture.

1994 - Ford Motor Company named Deborah Stewart Kent as Manager of the Ohio Assembly Plant in Avon Lake, she became the first African-American woman to manage an assembly plant in the firm's worldwide manufacturing system. After her appointment in Chicago, the Taurus/Sable became the bestselling car in the Nation.

On this Day in History...

December 30th

1870 - Mary Edmonia Lewis became the first African-American to achieve International fame and recognition as a Sculptor. After studying at Oberlin College, Ohio, she opened a studio in Boston and earned enough money to move to Europe. Lewis worked for most of her career in Rome, Italy. She received commissions for her Neoclassical Sculpture from all over the United States. Lewis also received National recognition at Philadelphia's Centennial Exhibition in 1876.

1892 - Miles Vandahurst Lynk became the first African-American to edit and publish a Medical Journal in the United States. "The Medical and Surgical Observer" was published in Jackson, TN. The first issue was thirty-two pages long, it was published regularly for eighteen months. Lynx was also the founder the University of West Tennessee College of Medicine and Surgery.

1966 - The first observance of the fifth day of Kwanzaa, "Nia" which means "Purpose" was observed. The celebration honors African Heritage in African-American Culture.

1984 - Julia Davidson-Randall became the first African-American woman State Registrar of Vital Records in the United States.

1997 - Actor, Tim Reid and his wife Daphne Maxwell Reid founded New Millennium Studios, the first full-service Hollywood film production studio in the State of Virginia. Reid formed New Millennium Studios Picture Corporation to concentrate on films and also Tim Reid Productions to concentrate on television.

On this Day in History...

December 31st

1951 - Hulan Jack became the first African-American Borough President of Manhattan, NYC. At the time, he was the highest ranking African-American elected official in the Nation.

1966 - The first observance of the sixth day of Kwanzaa, "Kuumba" which means "Creativity" was observed. The celebration honors African Heritage in African-American Culture.

1986 - William R. Harvey became the first African-American to be the sole Owner of a major soft-drink bottling franchise, a Pepsi plant in Houghton, Michigan. In 1978, Harvey became President of Hampton University.

1987 - Adam Clayton Powell III became the first African-American to Direct a Major National Radio News Network, National Public Radio (NPR). He has held a number of positions in the Communications Industry, including Manager and Producer for CBS News in New York City. Throughout his career, Powell was also became a New York City Councilman. After leaving NPR in 1990, he became a Producer for Quincy Jones Entertainment.

1995 - Carolyn Kennedy Worford became the first African-American woman to Chair the National Association of Television Program Executives (NATPE) International, the largest trade association of television programming executives in the world. Earlier in her career, she served as Station Manager and Vice President of Program Development at Detroit's WJBK-TV.

Index

A

Aaron, Hank. 12, 100, 181, 199, 215,
Abdul-Jabbar, Kareem. 322
Abel, Elijah. 162
Abrams, Stacey. 144
African-American Civil War Memorial. 302
African-American Museum of Iowa. 102
Agins, Michelle V. 239
Ailey, Alvin. 296, 365
Air Atlanta. 50
Alabama A&M University. 126
Alabama Penny Savings Bank. 325
Alabama State University. 39
Albany State University. 98
Alcorn University. 279
Aldridge, Ira F. 97
Alexander, Clifford. 335
Alexander, Joyce L. 335
Alexis, Marcus. 334
Ali, Laila. 161
Ali, Muhammad. 18, 58, 69, 161, 169, 199,
202, 215, 234, 243, 258, 260, 276, 305
Allen University. 45
Allen, Debbie. 286
Allen, Macon B. 125
Allen, Marcus. 346
Allen, Richard. 30, 165
Allensworth, Allen. 6
Alpha Kappa Alpha. 16

Alpha Phi Alpha. 340
AME Church. 30
American Negro Academy. 66
Amos, John. 361
Amos, Wallace "Wally". 71
Anderson, Charles A. 200
Anderson, Charles E. 162
Anderson, Charles W. 164
Anderson, Hubert. 223
Anderson, James. 235
Anderson, Marcia. 254
Anderson, Marian. 40, 342
Anderson, Mary A. 353
Anderson, Violette. 30
Andrews, Patrice. 323
Angelou, Maya. 7, 172
Apex Museum. 208
Apollo Theater. 12, 51,117
Archer, Dennis. 187
Archery, Oates. 164
Argrett, Loretta C. 306
Arlington, Richard J. 305
Armor, Vernice. 197
Armstrong, Henry. 123
Armstrong, Louis. 40, 53, 76
Ashe, Arthur. 132, 176
Ashford, Emmett. 56
Augusta, Alexander T. 78

B

Bailey, John H. 349
Bailey, Lawrence. 228
Bailey, Margaret F. 157
Bailey, Pearl. 353
Baker, Anita. 228
Baker, Ella J. 227
Baker, Gwendolyn C. 154
Baker, Josephine. 227
Baker, Vernon. 10
Bankhead, Dan. 240
Banks, Ernie. 211, 222
Banks, William V. 277
Banneker, Benjamin. 47, 144
Banning, James H. 92
Barden, Don H. 110
Barnett, Etta Moten. 31
Barry, Marion S. 192
Barthe, Richmond. 334
Barthelemy, Sidney J. 231
Basie, Count. 47, 59, 87, 126
Bass, Charlotta A. 129
Bass, Karen. 97
Bass, Sam. 181
Bateman, Mildred M. 247
Bath, Patricia. 139
Battle, Hinton. 285
Battle, Samuel. 67
Beard, Andrew. 138
BeBe and CeCe Winans. 296
Bechet, Sidney. 263
Beck, James G. 207
Becton, Julius W. 79
Belafonte, Harry. 40, 173
Bell, Derrick. 224

Bell, Robert M. 282
Bell, Travis. 177
Belton, Sharon S. 318
Benedict College. 78
Benjamin, Regina M. 152
Benjamin, Steve. 147
Bennett College. 275
Bennett, Adrienne. 222
Bennett, Marian C. 278
Benson, George. 264
Berry, Chuck. 23, 26, 283
Bethune-Cookman Univ. 43, 66, 278
Bethune, Mary McLeod. 43, 66, 77, 15
Bethune, Thomas G. 121
Billings, Cora. 156
Bismarck, Myrick. 122
Black Panther. 48, 188
Black Panther Party. 2, 278
Black Wall Street. 44, 125
Black, Joe. 275
Blackburn, Cleo W. 160
Blackwell, Utica. 308
Blair, Henry. 289
Blake, Eubie. 363
Bland, James. 119
Blanks, Lauren. 101
Blanton, Dain. 170
Bluford, Guion S. 244
Bluitt, Juliann. 193
Boardley, Diane. 253
Bolden, Charles "Buddy". 7
Bolden, Charles F. 198
Bolden, Lizzie. 229
Bolin, Jane M. 119

Bond, Horace J. 150
Bond, Horace M. 166
Bonds, Barry. 254, 279
Booker, Cory. 291
Booker, Simeon S. 301
Boone, Sarah. 118
Booze, Mary M. 325
Bouchet, Edward A. 118
Bounds, Mary. 198
Bowen, Clotilde D. 136
Bowen, Ruth J. 156
Bowie State University. 102
Boxley, Maude M. 285
Boyd, Tonya. 305
Boykin, Otis. 198
Boykins, Amber. 192
Boykins, Billie. 192
Bradley, Benjamin. 10
Bradley, Ed. 273
Bradley, Thomas. 282
Branch, Frederick C. 316
Brandford, Edward. 212
Brandon, Barbara. 181
Branham, George. 328
Brashear, Carl M. 279
Braun, Carol M. 309
Breen, London. 166
Brimmer, Andrew. 42
Bristow, Lonnie. 69
Britt, Catherine. 24
Brock, Lou. 211
Bronner, Arthur. 42
Bronner, Nathaniel. 42

Brooke, Edward. 314
Brooks, Charles. 113
Brooks, Gwendolyn. 123
Broussard, Allen E. 362
Brown, Alvin. 186
Brown, Antron. 48
Brown, Broadine M. 117
Brown, Cassandra D. 323
Brown, Cora M. 311
Brown-Chappell, Willa. 265
Brown, Dorothy L. 267
Brown, Elaine. 152
Brown, George. 311
Brown, Henry. 161
Brown, Henry. 308
Brown, James. 23, 57
Brown, Jesse. 112
Brown, Jesse L. 340
Brown, Jill. 68
Brown, Jim. 214, 250, 343
Brown, Kwame. 180
Brown, Lee P. 338
Brown, Marie Van B. 338
Brown, Marjorie L. 208
Brown, Paulette. 218
Brown, Ron. 72
Brown, Ronald H. 39
Brown, Tahirah L. 297
Brown, William W. 320
Brown, Willie L. 9
Brown, Wynston. 176
Browne, Rose B. 203
Bruce, Blanche K. 35

Buchanan, Calvin D. 336
Buffalo Soldiers. 136, 154
Bullard, Eugene. 241
Bunche, Ralph. 181, 267, 342
Burke, Selma H. 281
Burks, Ishmon F. 232
Burr, John A. 131
Burris, Roland. 182
Burrus, William. 105
Burton, Lavar. 303
Butler, Octavia. 100
Bynoe, Peter. 193

C

Cable, Theodore. 174
Cade, Henry. 182
Cadoria, Sherian G. 151
Caesar, Richard. 206
Cain, Richard H. 65
Callender, Clive O. 80
Calvary Baptist Church. 168
Calvin, Floyd J. 176
Campbell, Earl. 342
Campbell, Milt G. 336
Canady, Alexa. 218
Cannon, Katie G. 270
Cantrell, LaToya. 133
Cardozo, Francis L. 245
Carey, Archibald J. 333
Carlos, Ebenezer D. 10

Carlos, John. 291
Carn, Tameka. 237
Carney, William H. 201
Carroll, Diahann. 95, 321
Carroll, Vinnette J. 191
Carson, Julia. 323
Carson, Mary. 356
Carson, Samuel "Top". 234
Carson, Sanford. 58
Carter, Benny. 41
Carter, Eunice H. 186
Carter, Herbert. 254
Carter, Joseph C. 118
Carter, Pamela L. 272
Carter, Warrick L. 184
Carver, George W. 6, 197, 228
Cary, Sterling. 343
Catlett, Elizabeth. 185
Chamberlain, Wilt. 53, 63
Chaney, John. 163
Chapman, Charles P. 157
Chapman, Nathan A. 286
Chappell, Emma C. 287
Chappelle, Dave. 106
Charles, Ray. 23, 56, 120, 352
Charleston, Oscar. 223
Charlo, Jermall. 353
Charlo, Jermell. 353
Chase, John S. 246
Cheadle, Don. 161
Cheatham, Henry P. 315
Checker, Chubby. 317
Cheek, Donna M. 206
Chenault, Kenneth. 356

Cheswell, Wentworth. 60
Cheyney University. 56
Chisholm, Shirley. 25, 234
Christian, Barbara. 249
Christian, Charlie. 269
Church, Robert R. 130
Cinqué, Joseph. 240
Civil War. 104
Clark Septima P. 196
Clark, Kenneth B. 190, 361
Clark, Kwame. 292
Clark, Mamie P. 361
Clarke, Alyce G. 237
Clay, Cassius. 18, 57, 58, 243
Clay, Phillip L. 155
Clayton, Alonzo L. 72
Claytor, Helen. 205
Cleaver, Emanuel. 87
Clements, George H. 328
Clifton, Nathaniel. 294
Clyburn, Mignon. 266
Coachman, Alice. 215
Cobb, Jewel P. 176
Coffey, Cornelius. 229
Colbert, Judith A. 227
Cole, Johnnetta B. 359
Cole, Nat King. 53, 317
Cole, Rebecca J. 80
Coleman, Bessie. 119
Coles, Anna B. 339
Colin, Jade. 335
Collins, Cardiss. 158, 233
Collins, Janet. 339
Collins, Kathleen. 364

Colon, Nancy L. 247
Colston, James. 193
Congdon St. Baptist Church. 302
Congressional Black Caucus. 5
Conyers, Nathan G. 274
Cook, Mercer. 148
Cooke, Sam. 35
Cooper, Julia P. 345
Copeland, Misty. 284
Coppin State University. 293
Coppin, Fanny J. 47
Cornelius, Don. 275
Cornish, Samuel E. 111
Cothran, Ralph. 206
Cowings, Patricia S. 165
Cox, Minnie M. 83
Creer, Shayla. 309
Crockett, George W. 331
Cross, Dolores E. 226
Crosthwait, David. 127
Crumpler, Rebecca D. 72
Cuffe, John. 54
Cuffe, Paul. 54
Cullers, Vincent. 155
Curry, Michael. 203
Custis, Bernard. 306

D

Da Costa, Mathieu. 55
Dailey, Phyllis M. 68

Dalley, George A. 298
Dandridge, Dorothy. 79, 81
Dandridge, Ray. 209
Danenberg, Sophia. 128
Danielle, Lisa. 353
Daniels, Willie L. 177
Davenport, Willie. 56
Davidson, Ezra C. 306
Davis Jr., Benjamin O. 93
Davis Jr., Sammy. 66, 140
Davis Sr., Benjamin O. 29
Davis, Angela. 5
Davis, C.J. 323.
Davis, Darrell L. 153
Davis, Doris A. 97
Davis, Edward. 357
Davis, Ernie. 341
Davis, Errol B. 227
Davis, John H. 221
Davis, Kiko. 179
Davis, Miles. 51, 53
Davis, Shani. 50
Davis, Susan D. 188
Davis, Viola. 38
Dawes, Dominique. 108, 210
Dawson, William L. 5
Day, Leon. 213
Day, Thomas. 109
Days, Drew S. 60
De Sousa, Mathias. 43
Dean, Mark. 74
Dearing, James E. 112
DeGrasse, John V. 238
Del Rio, James. 166

Delany, Martin R. 54
Delany, Samuel R. 88
DeLarge, Robert C. 65
Delaware State University. 137
Denison, Franklin A. 231
DeShields, Andre. 285
DeVore-Mitchell, Ophelia. 17
Dickerson, Chris. 89
Dickerson, Mahala A. 114
Diddley, Bo. 22
Diggs, Hannah. 185
Diggs, Lucy. 137
Dilday, Judith N. 359
Dinkins, David. 2, 338
Dixon, Dean C. 270
Dixon, Irma. 213
Dixon, Margaret. 358
Dixon, Sharon P. 172
Doby, Larry. 188
Doley, Harold E. 27
Domino, Fats. 23
Donald, Bernice B. 264
Dorrington, Arthur. 320
Dorsett, Tony. 146, 345
Dorsey, Edmund S. 270
Dorsey, Thomas. 14
Douglas, "Gabby". 194, 216
Douglass, Frederick. 19, 46,
49, 96, 159, 224, 258
Downing, Philip. 302
Drake, Karen L. 325
Drew, Charles. 317
Drew, Howard P. 257
Drexel, Katherine M. 243

Du Bois, W.E.B. 32, 172, 211
Dumas, Charles E. 171
Dunbar, Paul L. 206, 250
Duncan, Robert M. 158
Duncanson, Robert S. 365
Dungey, Channing. 285
Dungy, Tony. 36
Dunham, Katherine. 365
Dunlap, James L. 202
Dunn, Oscar. 113
Dunnigan, Alice A. 37
Duplex, Edward P. 104
Durham, Diane. 222
Durham, James. 117
DuSable, Jean B.P. 52
Duvernay, Ava. 304
Dykes, Eva Beatrice. 167
Dymally, Mervyn. 311

Elizabeth City State University. 64
Elkins, Thomas. 310
Ellington, Duke. 58, 76, 121
Elliott, Robert B. 65, 149
Ellis, Clarence A. 205
Ellis, Harold. 79
Ellis, Larry. 280
Ender, Clara L. 118
Ervin, Anthony. 268
Erving, Julius "Dr. J". 256, 266
Espy, Mike. 27
Europe, James R. 115
Evans, Lydia A. 144
Evans, Melvin H. 153
Evans, Robert O. 276
Evers, James C. 135
Evers, Medgar. 36, 135
Exline, Brittney. 111

E

Early, Sarah J. 218
Earth, Wind and Fire. 259
Ebony Magazine. 307
Eckstine, William. 62
Edelman, Marian W. 274
Edmonds, Terry. 179
Edwards, Nelson J. 106
Edwards, Theresa. 216
Elder, Lee. 177
Elders, Joycelyn. 38

F

Fard, Wallace D. 187
Farley, James C. 97
Farmer, James. 16
Farmer, Karen. 350
Farmer, Sharon. 336
Farrakhan, Louis. 291
Fauset, Crystal B. 327
Fayetteville State University. 335
Fenwick, Lila. 147
Ferguson, Vernice. 163

Fidelin, Adrienne. 84
Fields, Carl. 275
Fields, Evelyn. 34
Fields, Virginia. 261
Fifteenth Amendment. 55, 92
Finney, Ernest A. 248
Finney, William K. 259
Fire Station No. 30. 78
Fishburne, Lillian. 199
Fisher, Gail. 131
Fisk Jubilee Singers. 36
Fisk University. 10, 75, 96
Fitch, Jacqueline. 220
Fitzgerald, Ella. 11, 126
Fitzhugh, Naylor. 83, 125
Flipper, Henry O. 168
Florida A&M (FAMU). 278
Flowers, Theodore. 59
Flowers, Vonetta. 52
Foote, Julia J. 265
Ford, Harold. 324
Ford, Justina L. 95
Foreman, George. 167, 293, 305, 311
Forsythe, Albert E. 200
Fort Valley State University. 312
Forten, James. 306
Foster, Andrew. 45
Foster, Bill. 217
Foxx, Jamie. 59
Frances, Henry M. 293
Frank, Shelly. 201
Franklin, Aretha. 22, 243
Franklin, Garromme P. 124
Franklin, John H. 190

Franklin, Shirley. 8
Frazier-Lyde, Jacqui. 161
Frazier, Joe. 69, 169, 292
Freedom National Bank. 175
Freedom Ride. 101, 126
Freeman, Algenia. 200
Freeman, Charles E. 326
Freeman, Morgan. 59, 79
Freeman, Thomas. 147
Fuhr, Grant. 165
Fuller, Solomon C. 76

G

Gadley, Jeff. 56
Gaines, Clarence. 39
Gans, Joe. 133
Gantt, Harvey B. 313
Garnet, Henry H. 44
Garnet, Sarah J. 249
Garrett, Michael L. 338
Garrison, William L. 144
Garrison, Zina L. 268
Garrott, Homer. 182
Garwood, George. 266
Gary, Willie E. 342
Gaskin, Walter E. 91
Gaston, "Cito." 300
Gatson, Dewey. 303
Gaye, Marvin. 22, 272
Gibbs, George. 27

Gibbs, Mifflin W. 134
Gibson, Althea. 88, 156, 208
Gibson, Benjamin F. 17
Gibson, Johnnie M. 15
Gibson, Josh. 221
Gibson, Paul. 194
Gibson, Reginald W. 124
Giddings, Helen G. 327
Gidron, Richard D. 155
Giles, Roscoe C. 157
Gillespie, Dizzy. 296
Gillum, Andrew. 242
Gilmore, Vanessa D. 295
Gittens, Charles. 332
Gladden, James R. 132
Glass, Robert D. 341
Glenn, Mildred. 105
Glover, John D. 122
Goldberg, Whoopi. 82
Goode, Sarah E. 197
Gordy, Berry. 13, 117, 299
Gossett Jr., Louis. 103, 142
Gould, William B. 244
Graham, Pamela T. 254
Graham, Rhea L. 153
Grambling State University. 307
Grandmaster Flash. 73
Grant, Edith. 53
Grant, George F. 318
Gravely, Samuel L. 60
Gray, Fred. 142
Green, A. C. 326
Green, Al. 13, 59
Green, James. 137

Green, Marlon. 84
Green, Nancy. 5
Green, Paul S. 152
Green, Tina S. 143
Green, Traci. 135
Greenberg, Reuben M. 335
Greene, Joe. 160
Greene, Maurice. 262
Greene, Petey. 161
Greener, Richard. 31
Greenfield, Elizabeth T. 132
Greenway, Jordan. 5
Greer, Cherie. 96
Gregg, Eric. 289
Gregory, Ann. 149
Gregory, Frederick D. 41, 233
Grier, Johnny. 241
Griffey Jr., Ken. 230, 245
Griffey Sr., Ken. 245
Griffin, Archie. 347
Griffin, Bessie B. 180
Guinier, Ewart. 230

H

Hagler, "Marvelous" Marvin. 107
Hairston, Harold. 269
Haley, Alex. 31, 328, 360
Haley, George. 114
Hall, Arsenio. 4, 313
Hall, Juanita. 116

Hall, Lloyd A. 72
Hall, Mary. 181
Hamer, Fannie Lou. 239
Hamilton, Jusan. 86
Hamilton, Virginia E. 156
Hammon, Jupiter. 37
Hammond, Wade. 269
Hampton University. 93
Hampton, Lionel. 21, 113
Handy, William C. 141
Haralson, Jeremiah. 315
Harlem Globetrotters. 49, 299
Harper, Thelma M. 229
Harris, Alfred W. 67
Harris, Bernard A. 41
Harris, Colleen. 304
Harris, Dave. 337
Harris, Irene T. 148
Harris, Kamala D. 314
Harris, Louisa. 163
Harris, Marcelite J. 131
Harris, Patrice. 170
Harris, Patricia R. 21
Harris, Reggie. 261
Harris, Robert L. 293
Harris, Walter. 283
Harrison, Alvin. 264
Harrison, Calvin. 264
Hart, Frank. 90
Hartshorn Memorial College. 325
Harvey, William R. 367
Hastie, William H. 87
Hatcher, Andrew T. 357
Hatchett, Joseph. 247

Hathaway, Isaac S. 352
Hawkins, Gina. 323
Hayes, Isaac. 108
Hayes, Roland. 255
Haynes, Lemuel. 9, 37
Haywood, Margaret A. 42
Healey, Patrick F. 209
Healy, James A. 163
Healy, Michael A. 115, 297
Healy, Patrick. 47
Hearns, Thomas "Hit Man". 92, 107
Hedgeman, Anna A. 329
Height, Dorothy. 51
Henderson, Alice M. 180
Henderson, George W. 180
Henderson, Thelton E. 324, 336
Hendrix, Jimi. 57, 232, 320
Henry, Robert C. 4
Henson, Josiah. 127
Henson, Matthew A. 12
Herenton, Willie W. 100
Heritage, John W. 341
Herriman, George. 209
Hewlett, James. 161
Hewlitt, Abraham M. 290
Higginbotham, Leon. 86
Hightower, Stephen L. 292
Hill, Henry A. 186
Hill, Jesse. 224
Hill, Oliver W. 330
Hill, Peter. 252
Hill, Tye. 213
Hillary, Barbara. 115
Hinchliffe Stadium. 77

Hinton, James S. 312
Hinton, William A. 78
Hip Hop. 225
Holbert, Breanna. 301
Holder, Eric. 34, 60
Holiday, Billie. 56, 99, 258
Holland, Jerome H. 16
Holland, John H. 244
Hollis, Michael. 50
Holloway, Josephine G. 238
Holmes, Dwight O. 208
Holmes, Oscar W. 102
Holmes, Tally. 137
Hooker, Olivia J. 44
Hooks, Benjamin L. 75
Hoover, Denise H. 240
Hopkins, Mary. 131
Horne, Lena. 54, 68, 130
Horton, George M. 94
Horton, Joann. 261
Horton, Odell. 283
Howard University. 63
Howard, Elston G. 164
Howard, Michelle J. 192
Howard, Robert B. 186
Howie, Kerri H. 303
Howroyd, Janice B. 298
Hubbard, Arnette R. 304
Hubbard, Marilyn F. 200
Hubbard, William D. 191
Hughes, Cathy. 306
Hughes, Dewey. 161
Hughes, Langston. 33, 299
Hunter, Alberta. 280

Hunton, Benjamin L. 212
Hyman, John A. 315

I

Irvin, Monfors. 217
Iverson, Allen. 85
Ivey, Phillip D. 90

J

Jack and Jill of America. 25
Jack, Hulan. 367
Jackson Jesse. 128
Jackson State University. 298
Jackson, Aprille E. 150
Jackson, Augustus. 83
Jackson, Bo. 348
Jackson, Gilda. 276
Jackson, Hal. 9
Jackson, Harry. 90
Jackson, Ida L. 208
Jackson, Janet. 112
Jackson, Levi. 316
Jackson, Lisa. 43
Jackson, Mahalia. 75, 76, 247
Jackson, Mary. 28, 267
Jackson, Maynard H. 8, 290
Jackson, Michael. 26, 326, 336, 356

Jackson, Perry B. 265
Jackson, Peter. 178
Jackson, Reggie. 215
Jackson, Robert T. 67
Jackson, Samuel L. 27, 169
Jackson, Shirley A. 84, 140
Jacobs, JoAnn. 355
James, Daniel H. 273
Jealous, Benjamin T. 140
Jefferson, Mildred F. 168
Jemisen, Mae C. 257
Jenkins, Augustus G. 227
Jenkins, Carolyn J. 248
Jennifer, Carol. 350
Jennings, Thomas. 64
Jet Magazine. 307
Johnson C. Smith University. 99
Johnson, Albert W. 285
Johnson, Bernette J. 224
Johnson, Beverly. 221
Johnson, Bob. 354
Johnson, Charles S. 233
Johnson, Earvin "Magic". 89, 174
Johnson, Francis. 48
Johnson, Gregory. 281
Johnson, Halle. 92
Johnson, Harry S. 329
Johnson, Harvey. 162
Johnson, Hazel W. 4
Johnson, I. S. Leevy. 223
Johnson, Jack. 47, 110, 362
Johnson, James A. 358
Johnson, James E. 186
Johnson, James W. 34, 211

Johnson, Jeh. 74
Johnson, John H. 307, 314
Johnson, Katherine. 240, 267
Johnson, Kevin. 338
Johnson, Mal. 272
Johnson, Michael. 104, 212
Johnson, Norma H. 123
Johnson, Rafer. 239
Johnson, Robert T. 263
Johnson, Stephanie. 79
Johnson, William. 35
Johnson, William "Judy". 230
Johnston, Joshua. 284
Jones Carlette "C.J". 287
Jones, Absalom. 307
Jones, Anna F. 349
Jones, Clara S. 349
Jones, Elaine R. 154
Jones, Eugene K. 12
Jones, Frederick M. 116
Jones, James Earl. 18
Jones, Lois M. 287
Jones, Quincy. 75, 204, 298
Jones, Samuel. 134
Jordan, Barbara C. 198, 225
Jordan, Carolyn D. 204
Jordan, George. 136
Jordan, Larry. 290
Jordan, Michael. 223, 322, 323
Josephis, Sadie R. 160
Joyner, Florence "Flo Jo". 199
Julian, Anna. 202
Juneteenth. 172
Just, Ernest Everett. 34

K

Kappa Alpha Psi. 6
Karenga, Maulana. 362
Kearse, Amalya L. 174
Keeble, Sampson W. 8
Keith, Karen C. 148
Kelly, Leontine T. 330
Kelly, Sharon P. 313
Kennard, William E. 313
Kennedy, Jayne. 85
Kent, Deborah S. 365
Kersey, Jackie J. 199
Kimbrell, Shawna R. 70
King B.B. 22, 235
King, Coretta Scott. 179, 211
King, Gwendolyn S. 299
King, Mabel. 285
King Jr., Martin Luther. 16, 17, 86, 96, 236, 242, 289
King, Suzie, 308
King, Teresa. 286
Kirk, Ron. 128
Kitzmiller, John. 127
Knight, Gladys. 180
Knox, Clinton E. 75
Knox, Simmie. 349
Koontz, Duncan. 364
Kountz, Samuel L. 61
Kwanzaa. 362

L

LaBelle, Patti. 68
Lafontant, Jewel S. 73
Lofton, William. 192
Lomax, Louis L. 342
Long, Jefferson F. 32
Loudd, Rommie. 225
Louis, Joe. 175
Loving, Alvin D. 251
Lowe, Ann C. 351
Lu Valle, James E. 266
Lucas, Ruth. 292
Lunsford, Lisa. 288
Lushington, Augustus N. 87
Lymon, Frankie. 62, 260
Lynch, John R. 65
Lynk, Miles V. 366
Lytle, Lutie A. 196

M

Mabley Jackie "Moms". 12
Mack, Kelvin. 70
Madison, Floyd. 201
Mahone, Barbara J. 304
Mahone, Paula R. 325
Mahoney, Charles H. 221
Mahoney, Mary E. 216
Malcolm X. 20, 68, 265
Mallett, Conrad L. 351
Malone, Moses. 166
Mandela, Nelson. 43
Manley, Albert E. 168
Manley, Audrey Forbes. 80

Mann, Thomas J. 111
Manning, Madeline. 294
March on Washington. 242
Markle, Meghan. 141
Marsalis, Wynton. 151
Marsh, Henry L. 69
Marshall Jr., Thurgood. 76
Marshall, John. 289
Marshall, Thurgood. 131, 139, 244
Mason, Bridget "Biddy". 109
Massey, Walter E. 111
Mathis, Johnny. 154
Mattox, Bernadette L. 206
Matzeliger, Jan E. 260
Mauldin, Al. 140
Maxwell, Sherman. 182
Maynard Robert C. 326
Maynard, Nancy H. 326
Maynor, Dorothy. 21
Mays, Benjamin. 282
Mays, Willie. 219
Mayweather, Floyd. 240
McAfee, Walter S. 83
McAllister, Jane E. 112
McAlpin, Harry S. 41
McCall Jr., Leander "Frank". 116
McCormick, Larry W. 342
McCoy, Elijah. 194
McCray, Robert. 309
McDaniel, Hattie. 61
McDemmond, Marie V. 200
McFarlane, Victor B. 91
McGee, Henry W. 311
McKenzie, Vashti M. 339

McKinney, Gene C. 177
McKissick, Floyd B. 130
McLeod, Gustavus "Gus". 109
McMichael, Alford L. 67
McNair, Lily D. 184
McNair, Ronald. 251
McNeil, Lori M. 173
McPherson, Gertrude E. 88
Medley, Tyrone E. 202
Melvin, Leland. 300
Menard, John W. 325
Menze, Jeanine. 175
Mercer, William R. 358
Meredith, James. 255
Metcalfe, Ralph H. 165
Meyzeek, Albert E. 35
Micheaux, Oscar. 49
Miles, Alexander. 286
Miller, Dorie. 246
Miller, Harriet A. 325
Miller, Ross M. 70
Miller, Thomas E. 315
Million Man March. 291
Million Woman March. 301
Mills, Florence. 286
Mills, Stephanie. 285
Mines, Janie L. 154
Mitchell, Arthur. 333
Mitchell, Bert N. 308
Mitchell, Clarence M. 108
Mitchell, John R. 191
Mitchell, Juanita E. 144
Mitchell, Michelle B. 226
Mitchell, Naomi. 335

Mollison, Irving C. 329
Monk, Thelonious. 355
Moon, Mollie. 233
Moon, Warren. 36
Moore, Ben. 268
Moore, Charles. 188
Moore, Juanita. 122
Moore, Matthew F. 268
Moore, Minyon. 327
Moore, Roscoe M. 124
Moore, Willie H. 191
Morehouse College. 50
Morgan State University. 321
Morgan, Aletha. 354
Morgan, Garrett. 295, 326
Morial, Ernest N. 318
Moron, Alonzo G. 121
Morris Brown College. 290
Morris, Raheem. 149
Morrison, Toni. 30
Mosley, Donna L. 205
Moss, Elizabeth B. 267
Mossell, Nathan F. 250
Mossell, Sadie T. 129, 167
Motley, Constance B. 244
Motley, Pearline. 360
Motown Records. 13, 299
Mulzac, Hugh. 363
Murphy, Eddie. 179
Murphy, Isaac. 135
Murray, Daniel A. 114
Murray, George. 158
Murray, Jacqueline. 231
Murray, Pauli. 331

Murray, Peter M. 192
Muse, Clarence. 55

N

NAACP. 44
Nabrit, Samuel M. 361
Nash, Charles E. 315
National Black Arts Festival. 146
National Urban League. 274
Nell, William C. 74
Nelson, "Prince" R. 360
Newcombe, Don. 41, 293
Newman, Theodore R. 340
Newton, Huey P. 2, 278
Newton, Lloyd "Fig". 271
Nichols, Nichelle. 58
Nix, Robert N. 7
Noble, Ronald K. 27
Norfolk State University. 200, 263
Norford, George E. 166
North Carolina A&T Univ. 70
North Carolina Central Univ. 302
Norton, Eleanor H. 229
Nutter, Adele. 350

O

O'Hara, James E. 315
O'Leary, Hazel R. 75

O'Neil, John "Buck". 16
O'Ree, Willie. 290
Obama, Barack. 4, 21, 38, 171, 210, 242, 310, 346
Obama, Michelle. 18
Oblate Sisters of Providence. 185
Olden, George. 230
Olive, Milton L. 142
Omega Psi Phi. 34, 323
Organ, Claude H. 152
Ormes, Zelda J. 254
Orr, Wallace E. 358
Outlaw, Danielle. 303
Overby, Ethel T. 256
Owens, Dana. 5
Owens, George A. 155
Owens, Jesse. 181, 189, 217

P

Page, Alan Cedric. 28
Page, Clarence. 280
Paige, "Satchel". 223, 234
Paige, Roderick R. 24
Palmer, Violet. 118
Parchment, Cora I. 7
Parham, Thomas D. 357
Paris, John. 223
Parker, Charlie. 60
Parker, Dave. 158
Parker, Kellis E. 212

Parks Sausage Company. 20
Parks, Gordon A. 331
Parks, Rosa. 337, 359
Parsons, James B. 309
Paterson, David A. 239
Patrick, Deval. 313
Patrick, Jennie R. 147
Patterson, Arthur J. 245
Patterson, Darin. 245
Patterson, Darius. 245
Patterson, Floyd. 173
Patterson, Frederick D. 268
Patterson, James O. 343
Patterson, Mary J. 151
Patterson, Sandra C. 245
Patton, Vincent W. 69
Paul, Thomas. 336
Payne, Daniel A. 71
Payton, Carolyn R. 269
Payton, Walter. 38, 203
Peck, Carolyn. 89
Pendleton, Clarence M. 246
Penn, Robert. 202
Penniman, Richard. 23, 174, 354
Perkins, Edward J. 343
Perry, Harold R. 273
Perry, Lowell W. 351
Perry, Matthew J. 266
Perry, Tyler. 279
Person, Waverly. 360
Peters, Aulana L. 247
Petersen, Frank E. 147
Peterson, Thomas M. 92
Petry, Ann. 91

Petty, Dana. 295
Phi Beta Kappa. 96, 180, 190
Phi Beta Sigma. 10
Phillips, Charles H. 145
Phillips. Vel R. 332
Pickett, Bill. 106
Pickett, Tydie. 201
Pickett, Wilson. 17
Pierce, Samuel R. 73
Pierre, Percy A. 197
Pilgrim Baptist Church. 320
Pinchback, Pinckney B. 345
Pinckney, Leo. 141
Pinkney, William "Bill". 220
Pipkins, Robert E. 39
Pittman, William S. 98
Player, Willa B. 196
Pleasant, Mary E. 3
Plummer, Henry V. 353
Poage, George C. 184
Poitier, Sidney. 32, 72, 105
Polk, Anthony J. 150
Polk, William. 269
Pollard, Fritz. 297
Poole, Cecil F. 194
Porter, Edward M. 190
Powell, Adam C. 367
Powell, Clilan B. 157
Powell, Renee. 203
Powell, William J. 66
Powers, Georgia M. 119
Prairie View A&M Univ. 228
Prestage, Jewel L. 144
Pride, Charley. 67

Prince, Art. 39
Prince, Hall. 153
Procope, Ernesta G. 358
Proctor, Barbara G. 292
Pryor, Richard. 142, 295
Puckett, Kirby. 183, 219
Purvis, Charles B. 359
Purvis, William. 8

Q

Quince, Peggy A. 361

R

Radio One. 306
Raines, Franklin D. 178
Rainey, Joseph H. 348
Randall, Julia D. 366
Randolph, Asa P. 329
Randolph, Joseph. 32
Raney, Della. 134
Ransier, Alonzo J. 65
Rapier, James T. 65
Rashad, Phylicia. 159
Raveling, George H. 155
Rawls, Lou. 351
Ray, Charlotte E. 63
Rayfield, Wallace A. 182

Ready, Stephanie. 85
Reason, Joseph P. 308
Rector, Sarah. 37
Redding, Louis L. 111
Redding, Otis. 19
Reed, Rosalie A. 157
Reese, Della. 162
Reeves, Bass. 76
Reeves, Frank D. 92
Reid, Daphne M. 366
Reid, Tim. 366
Renfro, Earl W. 298
Revels, Hiram. 57
Rhimes, Shonda. 321
Rhodes, Ray. 170
Rhodman, William. 325
Ribbs, Willie T. 62
Rice, Jerry. 250
Rice, Norman B. 252
Rice, Susan. 184
Richards, Beah. 241
Richie, Lionel. 64, 173
Richmond, William. 190
Rickey, Henderson. 117
Rillieux, Norbert. 271
Rivers, Johnny. 361
Roberts, Robin. 105
Robinson, "Sugar" Ray. 351
Robinson, Bishop. 261
Robinson, Cleveland. 101
Robinson, Eddie. 314
Robinson, Frank. 215, 262
Robinson, Georgia A. 7

Robinson, Ida B. 297
Robinson, Isaiah E. 207
Robinson, Jackie. 15, 25, 107, 187, 216
Robinson, Max. 38
Robinson, Oscar. 96
Robinson, Randall. 252
Robinson, Roscoe. 143
Robinson, Smokey. 54
Robinson, Spottswood W. 212
Rock, Chris. 73, 131
Rock, John S. 33
Rodgers, Timmie. 333
Rogan, Bullet. 209
Rollins, Ida. 150
Roman, Carl T. 30
Roman, Charles V. 156
Rose, Lucille M. 359
Ross, Diana. 128, 322
Ross, Ted. 285
Ross, William H. 182
Rozier, Mike. 344
Rucker, Darius. 282
Rudd, Daniel. 135
Rudolph, Wilma. 245
Ruffin, George L. 133
Ruffin, Paulette F. 270
Rundles, LaShunda. 204
Runge, Mary. 303
Rush, Gertrude E. 113
Russell, Bill. 110, 127, 163
Russell, Herman J. 203
Russwurm, John B. 246

Rust College. 330
Rust, Art. 199
Rustin, Bayard. 329

S

Sampson, Charles. 91
Sampson, Edith S. 124
Sampson, George T. 160
Sampson, Henry T. 189
Sanders, Barry. 340, 352
Santiago, Margaret. 158
Satcher, David. 236
Savage, Augusta C. 284
Savannah State University. 321
Savary, Joseph. 350
Schmoke, Kurt L. 344
Scott, Danielle. 186
Scott, Gloria D. 196
Scott, Jimmy. 113
Scott, Regina. 195
Scott, Wendell O. 334
Scurry, Briana. 193, 218
Seale, Bobby. 2, 278
Searles, Joseph L. 55
Second Baptist Church. 207
Seymore, Leslie. 202
Shabazz, Betty. 265
Shanks, Simon. 175
Sharpe, Ronald M. 248
Shaw University. 337

Shaw, Leander J. 332
Shaw, Leslie N. 149
Shippen, John. 13
Sifford, Charlie. 316
Simmons, Joseph "Jake". 109
Simmons, Lauren. 81
Simmons, Ron. 88
Simmons, Ruth J. 317
Simone, Nina. 55
Simpson, Georgiana. 167
Sims, Billy. 343
Sinkford, Jeanne. 331
Sivart Mortgage Company. 175
Sklarek, Norma M. 11
Slater, Frederick. 346
Slater, Rodney E. 46
Sleet, Gregory M. 207
Sleet, Moneta. 149
Small, Mary J. 74
Smalls, Robert E. 45, 315
Smith, Bessie. 274
Smith, Charles. 249
Smith, Chester. 249
Smith, Emmitt. 302, 310
Smith, Hilton. 219
Smith, J. Clay. 11
Smith, James M. 71
Smith, Louise. 284
Smith, Lucy M. 101
Smith, Mamie. 46
Smith, Merle J. 176
Smith, Orlando "Tubby". 287
Smith, Ozzie. 129, 211
Smith, Patricia G. 138

Smith, Tommie. 291
Smith, Virginia L. 288
Smith, Will. 63
Smoke Jumpers. 355
Snipes, Wesley. 235
Snowden, Mareena R. 161
Solomon, Allyson. 99
Sorrell, Maurice. 363
Soul Train. 275
South Carolina State Univ. 65
Southern Univ. 93
Spanish-American War. 113
Spaulding, Charles C. 236
Spears, Doris E. 110
Spelman College. 103, 143
Spencer, Anne. 347
Spencer, Chauncey. 347
Spencer, Edward. 347
Spigner, Marcus E. 299
Spikes, Dolores. 232
Spikes, Richard. 342
Spingarn, Joel E. 361
St. George Camp Meeting. 277
St. Philip's Episcopal Church. 114
Stahl, Jesse. 341
Stallings, George A. 271
Stanley, Frank L. 191
Stanton, Alysa. 159
Stanton, Lucy A. 344
Stanton. Robert G. 238
Stargell, Willie. 214
Starkes, Virgil A. 281
Staton, Candi. 178
Stearnes, Norman. 206

Stephan, Martin. 153
Stephens, Charlotte A. 283
Stephens, David. 100
Stephens, Joyce. 317
Stephens, Paul A. 265
Steward, Susan M. 85
Stewart, Ella P. 104
Stewart, James "Bubba". 90
Stewart, Melodie M. 273
Still, William G. 9
Stith, Deborah P. 233
Stokes, Charles M. 236
Stokes, Louise. 201
Stone, James. 237
Stringer, Vivian. 97
Stringfield, Bessie. 332
Sudarkasa, Niara. 249
Suffren, Angelica. 186
Summer, Cree. 251
Summer, Donna. 79
Swoopes, Sheryl. 189

T

Talbert, Mary B. 123
Talbot, Gerald E. 228
Tandy, Vertner W. 253
Tanner, Henry O. 255
Tanner, Jack. 309
Taylor, Anna D. 321
Taylor, Azie. 257

Taylor, Charles H. 128
Taylor, Dorothy M. 320
Taylor, George E. 3
Taylor, John B. 188
Taylor, Lawrence. 120
Taylor, Marshall W. 84
Taylor, Ruth C. 43
Taylor, Susie K. 94
Temple, Edward S. 195
Terrell, Mary C. 241
Terrell, Robert H. 334
Texas State University. 252
Tharpe, Rosetta. 42
The Fair Housing Act. 103
The Four Tops. 18, 115
The Gaither Quintuplets. 217
The Jackson Five. 17, 326
The Jeffersons. 19
The Platters. 18
The Sugar Hill Gang. 20, 214
The Supremes. 20, 128
The Temptations. 19, 259
The Wiz. 285
Thomas, Alfred J. 269
Thomas, Alma W. 294
Thomas, Debi. 59
Thomas, Frank. 319
Thomas, John C. 309
Thompson, Catrina A. 320
Thompson, Egbert. 269
Thompson, Frazier L. 176
Thompson, John. 95
Thompson, Marie. 90

Thompson, William H. 210
Thornton, Benjamin F. 316
Thurman, Howard. 137
Tillman, Harold G. 266
Todman, Terence A. 96
Tomes, Henry. 238
Travis, Dempsey J. 175
Trigg, Harold L. 238
Trigg, Joseph E. 74
Triplett, Wallace. 357
True Reformers Bank. 95
Truth, Sojourner. 151
Tubman, Harriet. 33, 54, 160, 262
Tucker, William. 4
Tunnel, Emlen. 46
Tupper, Henry. 337
Turner, Benjamin S. 65
Turner, Emmett. 272
Turner, Henry M. 256
Turner, Nat. 235
Turner, Tina. 29, 242
Tuskegee University. 187, 254
TV One. 20
Twilight, Alexander L. 130
Tyler, Dana. 261
Tyler, Ralph W. 134
Tyson, Cicely. 235, 250, 322
Tyson, Mike. 328
Tyus, Wyomia. 296

U

United Negro College Fund. 116
Univ. of Arkansas at Pine Bluff. 117
Univ. of Maryland Eastern Shore. 258
UniverSoul Circus. 255

V

Van Horne, Mahlon. 333
Vaughan, Dorothy. 28
Vaughan, Sarah. 214
Vaughn, Jacqueline B. 227
Virginia State University. 67
Virginia Union University. 95

W

Waddy, Harriet M. 360
Wade, Adam. 168
Walden, Austin T. 347
Walker, Alice. 106
Walker, Dorothy. 183
Walker, George T. 142
Walker, George. 365
Walker, Herschel. 345
Walker, Leroy T. 164
Walker, Madam C.J. 29
Walker, Moses F. 339
Wallace, Carolynn R. 206

Wallace, Joan S. 83
Wallis, Quvenzhané. 30
Walls, Josiah. 65
Ward, Charlie. 350
Ward, Joseph H. 300
Ward, Lloyd D. 283
Warwick, Dionne. 348
Washington, Booker T. 94, 99, 277, 291, 352
Washington, Denzel. 38, 85
Washington, Harold. 104
Washington, Huel. 145
Washington, Katie. 138
Washington, Kenneth S. 82
Washington, Leonard. 259
Washington, Mary T. 194
Washington, Ora. 174
Washington, Walter. 3
Waters, "Muddy". 364
Waters, Ethel. 13, 28
Watley, William. 201
Watson, Barbara M. 70
Wattleton, Faye. 148
Weaver, Robert C. 19, 351
Webb, Wellington. 171
Weddington, Elaine C. 339
Wells, Ida B. 33, 276
Wells, Willie. 214
Wentworth, Thomas. 308
Wesley, Carter W. 191
West, Gladys. 330
West, Togo D. 82
Wharton Jr., Clifton R. 110

Wharton Sr., Clifton R. 324
Wheatley, Phillis. 12
Whitaker, Forest. 57
White, Barry. 265
White, Bill. 354
White, Charline. 344
White, Cheryl. 195
White, Ronnie L. 231
White, Ruth C. 105
White, Walter. 237
Whitehead, James T. 52
Whitfield, Fred. 102
Wilkens, Lenny. 8
Wilkins, Jesse E. 64
Wilkins, Roy. 327
William, Marcus D. 357
Williams, Ann C. 200
Williams, Anthony A. 195
Williams, Bert. 47, 365
Williams, Billy. 209
Williams, Billy D. 88
Williams, Camilla E. 243
Williams, Cathay. 320
Williams, Daniel H. 24, 319
Williams, Dixie E. 325
Williams, Doug. 241
Williams, Herman. 264
Williams, Hosea. 133
Williams, James E. 98
Williams, Joe. 218
Williams, Lorraine. 236
Williams, Lucie C. 264
Williams, Marguerite T. 204
Williams, Marie S. 55

Williams, Patricia. 303
Williams, Paul R. 256
Williams, Peter. 178
Williams, Samuel L. 210
Williams, Serena. 257
Williams, Vanessa. 259
Williams, Venus. 257
Williams, Wesley A. 9
Williams, Willie L. 253
Willis, Billie A. 268
Wilson, August. 98
Wilson, Barbara J. 304
Wilson, Blenda J. 297
Wilson, Flip. 262
Wilson, Jackie. 22
Wilson, John L. 112
Wilson, Margaret B. 50
Wilson, Nancy. 356
Wilson, Norries. 171
Winfield, Dave. 219, 271
Winfrey, Oprah. 2, 6, 40, 172
Winston Salem State Univ. 273
Winters, Joseph. 129
Witcher, Veroman D. 260
Witherspoon, Fredda. 228
Wonder, Stevie. 19, 62
Woodard, Lynette. 299
Woods, Granville T. 272
Woodson, Carter G. 2, 33
Woodson, George H. 193
Worford, Carolyn K. 367
Worthington, Wyatt. 334
Wright, Brie. 189

Wright, Jonathan J. 248
Wright, Samuel D. 152

X

Xavier University. 285

Y

Yarbrough, Emanuel. 170
Yarbrough, Marilyn V. 324
Yardley, William F. 142
Yates, Josephine S. 164
Yerby, Frank G. 106
Young, Andrew. 312
Young, Charles. 18
Young, Coleman A. 312
Young, Lee R. 251
Young, Roger A. 201

Sources

African-American Inventions That Changed The World, Michael A. Carson. Catherine Britt, Sandra Patterson, Leander "Frank" McCall Jr., Mary Carson, Samuel "Top Carson, Sanford Carson, Dana Petty, Lisa Danielle, Brie Wright, Tameka Carn, African-American Athletes. Afro-American History. New York: Franklin Watts, 1969. Hornsby, Alton, Jr., Chronology of African-American History. Detroit: Gale, 1991. Jet Magazine,Civil Rights: A Current Guide to the People, Organizations, and Events. New York: Bowker, 1970. Adams, James Truslow, ed. Dictionary of American History. 7 vols. 2nd ed. New York: Charles Scribner's, 1968. The African-American Education Databook. Volume I: Higher and Adult Education. African-American Legislators 1893-2002: 109 years of Service. Lansing: Michigan Legislative Black Caucus, 2002. Ebony Magazine, Black First, Jessie Smith, Rock & Roll Hall of Fame, Rodeo Hall of Fame, Professional Football Hall of Fame, Professional Baseball Hall of Fame, Jockey Hall of Fame,Afro-American Encyclopedia. North Miami, FL: Educational Book Publishers, 1974. National Inventors Hall of Fame, Alford, Sterling G. Famous First Blacks. New York: Vantage, 1974. Grammy Hall of Fame, They Had a Dream: The Civil Rights Struggle from Frederick Douglass to Martin Luther King, Jr., College Football Hall of Fame, Scribner, 1971. Richards, Larry. African-American Films through 1959: Comprehensive, Illustrated Filmography. Jefferson, NC: McFarland, 1998. Richardson, Joe M. A History of Fisk University, 1865-1946. The Book of Firsts. New York: Clarkson N. Potter, 1974. Washington, DC: Acropolis Books, 1988. Robinson, Wilhelmina S. Historical Negro Biographies. New York: Publishers Company, 1970. Randolph, Elizabeth S., ed. An African-American Album. Charlotte, NC, Richards, Larry. African-American Films through 1959.

ACKNOWLEDGEMENTS

As always, I have to begin by giving thanks to God, for guiding my life and giving my family and I his infinite blessings.

To my lovely wife Shenika and our son Matthew.

To my parents, Mary and Sam, who gave me life and taught me how to love God and Family.

To my sister and brother-in-law, Sandra and Arthur.
To my brother and sister-in-law, Sanford and Brigette.
Thank you for your love and support.

To my nieces and nephews, Serena, Stephanie, Shayla, Jayda, Keiana, Darius, Darin and Austin.

To the entire Carson, Street, Hall and Bolden families.
Much love to all of you.

ABOUT THE AUTHOR

Michael A. Carson is a husband and father. He was born and raised in Queens, New York. He has a Bachelors Degree in Psychology from Virginia State University. He now resides with his family in Atlanta, Georgia working as a Government Analyst.

Along with his first publication: "African-American Inventions That Changed The World," Michael continues to educate the next generation about the many significant contributions African-Americans have made in our society and throughout the world.

Michael and his wife Shenika co-founded Double Infinity Publishing. Their goal is to publish high quality literature that represents historical facts as well as provide a voice and platform for educating readers.

CPSIA information can be obtained
at www.ICGtesting.com
Printed in the USA
LVHW101444200219
608186LV00008B/139/P